**Houghton
Mifflin
Harcourt**

© Houghton Mifflin Harcourt Publishing Company • Cover Image Credits: (Moose) ©Richard Wear/Design Pics/ Corbis; (Field, Delaware) ©Brian E. Kushner/Flickr Open/Getty Images

GO MATH!

Volume 1

Made in the United States
Text printed on 100%
recycled paper

Houghton Mifflin Harcourt

ISBN 978-0-544-43275-8

11 12 13 14 0029 22 21 20 19 18

4500713600   E F G

Dear Students and Families,

Welcome to **Go Math!**, Grade 3! In this exciting mathematics program, there are hands-on activities to do and real-world problems to solve. Best of all, you will write your ideas and answers right in your book. In **Go Math!**, writing and drawing on the pages helps you think deeply about what you are learning, and you will really understand math!

By the way, all of the pages in your **Go Math!** book are made using recycled paper. We wanted you to know that you can Go Green with **Go Math!**

Sincerely,

The Authors

Made in the United States
Text printed on 100% recycled paper

GO MATH!

Authors

Juli K. Dixon, Ph.D.
Professor, Mathematics Education
University of Central Florida
Orlando, Florida

Edward B. Burger, Ph.D.
President, Southwestern University
Georgetown, Texas

Steven J. Leinwand
Principal Research Analyst
American Institutes for
    Research (AIR)
Washington, D.C.

Contributor

Rena Petrello
Professor, Mathematics
Moorpark College
Moorpark, CA

Matthew R. Larson, Ph.D.
K-12 Curriculum Specialist for
    Mathematics
Lincoln Public Schools
Lincoln, Nebraska

Martha E. Sandoval-Martinez
Math Instructor
El Camino College
Torrance, California

English Language Learners Consultant

Elizabeth Jiménez
CEO, GEMAS Consulting
Professional Expert on English
    Learner Education
Bilingual Education and
    Dual Language
Pomona, California

Whole Number Operations

 Critical Area Developing understanding of multiplication and division and strategies for multiplication and division within 100

Critical Area

GO DIGITAL

Go online! Your math lessons are interactive. Use *i*Tools, Animated Math Models, the Multimedia eGlossary, and more.

Essential Question
How can you use properties to explain patterns on the addition table?
Start

1 Addition and Subtraction Within 1,000   **3**

Domains Operations and Algebraic Thinking
Number and Operations in Base Ten
COMMON CORE STATE STANDARDS 3.OA.D.8, 3.OA.D.9, 3.NBT.A.1, 3.NBT.A.2

Chapter 1 Overview

In this chapter, you will explore and discover answers to the following **Essential Questions**:

• How can you add and subtract whole numbers and decide if an answer is reasonable?

• How do you know when an estimate will be close to an exact answer?

• When do you regroup to add or subtract whole numbers?

• How might you decide which strategy to use to add or subtract?

2 Represent and Interpret Data   **85**

Domains Operations and Algebraic Thinking
Number and Operations in Base Ten
Measurement and Data
COMMON CORE STATE STANDARDS 3.OA.D.8, 3.NBT.A.2, 3.MD.B.3, 3.MD.B.4

Chapter 3 Overview

In this chapter, you will explore and discover answers to the following **Essential Questions**:

• How can you use multiplication to find how many in all?

• What models can help you multiply?

• How can you use skip counting to help you multiply?

• How can multiplication properties help you find products?

• What types of problems can be solved by using multiplication?

Practice and Homework

Lesson Check and Spiral Review in every lesson

Chapter 4 Overview

In this chapter, you will explore and discover answers to the following **Essential Questions**:

• What strategies can you use to multiply?

• How are patterns and multiplication related?

• How can multiplication properties help you find products?

• What types of problems can be solved by using multiplication?

Chapter 5 Overview

In this chapter, you will explore and discover answers to the following **Essential Questions**:

• How can you use multiplication facts, place value, and properties to solve multiplication problems?
• How are patterns and multiplication related?
• How can multiplication properties help you find products?
• What types of problems can be solved by using multiplication?

Chapter 6 Overview

In this chapter, you will explore and discover answers to the following **Essential Questions**:

• How can you use division to find how many in each group or how many equal groups?
• How are multiplication and division related?
• What models can help you divide?
• How can subtraction help you divide?

Chapter 7 Overview

In this chapter, you will explore and discover answers to the following **Essential Questions:**

- What strategies can you use to divide?
- How can you use a related multiplication fact to divide?
- How can you use factors to divide?
- What types of problems can be solved by using division?

⑦ Division Facts and Strategies **363**

Domain Operations and Algebraic Thinking

COMMON CORE STATE STANDARDS 3.OA.A.3, 3.OA.A.4, 3.OA.C.7, 3.OA.D.8

Critical Area

GO DIGITAL

Go online! Your math lessons are interactive. Use *i*Tools, Animated Math Models, the Multimedia *e*Glossary, and more.

Essential Question
What are equal parts of a whole?
Start

Chapter 8 Overview

In this chapter, you will explore and discover answers to the following **Essential Questions**:

• How can you use fractions to describe how much or how many?

• Why do you need to have equal parts for fractions?

• How can you solve problems that involve fractions?

Chapter 9 Overview

In this chapter, you will explore and discover answers to the following **Essential Questions**:

• How can you compare fractions?

• What models can help you compare and order fractions?

• How can you use the size of the pieces to help you compare and order fractions?

• How can you find equivalent fractions?

Critical Area

GO DIGITAL

Go online! Your math lessons are interactive. Use *i*Tools, Animated Math Models, the Multimedia *e*Glossary, and more.

Chapter 10 Overview

In this chapter, you will explore and discover answers to the following **Essential Questions**:

• How can you tell time and use measurement to describe the size of something?

• How can you tell time and find the elapsed time, starting time, or ending time of an event?

• How can you measure the length of an object to the nearest half or fourth inch?

Chapter 11 Overview

In this chapter, you will explore and discover answers to the following **Essential Questions**:

• How can you solve problems involving perimeter and area?

• How can you find perimeter?

• How can you find area?

• What might you need to estimate or measure perimeter and area?

Measurement

 Common Core **Critical Area** Developing understanding of the structure of rectangular arrays and of area

10 Time, Length, Liquid Volume, and Mass **559**

Domain Measurement and Data
COMMON CORE STATE STANDARDS 3.MD.A.1, 3.MD.A.2, 3.MD.B.4

11 Perimeter and Area **623**

Domain Measurement and Data
COMMON CORE STATE STANDARDS 3.MD.C.5, 3.MD.C.5a, 3.MD.C.5b, 3.MD.C.6, 3.MD.C.7, 3.MD.C.7a, 3.MD.C.7b, 3.MD.C.7c, 3.MD.C.7d, 3.MD.D.8

Geometry

Critical Area Describing and analyzing two-dimensional shapes

Critical Area

GO DIGITAL

Go online! Your math lessons are interactive. Use *i*Tools, Animated Math Models, the Multimedia *e*Glossary, and more.

Chapter 12 Overview

In this chapter, you will explore and discover answers to the following **Essential Questions**:

- What are some ways to describe and classify two-dimensional shapes?

- How can you describe the angles and sides in polygons?

- How can you use sides and angles to describe quadrilaterals and triangles?

- How can you use properties of shapes to classify them?

- How can you divide shapes into equal parts and use unit fractions to describe the parts?

Personal Math Trainer
Online Assessment and Intervention

Whole Number Operations

Common Core

CRITICAL AREA Developing understanding of multiplication and division and strategies for multiplication and division within 100

Some Baby Abuelita dolls sing Spanish rhymes and lullabies.

Inventing Toys

The dolls in the picture are called Abuelitos. Some of them are grandmother and grandfather dolls that were designed to sing lullabies. They and the grandchildren dolls have music boxes inside them. You squeeze their hands to start them singing!

Get Started  **WRITE** ▸ *Math*

Suppose you and a partner work in a toy store. You want to order enough dolls to fill two shelves in the store. Each shelf is 72 inches long. How many cartons of dolls will fill the two shelves? Use the Important Facts to help you.

Important Facts

- Each Abuelita doll comes in a box that is 8 inches wide.
- There are 4 boxes in 1 carton.
- Abuelita Rosa sings 6 songs.
- Abuelito Pancho sings 4 songs.
- Javier sings 5 songs.
- Baby Andrea and Baby Tita each sing 5 songs.
- Baby Mimi plays music but does not sing.

8 in.

_____

_____

_____

_____

_____

_____

Completed by _____

Addition and Subtraction Within 1,000

✓ Show What You Know

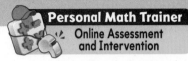
Personal Math Trainer
Online Assessment and Intervention

Check your understanding of important skills.

Name _____

▶ **Think Addition to Subtract** **Write the missing numbers.** (1.OA.A.1)

1. $9 - 4 = $ ■

Think: $4 + $ ■ $ = 9$

$4 + $ _____ $ = 9$

So, $9 - 4 = $ _____.

2. $13 - 7 = $ ■

Think: $7 + $ ■ $ = 13$

$7 + $ _____ $ = 13$

So, $13 - 7 = $ _____.

3. $17 - 9 = $ ■

Think: $9 + $ ■ $ = 17$

$9 + $ _____ $ = 17$

So, $17 - 9 = $ _____.

▶ **Addition Facts** **Find the sum.** (1.OA.C.6)

4. $\begin{array}{r} 4 \\ + 3 \\ \hline \end{array}$

5. $\begin{array}{r} 2 \\ + 7 \\ \hline \end{array}$

6. $\begin{array}{r} 8 \\ + 6 \\ \hline \end{array}$

7. $\begin{array}{r} 9 \\ + 4 \\ \hline \end{array}$

8. $\begin{array}{r} 7 \\ + 9 \\ \hline \end{array}$

▶ **Subtraction Facts** **Find the difference.** (1.OA.C.6)

9. $\begin{array}{r} 8 \\ - 5 \\ \hline \end{array}$

10. $\begin{array}{r} 11 \\ - 2 \\ \hline \end{array}$

11. $\begin{array}{r} 10 \\ - 6 \\ \hline \end{array}$

12. $\begin{array}{r} 18 \\ - 9 \\ \hline \end{array}$

13. $\begin{array}{r} 15 \\ - 7 \\ \hline \end{array}$

Manuel's puppy chewed part of this homework paper. Two of the digits in his math problem are missing. Help Manuel figure out the missing digits. What digits are missing?

Vocabulary Builder

▶ **Visualize It** ••••••••••••••••••••••••••••••

Sort the review words with a ✓ into the Venn diagram.

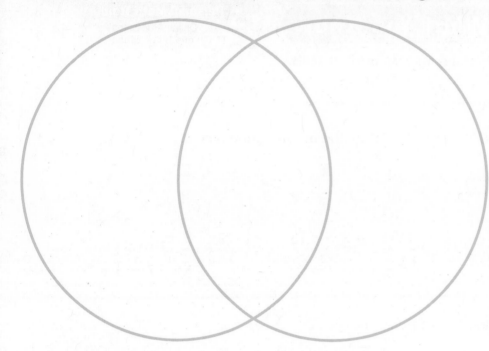

Addition Words   **Subtraction Words**

Review Words

✓ add
✓ difference
  even
✓ hundreds
  odd
✓ ones
✓ regroup
✓ subtract
✓ sum
✓ tens

Preview Words

Associative Property
  of Addition
Commutative
  Property of Addition
compatible numbers
estimate
Identity Property
  of Addition
pattern
round

▶ **Understand Vocabulary** ••••••••••••••••••••

Complete the sentences by using preview words.

1. A number close to an exact number is called
   an _____.

2. You can _____ a number to the
   nearest ten or hundred to find a number that tells *about*
   how much or *about* how many.

3. _____ are numbers that are easy to
   compute mentally.

4. The _____ states that you
   can add two or more numbers in any order and get the
   same sum.

GO DIGITAL • **Interactive Student Edition**
  • **Multimedia eGlossary**

Chapter 1 Vocabulary

Associative Property of Addition

Propiedad asociativa de la suma

5

Commutative Property of Addition

Propiedad conmutativa de la suma

8

compatible numbers

números compatibles

10

difference

diferencia

12

estimate

estimar

24

Identity Property of Addition

Propiedad de identidad de la suma

34

Pattern

patrón

57

round

redondear

72

The property that states that you can add two or more numbers in any order and get the same sum

Example: 6 + 7 = 7 + 6

The property that states that you can group addends in different ways and still get the same sum

Example: (2 + 3) + 4 = 2 + (3 + 4)

The answer to a subtraction problem

Example: 6 − 3 = 3

difference

Numbers that are easy to compute with mentally

The property that states that when you add zero to a number, the result is that number

Example: 17 + 0 = 17

To find about how many or how much

To replace a number with another number that tells about how many or how much

Example:

42 → 40
+16 → +20
58   60

An ordered set of numbers or objects in which the order helps you predict what will come next

Examples: 2, 4, 6, 8, 10, 2, 4, 6, 8, 10

Going to New York City

For 2 to 4 players

Materials

- 1 red playing piece
- 1 blue playing piece
- 1 green playing piece
- 1 yellow playing piece
- 1 number cube
- Clue Cards

How to Play

1. Each player puts a playing piece on START.

2. If you land on these spaces:

   Green Space Follow the directions printed in the space.

   Blue Space Round the number to the nearest hundred. If you round it correctly, move ahead 1.

   Red Space The player to your right draws a Clue Card and reads you the question. If you answer correctly, move ahead 1. Return the Clue Card to the bottom of the pile.

3. The first player to reach FINISH wins.

Word Box

Associative Property of Addition

Commutative Property of Addition

compatible numbers

difference

estimate

Identity Property of Addition

pattern

round

START

Visit the Empire State Building. Move ahead 1.

New York, NY

149

CLUE CARD

Get lost in Central Park. Lose 1 turn.

CLUE CARD

Visit the Statue of Liberty. Take another turn.

285

CLUE CARD

424

FINISH

CLUE CARD

777

Visit the American Museum of Natural History. Move ahead 1.

CLUE CARD

BROADWAY

See a Broadway show. Trade places with another player.

CLUE CARD

CONCERT

Hear a concert at Madison Square Garden. Go back 1.

561

CLUE CARD

The Write Way

Reflect

Choose one idea. Write about it.

- Draw and explain two ways to add 3-digit numbers. Use a separate piece of paper for your drawing.
- Elena and Han rounded 469 to the nearest hundred. Which solution is correct? Tell how you know.
- *Elena's solution*: 470, because 469 is closer to 470 than 460 on a number line.
- *Han's solution*: 500, 469 is closer to 500 than 400 because the tens digit is 6.
- Explain the Associative Property of Addition so a younger child would understand it.

Name _____

Number Patterns

Essential Question How can you use properties to explain patterns on the addition table?

Common Core **Operations and Algebraic Thinking—3.OA.D.9**
MATHEMATICAL PRACTICES
MP2, MP6, MP7

🔑 Unlock the Problem

A **pattern** is an ordered set of numbers or objects. The order helps you predict what will come next.

You can use the addition table to explore patterns.

🔑 Activity 1

Materials ■ orange and green crayons

- Look across each row and down each column. What pattern do you see?

_____

_____

- Shade the row and column orange for the addend 0. Compare the shaded squares to the yellow row and the blue column. What pattern do you see?

_____

What happens when you add 0 to a number?

_____

- Shade the row and column green for the addend 1. What pattern do you see?

_____

What happens when you add 1 to a number?

_____

_____

+	0	1	2	3	4	5	6	7	8	9	10
0	0	1	2	3	4	5	6	7	8	9	10
1	1	2	3	4	5	6	7	8	9	10	11
2	2	3	4	5	6	7	8	9	10	11	12
3	3	4	5	6	7	8	9	10	11	12	13
4	4	5	6	7	8	9	10	11	12	13	14
5	5	6	7	8	9	10	11	12	13	14	15
6	6	7	8	9	10	11	12	13	14	15	16
7	7	8	9	10	11	12	13	14	15	16	17
8	8	9	10	11	12	13	14	15	16	17	18
9	9	10	11	12	13	14	15	16	17	18	19
10	10	11	12	13	14	15	16	17	18	19	20

The **Identity Property of Addition** states that the sum of any number and zero is that number.

$$7 + 0 = 7$$

Math Talk

MATHEMATICAL PRACTICES ⑦

Look for a Pattern What other patterns can you find in the addition table?

Activity 2

Materials ■ orange crayon

- Shade all the sums of 5 orange. What pattern do you see?

  _____

  _____

- Write two addition sentences for each sum of 5. The first two are started for you.

  5 + 0 = _____   and   0 + 5 = _____

  _____ + _____ = _____   and   _____ + _____ = _____

  _____ + _____ = _____   and   _____ + _____ = _____

- What pattern do you see?

  _____

  _____

+	0	1	2	3	4	5	6	7	8	9	10
0	0	1	2	3	4	5	6	7	8	9	10
1	1	2	3	4	5	6	7	8	9	10	11
2	2	3	4	5	6	7	8	9	10	11	12
3	3	4	5	6	7	8	9	10	11	12	13
4	4	5	6	7	8	9	10	11	12	13	14
5	5	6	7	8	9	10	11	12	13	14	15
6	6	7	8	9	10	11	12	13	14	15	16
7	7	8	9	10	11	12	13	14	15	16	17
8	8	9	10	11	12	13	14	15	16	17	18
9	9	10	11	12	13	14	15	16	17	18	19
10	10	11	12	13	14	15	16	17	18	19	20

> The **Commutative Property of Addition** states that you can add two or more numbers in any order and get the same sum.
>
> $$3 + 4 = 4 + 3$$
> $$7 = 7$$

Activity 3

Materials ■ orange and green crayons

- Shade a diagonal from left to right orange. Start with a square for 1. What pattern do you see?

  _____

- Shade a diagonal from left to right green. Start with a square for 2. What pattern do you see?

  _____

- Write addition sentences for the shaded boxes. Write *even* or *odd* under each addend.

Remember

Even numbers end in 0, 2, 4, 6, or 8. Odd numbers end in 1, 3, 5, 7, or 9.

Math Talk

MATHEMATICAL PRACTICES ⑥

Describe how you know when the sum of two numbers will be odd.

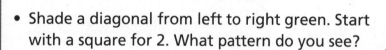

_____ + _____ = 6   _____ + _____ = 7   _____ + _____ = 8

↑   ↑   ↑   ↑   ↑   ↑   ↑   ↑   ↑

_____ + _____ = even   _____ + _____ = odd   _____ + _____ = even

Name _____

Use the addition table on page 6 for 1–9.

1. Complete the addition sentences to show the Commutative Property of Addition.

$3 +$ ____ = ____ $4 +$ ____ = ____

Math Talk

MATHEMATICAL PRACTICES ②

Reason Abstractly Explain why you can use the Commutative Property of Addition to write a related addition sentence.

Find the sum. Then use the Commutative Property of Addition to write the related addition sentence.

☑ 2. 8 + 5 = ____   3. 7 + 9 = ____   4. 10 + 4 = ____

____ + ____ = ____   ____ + ____ = ____   ____ + ____ = ____

Is the sum even or odd? Write *even* or *odd*.

5. $8 + 1$ _____   6. $3 + 9$ _____   ☑ 7. $4 + 8$ _____

Problem Solving • Applications Real World

8. *THINK SMARTER* Look back at the shaded diagonals in Activity 2. Why does the orange diagonal show only odd numbers? Explain.

_____

_____

9. *GO DEEPER* Find the sum $15 + 0$. Then write the name of the property that you used to find the sum.

_____

10. *THINK SMARTER* Select the number sentences that show the Commutative Property of Addition. Mark all that apply.

Ⓐ $27 + 4 = 31$ Ⓒ $27 + 0 = 0 + 27$

Ⓑ $27 + 4 = 4 + 27$ Ⓓ $27 + (4 + 0) = (27 + 4) + 0$

Sense or Nonsense?

11. **MATHEMATICAL PRACTICE ③ Make Arguments** Whose statement makes sense? Whose statement is nonsense? Explain your reasoning.

The sum of an odd number and an odd number is odd.

The sum of an even number and an even number is even.

| Joey's Work | Kayley's Work |

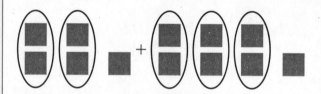

odd + odd = odd
5 + 7

I can circle pairs of tiles in each addend and there is 1 left over in each addend. So, the sum will be odd.

_____

_____

_____

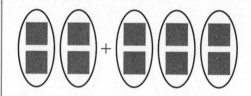

even + even = even
4 + 6

I can circle pairs of tiles with no tiles left over. So, the sum is even.

_____

_____

_____

• For the statement that is nonsense, correct the statement.

_____

Number Patterns

Common Core **COMMON CORE STANDARD—3.0A.D.9**
Solve problems involving the four operations,
and identify and explain patterns in arithmetic.

Find the sum. Then use the Commutative Property of Addition to write the related addition sentence.

1. $9 + 2 = \underline{\ 11\ }$ 3. $3 + 10 = \underline{\ \ \ \ }$ 5. $8 + 9 = \underline{\ \ \ \ }$

   $\underline{\ 2\ } + \underline{\ 9\ } = \underline{\ 11\ }$ $\underline{\ \ \ } + \underline{\ \ \ } = \underline{\ \ \ }$ $\underline{\ \ \ } + \underline{\ \ \ } = \underline{\ \ \ }$

2. $4 + 7 = \underline{\ \ \ \ }$ 4. $6 + 7 = \underline{\ \ \ \ }$ 6. $0 + 4 = \underline{\ \ \ \ }$

   $\underline{\ \ \ } + \underline{\ \ \ } = \underline{\ \ \ }$ $\underline{\ \ \ } + \underline{\ \ \ } = \underline{\ \ \ }$ $\underline{\ \ \ } + \underline{\ \ \ } = \underline{\ \ \ }$

Is the sum even or odd? Write *even* or *odd*.

7. $5 + 2$ _____   8. $6 + 4$ _____   9. $1 + 0$ _____

10. $5 + 5$ _____   11. $3 + 8$ _____   12. $7 + 7$ _____

Problem Solving

13. Ada writes $10 + 8 = 18$ on the board. Maria wants to use the Commutative Property of Addition to rewrite Ada's addition sentence. What number sentence should Maria write?

_____

_____

_____

14. Jackson says he has an odd number of model cars. He has 6 cars on one shelf and 8 cars on another shelf. Is Jackson correct? **Explain**.

_____

_____

_____

15. **WRITE** ▸*Math* Write the definitions of the Identity Property of Addition and the Commutative Property of Addition. Use the addition table to provide examples of each.

_____

_____

Lesson Check (3.OA.D.9)

1. Marvella writes the addition problem 5 + 6. Is this sum even or odd?

_____

2. What related number sentence shows the Commutative Property of Addition?

$$3 + 9 = 12$$

_____

Spiral Review (Reviews 2.MD.A.3, 2.MD.C.8, 2.MD.D.10)

3. Amber has 2 quarters, 1 dime, and 3 pennies. How much money does Amber have?

_____

_____

4. Josh estimates the height of his desk. What is a reasonable estimate?

_____

_____

Use the bar graph for 5–6.

5. Who read the most books?

_____

6. Who read 3 more books than Bob?

_____

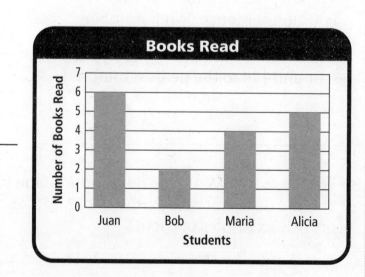

FOR MORE PRACTICE GO TO THE Personal Math Trainer

Round to the Nearest Ten or Hundred

Essential Question How can you round numbers?

 Common Core Number and Operations in Base Ten—
3.NBT.A.1
MATHEMATICAL PRACTICES
MP1, MP2, MP3, MP6

? Unlock the Problem

When you **round** a number, you find a number that tells you *about* how much or *about* how many.

Mia's baseball bat is 32 inches long. What is its length rounded to the nearest ten inches?

🔑 One Way Use a number line to round.

Ⓐ Round 32 to the nearest ten.

Find which tens the number is between.

32 is between _____ and _____.

32 is closer to _____ than it is to _____.

32 rounded to the nearest ten is _____.

So, the length of Mia's bat rounded to the

nearest ten inches is _____ inches.

Ⓑ Round 174 to the nearest hundred.

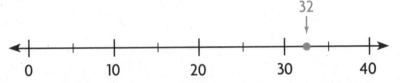

Find which hundreds the number is between.

174 is between _____ and _____.

174 is closer to _____ than it is to _____.

So, 174 rounded to the nearest hundred is _____.

Math Talk

MATHEMATICAL PRACTICES ①

Analyze Relationships How is rounding to the nearest ten similar to rounding to the nearest hundred?

Try This! Round 718 to the nearest ten and hundred.
Locate and label 718 on the number lines.

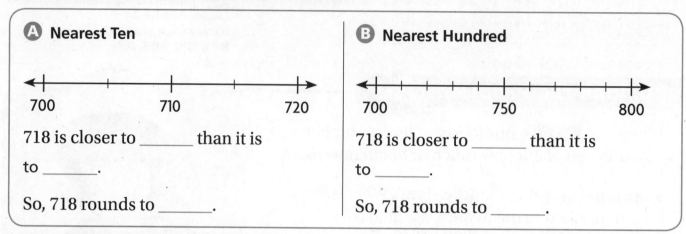

A Nearest Ten

700   710   720

718 is closer to _____ than it is

to _____.

So, 718 rounds to _____.

B Nearest Hundred

700   750   800

718 is closer to _____ than it is

to _____.

So, 718 rounds to _____.

🔑 Another Way Use place value.

A **Round 63 to the nearest ten.**

Think: The digit in the ones place tells if
the number is closer to 60 or 70.

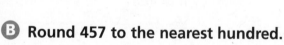 3 ◯ 5

63
↑

So, the tens digit stays the same. Write 6 as the
tens digit.

Write zero as the ones digit.

So, 63 rounded to the nearest ten

is _____.

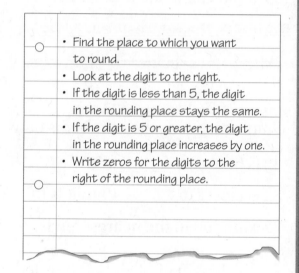

- Find the place to which you want
  to round.
- Look at the digit to the right.
- If the digit is less than 5, the digit
  in the rounding place stays the same.
- If the digit is 5 or greater, the digit
  in the rounding place increases by one.
- Write zeros for the digits to the
  right of the rounding place.

B **Round 457 to the nearest hundred.**

Think: The digit in the tens place tells if
the number is closer to 400 or 500.

 5 ◯ 5

457
↑

So, the hundreds digit increases by one.
Write 5 as the hundreds digit.

Write zeros as the tens and ones digits.

So, 457 rounded to the nearest hundred

is _____.

Math Talk

MATHEMATICAL PRACTICES ⑥

Make Connections
Explain how using
place value is similar to
using a number line.

Name _____

Locate and label 46 on the number line.
Round to the nearest ten.

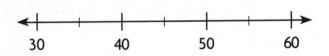

30   40   50   60

Math Talk

Use Reasoning What is the greatest number that rounds to 50 when rounded to the nearest ten? What is the least number? Explain.

1. 46 is between _____ and _____.

2. 46 is closer to _____ than it is to _____.

3. 46 rounded to the nearest ten is _____.

Round to the nearest ten.

4. 19 _____

5. 66 _____

6. 51 _____

Round to the nearest hundred.

7. 463 _____

8. 202 _____

9. 658 _____

On Your Own

Locate and label 548 on the number line.
Round to the nearest hundred.

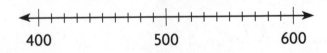

400   500   600

10. 548 is between _____ and _____.

11. 548 is closer to _____ than it is to _____.

12. 548 rounded to the nearest hundred is _____.

13. **Go DEEPER** There are 372 workers at a software company. There are 483 workers at a lumber company. When rounding to the nearest hundred, which company has 400 workers?

Problem Solving · Applications

Use the table for 14–16.

14. On which day did about 900 visitors come to the giraffe exhibit?

    _____

15. **GO DEEPER** On which two days did about 400 visitors come to the giraffe exhibit each day?

    _____

16. **GO DEEPER** On which two days did about 800 visitors come to the giraffe exhibit each day?

    _____

Visitors to the Giraffe Exhibit	
Day	**Number of Visitors**
Sunday	894
Monday	793
Tuesday	438
Wednesday	362
Thursday	839
Friday	725
Saturday	598

17. **MATHEMATICAL PRACTICE ③ Make Arguments** Cole said that 555 rounded to the nearest ten is 600. What is Cole's error? Explain.

    _____

    _____

    _____

WRITE ▸*Math* · **Show Your Work**

18. **THINK SMARTER** Write five numbers that round to 360 when rounded to the nearest ten.

    _____

    _____

19. **THINK SMARTER** Select the numbers that round to 100. Select all that apply.

    (A) 38   (C) 109

    (B) 162   (D) 83

Round to the Nearest Ten or Hundred

COMMON CORE STANDARD—3.NBT.A.1
Use place value understanding and properties of operations to perform multi-digit arithmetic.

Locate and label 739 on the number line.
Round to the nearest hundred.

600   700   800   900

1. 739 is between __700__ and __800__.

2. 739 is closer to _____ than it is to _____.

3. 739 rounded to the nearest hundred is _____.

Round to the nearest ten and hundred.

4. 66 _____

5. 829 _____

6. 572 _____

_____

_____

_____

7. 209 _____

8. 663 _____

9. 949 _____

_____

_____

_____

Problem Solving Real World

10. The baby elephant weighs 435 pounds. What is its weight rounded to the nearest hundred pounds?

_____

11. Jayce sold 218 cups of lemonade at his lemonade stand. What is 218 rounded to the nearest ten?

_____

12. **WRITE** ▸Math Describe how to round 678 to the nearest hundred.

_____

_____

Lesson Check (3.NBT.A.1)

1. One day, 758 people visited the Monkey House at the zoo. What is 758 rounded to the nearest hundred?

2. Sami ordered 132 dresses for her store. What is 132 rounded to the nearest ten?

Spiral Review (Reviews 2.G.A.1, 2.G.A.3, 3.OA.D.9)

3. What property describes the number sentence?

$$6 + 0 = 6$$

4. Is the sum even or odd?

$$2 + 6$$

5. What name describes this shape?

6. What word describes the equal shares of the shape?

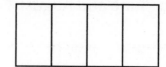

FOR MORE PRACTICE
GO TO THE
Personal Math Trainer

Name _____

Estimate Sums

Essential Question How can you use compatible numbers and rounding to estimate sums?

 Common Core Number and Operations in Base Ten—
3.NBT.A.1 Also 3.NBT.A.2
MATHEMATICAL PRACTICES
MP1, MP2, MP4

Unlock the Problem · Real World

The table shows how many dogs went to Pine Lake Dog Park during the summer months. About how many dogs went to the park during June and August?

You can estimate to find *about* how many or *about* how much. An **estimate** is a number close to an exact amount.

Pine Lake Dog Park

Month	Number of Dogs
June	432
July	317
August	489

One Way Use compatible numbers.

Compatible numbers are numbers that are easy to compute mentally and are close to the real numbers.

$$
\begin{array}{ccc}
432 & \rightarrow & 425 \\
+\ 489 & \rightarrow & +\ 475 \\
\end{array}
$$

So, about _____ dogs went to Pine Lake Dog Park during June and August.

 Math Talk

 MATHEMATICAL PRACTICES ②

Reason Quantitatively Will the sum of the compatible numbers 425 and 475 be greater than or less than the exact sum? Explain.

1. What other compatible numbers could you have used?

_____

2. About how many dogs went to the park during July and August? What compatible numbers could you use to estimate?

_____

Another Way Use place value to round.

432 + 489 = ▮

First, find the place to which you want to round.
Round both numbers to the same place.
The greatest place value of 432 and 489 is
hundreds. So, round to the nearest hundred.

Remember

When you round a number,
you find a number that tells
about how many or *about*
how much.

STEP 1   Round 432 to the nearest hundred.

- Look at the digit to the right of the
  hundreds place.

- Since 3 < 5, the digit 4 stays the same.

- Write zeros for the tens and ones digits.

$$4\ 3\ 2 \qquad \begin{array}{r} 4\ 3\ 2 \\ +\ 4\ 8\ 9 \end{array} \rightarrow \begin{array}{r} \\ + \end{array}$$

STEP 2   Round 489 to the nearest hundred.

- Look at the digit to the right of the
  hundreds place.

- Since 8 > 5, the digit 4 increases by one.

- Write zeros for the tens and ones digits.

$$4\ 8\ 9 \qquad \begin{array}{r} 4\ 3\ 2 \\ +\ 4\ 8\ 9 \end{array} \begin{array}{l} \rightarrow \\ \rightarrow \end{array} \begin{array}{r} 4\ 0\ 0 \\ + \end{array}$$

STEP 3   Find the sum of the rounded numbers.

$$\begin{array}{r} 4\ 3\ 2 \\ +\ 4\ 8\ 9 \end{array} \begin{array}{l} \rightarrow \\ \rightarrow \end{array} \begin{array}{r} 4\ 0\ 0 \\ +\ 5\ 0\ 0 \end{array}$$

So, 432 + 489 is about _____.

Math Talk   MATHEMATICAL PRACTICES ②

Use Reasoning   How can a
number rounded to the nearest
ten be greater than the same
number rounded to the nearest
hundred?

Try This! Estimate the sum.

A Use compatible numbers.

$$\begin{array}{r} 47 \\ +23 \end{array} \begin{array}{l} \rightarrow \\ \rightarrow \end{array} \begin{array}{r} \\ +25 \end{array}$$

B Use rounding.

$$\begin{array}{r} 304 \\ +494 \end{array} \begin{array}{l} \rightarrow \\ \rightarrow \end{array} \begin{array}{r} 300 \\ + \end{array}$$

Name _____

1. Use compatible numbers to complete the problem. Then estimate the sum.

$$428 \rightarrow \underline{\hspace{2cm}}$$
$$+286 \rightarrow + \underline{\hspace{2cm}}$$

Math Talk

MATHEMATICAL PRACTICES ❶

Evaluate What other compatible numbers could you use for 428 and 286?

Use rounding or compatible numbers to estimate the sum.

2. 65
   +23   + _____

☑ 3. 421
   +218   + _____

☑ 4. 369
   +480   + _____

On Your Own

Use rounding or compatible numbers to estimate the sum.

5. 19
   +54   + _____

6. 39
   +42   + _____

7. 327
   +581   + _____

8. Seth bought a pair of sneakers for $48 and a jacket for $64. Explain how you can estimate to find the total amount that he spent for the sneakers and jacket.

_____

_____

9. Elena drove 255 miles last week and 342 miles this week. About how many miles did Elena drive for the two weeks, rounded to the nearest hundred?

_____

10. **GO DEEPER** There are 187 kindergarten students, 203 first-grade students, and 382 second-grade students. About how many students are in the three grades, rounded to the nearest ten? How does the answer change if you round each number to the nearest hundred?

_____

Problem Solving • Applications

Use the table for 11–13.

Dan's Pet Supplies Sold

Month	Pet Bowls	Bags of Pet Food
June	91	419
July	57	370
August	76	228

11. **MATHEMATICAL PRACTICE 2** **Use Reasoning** About how many pet bowls were sold in June and July altogether?

_____

12. **GO DEEPER** Would you estimate there were more pet bowls sold in June or in July and August combined? Explain.

_____

_____

13. **THINK SMARTER** Dan estimated the lowest-monthly sales of both pet bowls and bags of pet food to be about 300. What month had the lowest sales? Explain.

_____

_____

_____

14. **THINK SMARTER** Write each number sentence in the box below the better estimate of the sum.

263 + 189 = ▧   305 + 72 = ▧   195 + 238 = ▧   215 + 289 = ▧

400	500

Estimate Sums

COMMON CORE STANDARD—3.NBT.A.1
Use place value understanding and properties of
operations to perform multi-digit arithmetic.

**Use rounding or compatible numbers
to estimate the sum.**

1. $\begin{array}{r} 171 \\ + 727 \\ \hline \end{array}$ $\begin{array}{r} 175 \\ + 725 \\ \hline 900 \end{array}$

2. $\begin{array}{r} 87 \\ + 34 \\ \hline \end{array}$ $\begin{array}{r} \underline{} \\ + \underline{} \\ \hline \end{array}$

3. $\begin{array}{r} 222 \\ + 203 \\ \hline \end{array}$ $\begin{array}{r} \underline{} \\ + \underline{} \\ \hline \end{array}$

4. $\begin{array}{r} 52 \\ + 39 \\ \hline \end{array}$ $\begin{array}{r} \underline{} \\ + \underline{} \\ \hline \end{array}$

5. $\begin{array}{r} 256 \\ + 321 \\ \hline \end{array}$ $\begin{array}{r} \underline{} \\ + \underline{} \\ \hline \end{array}$

6. $\begin{array}{r} 302 \\ + 412 \\ \hline \end{array}$ $\begin{array}{r} \underline{} \\ + \underline{} \\ \hline \end{array}$

7. $325 + 458$

_____ + _____ = _____

8. $620 + 107$

_____ + _____ = _____

 Problem Solving Real World

9. Stephanie read 72 pages on Sunday
and 83 pages on Monday. About how
many pages did Stephanie read during
the two days?

10. Matt biked 345 miles last month.
This month he has biked 107 miles.
Altogether, about how many miles
has Matt biked last month and
this month?

_____

_____

11. **WRITE** ▸Math Explain how to estimate $368 + 231$
two different ways.

_____

_____

Lesson Check (3.NBT.A.1)

1. The McBrides drove 317 miles on one day and 289 miles on the next day. Estimate the number of miles the McBrides drove during the two days.

_____

_____

2. Ryan counted 63 birds in his backyard last week. This week, he counted 71 birds in his backyard. About how many birds did Ryan count?

_____

_____

Spiral Review (Reviews 2.G.A.1, 3.NBT.A.1, 3.OA.D.9)

3. What name describes this shape?

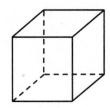

_____

4. Is the sum even or odd?

$$6 + 7$$

_____

5. What is 503 rounded to the nearest hundred?

_____

6. What is 645 rounded to the nearest ten?

_____

FOR MORE PRACTICE
GO TO THE
Personal Math Trainer

Name _____

Mental Math Strategies for Addition

Essential Question What mental math strategies can you use to find sums?

Common Core Number and Operations in Base Ten—
3.NBT.A.2
MATHEMATICAL PRACTICES
MP1, MP4, MP6, MP8

♪ Unlock the Problem (Real World)

The table shows how many musicians are in each section of a symphony orchestra. How many musicians play either string or woodwind instruments?

Orchestra Musicians	
Section	**Number**
Brass	12
Percussion	13
String	57
Woodwind	15

🔑 One Way Count by tens and ones to find 57 + 15.

A Count on to the nearest ten. Then count by tens and ones.

Think: 3 + ■ = 15

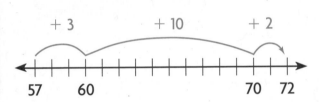

+ 3   + 10   + 2

57   60   70   72

57 + 15 = _____

So, _____ musicians play either string or woodwind instruments.

B Count by tens. Then count by ones.

Think: 10 + 5 = 15

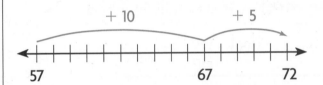

+ 10   + 5

57   67   72

Math Idea
Count on from the greater addend, 57.

Try This! Find 43 + 28. Draw jumps and label the number line to show your thinking.

<--->

So, 43 + 28 = _____.

Math Talk

MATHEMATICAL PRACTICES ④

Use Diagrams Explain another way you can draw the jumps.

Other Ways

A Use compatible numbers to find 178 + 227.

STEP 1 Break apart the addends to make them compatible.

Think: 178 = 175 + 3
227 = 225 + 2

175 and 225 are compatible numbers.

Remember
Compatible numbers are easy to compute mentally and are close to the real numbers.

STEP 2 Find the sums.

178	→	175	+	3
+ 227	→	225	+	2
			+	

STEP 3 Add the sums. _____ + _____ = _____

So, 178 + 227 = _____ .

 Math Talk

MATHEMATICAL PRACTICES ①
Describe another way to use friendly numbers to find the sum.

B Use friendly numbers and adjust to find 38 + 56.

STEP 1 Make a friendly number.

38 + 2 = _____

Think: Add to 38 to make a number with 0 ones.

STEP 2 Since you added 2 to 38, you have to subtract 2 from 56.

56 − 2 = _____

STEP 3 Find the sum. _____ + _____ = _____

So, 38 + 56 = _____ .

Share and Show **MATH BOARD**

1. Count by tens and ones to find 63 + 27. Draw jumps and label the number line to show your thinking.

Think: Count by tens and ones from 63.

```
←————|—————————————————————→
     63
```

63 + 27 = _____

Name _____

2. Use compatible numbers to find 26 + 53.

Think: 26 = 25 + 1   26 + 53 = _____
         53 = 50 + 3

MATHEMATICAL PRACTICES ⑧

Generalize Explain when it is most helpful to use compatible numbers to solve a problem.

Count by tens and ones to find the sum.
Use the number line to show your thinking.

3. 34 + 18 = _____

4. 22 + 49 = _____

On Your Own

Use mental math to find the sum.
Draw or describe the strategy you use.

5. 116 + 203 = _____

6. 18 + 57 = _____

7. MATHEMATICAL PRACTICE ⑥ **Explain a Method** On Friday, 376 people attended the school concert. On Saturday, 427 people attended. On Sunday, 254 people attended. Explain how you can use mental math to find which two nights more people attended the concert.

_____

_____

_____

8. GO DEEPER There are 14 more girls than boys in the school orchestra. There are 19 boys. How many students are in the school orchestra?

_____

Problem Solving • Applications

Use the table for 9–12

9. **MATHEMATICAL PRACTICE ①** **Analyze** How many girls attended school on Monday and Tuesday?

_____

10. **What's the Question?** The answer is 201 students.

_____

_____

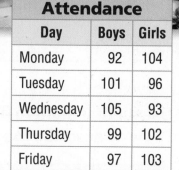

Harrison School Attendance		
Day	Boys	Girls
Monday	92	104
Tuesday	101	96
Wednesday	105	93
Thursday	99	102
Friday	97	103

11. **THINK SMARTER** How many students attended school on Tuesday and Wednesday? Explain how you can find your answer.

_____

_____

_____

_____

12. **GO DEEPER** On which day did the most students attend school?

_____

13. **THINK SMARTER** On Monday, 46 boys and 38 girls bought lunch at school. How many students bought lunch? Explain one way to solve the problem.

_____

_____

Mental Math Strategies
for Addition

 COMMON CORE STANDARD—3.NBT.A.2
*Generalize place value understanding for
multi-digit whole numbers.*

**Count by tens and ones to find the sum.
Use the number line to show your thinking.**

1. $29 + 14 =$ ___43___

2. $36 + 28 =$ _____

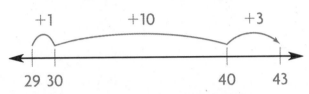

**Use mental math to find the sum.
Draw or describe the strategy you use.**

3. $52 + 19 =$ _____

4. $122 + 306 =$ _____

 Problem Solving (Real World)

5. Shelley spent 17 minutes washing the dishes. She spent 38 minutes cleaning her room. **Explain** how you can use mental math to find how long Shelley spent on the two tasks.

_____

_____

_____

_____

6. It took Marty 42 minutes to write a book report. Then he spent 18 minutes correcting his report. **Explain** how you can use mental math to find how long Marty spent on his book report.

_____

_____

_____

_____

7. **WRITE** ▸*Math* Which method do you prefer to use to find sums—count by tens and ones, use compatible numbers, or use friendly numbers and adjust? Explain why.

_____

Lesson Check (3.NBT.A.2)

1. Sylvia spent 36¢ for a pencil and 55¢ for a notepad. Use mental math to find how much she spent.

2. Will spent 24 minutes putting together a model plane. Then he spent 48 minutes painting the model. How long did Will spend working on the model plane?

_____

_____

Spiral Review (Reviews 2.G.A.1, 2.G.A.3, 3.OA.D.9, 3.NBT.A.1)

3. What name describes this shape?

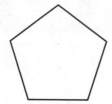

4. What word describes the equal shares of the shape?

_____

_____

5. Tammy wrote the addition problem 5 + 6. Is this sum even or odd?

6. Greg counted 83 cars and 38 trucks in the mall parking lot. Estimate the total number of cars and trucks Greg counted.

_____

_____

_____

_____

FOR MORE PRACTICE
GO TO THE
Personal Math Trainer

Name _____

Use Properties to Add

Essential Question How can you add more than two addends?

CONNECT You have learned the Commutative Property of Addition. You can add two or more numbers in any order and get the same sum.

$$16 + 9 = 9 + 16$$

The **Associative Property of Addition** states that you can group addends in different ways and still get the same sum. It is also called the Grouping Property.

$$(16 + 7) + 23 = 16 + (7 + 23)$$

Common Core — Number and Operations in Base Ten—3.NBT.A.2
MATHEMATICAL PRACTICES
MP2, MP6

Math Idea

You can change the order or the grouping of the addends to make combinations that are easy to add.

Unlock the Problem

Mrs. Gomez sold 23 cucumbers, 38 tomatoes, and 42 peppers at the Farmers' Market. How many vegetables did she sell in all?

Find 23 + 38 + 42.

• Will the sum be closer to 90 or 100?

_____

 Look for an easy way to add.

STEP 1 Line up the numbers by place value.

```
  2 3
  3 8
+ 4 2
─────
```

STEP 2 Group the ones to make them easy to add.

Think: Make a ten.

```
  ¹
  2 3
  3 8 ⎤
+ 4 2 ⎦ 10
─────
    3
```

STEP 3 Group the tens to make them easy to add.

Think: Make doubles.

```
      ¹
  5 < 5 < 2 3
          3 8
        + 4 2
        ─────
        1 0 3
```

Math Talk MATHEMATICAL PRACTICES ②

Reason Abstractly Explain how to group the digits to make them easy to add.

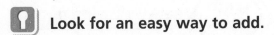
23 + 38 + 42 = _____

So, Mrs. Gomez sold _____ vegetables in all.

Example Use properties to find 36 + 37 + 51.

STEP 1 Line up the numbers by place value.	**STEP 2** Change the grouping.	**STEP 3** Add.
	Think: Adding 37 + 51 first would be easy because there is no regrouping needed.	
3 6 3 7 + 5 1	3 6 3 7 ⟩ 88 + 5 1 ⟩	3 6 + 8 8

So, 36 + 37 + 51 = _____.

Try This! **Use properties to add.**

Ⓐ Find 11 + 16 + 19 + 14.

Think: Use the Commutative Property of Addition to change the order.

1 1   1 1 ⟩ 10
1 6 → 1 9
1 9   1 6 ⟩ 10
+ 1 4   + 1 4

Ⓑ Find 17 + (33 + 45).

Think: Use the Associative Property of Addition to change the grouping.

1 7 ⟩ 50
3 3
+ 4 5 → 5 0
        + 4 5

Share and Show

Math Talk

MATHEMATICAL PRACTICES ⑥

Explain how the Commutative and Associative Properties of Addition are alike and how they are different.

1. Find the sum. Write the addition property you used.

STEP 1	STEP 2	STEP 3	STEP 4
4 6 5 5 + 2 4	5 5 + 2 4	5 5 4 6 ⟩ + 2 4	5 5 + 7 0
_____ Property of Addition		_____ Property of Addition	

Use addition properties and strategies to find the sum.

✓ **2.** $13 + 26 + 54 =$ _____

✓ **3.** $57 + 62 + 56 + 43 =$ _____

On Your Own

Use addition properties and strategies to find the sum.

4. $18 + 39 + 32 =$ _____

5. $13 + 49 + 87 =$ _____

6. GO DEEPER There was a food drive at the school fair. Two local grocery stores each donated 75 boxes of pasta and 30 cans of soup. How many packages of food did both stores donate altogether?

_____

7. GO DEEPER Mrs. Jackson and Mrs. Reed each brought 25 packages of cups, 32 packages of plates, and 25 packages of napkins for the school picnic. How many packages of paper goods did the two mothers bring to the school picnic?

_____

8. Change the order and the grouping of the addends so that you can use mental math to find the sum. Then find the sum.

$43 + 39 + 43 + 11 =$ _____

_____ + _____ + _____ + _____ = _____

Problem Solving • Applications Real World

9. **GO DEEPER** Mr. Arnez bought 32 potatoes, 29 onions, 31 tomatoes, and 28 peppers to make salads for his deli. How many vegetables did he buy?

_____

10. **GO DEEPER** A local community donated books to a school to sell at the school fair. On Wednesday, 74 books were donated. On Thursday, 62 books were donated. On Friday, 36 books were donated. Were more books donated on Wednesday and Thursday or on Thursday and Friday?

_____

11. **MATHEMATICAL PRACTICE ②** **Reason Abstractly** What is the unknown number? Which property did you use?

$$(\blacksquare + 8) + 32 = 49$$

_____

12. **THINK SMARTER** Change the order or grouping to find the sum. Explain how you used properties to find the sum.

$$63 + 86 + 77$$

_____

_____

13. **THINK SMARTER** For numbers 13a–13d, choose Yes or No to tell whether the number sentence shows the Associative Property of Addition.

13a. $(86 + 7) + 93 = 86 + (7 + 93)$ ○ Yes   ○ No

13b. $86 + 7 = 7 + 86$ ○ Yes   ○ No

13c. $86 + 0 = 86$ ○ Yes   ○ No

13d. $86 = 80 + 6$ ○ Yes   ○ No

Use Properties to Add

Common Core
COMMON CORE STANDARD—3.NBT.A.2
Use place value understanding and properties of operations to perform multi-digit arithmetic.

Use addition properties and strategies to find the sum.

1. $34 + 62 + 51 + 46 =$ ___193___

$$
\begin{array}{r}
34 \\
46 \\
62 \\
+51 \\
\hline
193
\end{array}
$$

2. $27 + 68 + 43 =$ _____

3. $42 + 36 + 18 =$ _____

4. $74 + 35 + 16 + 45 =$ _____

Problem Solving (Real World)

5. A pet shelter has 26 dogs, 37 cats, and 14 gerbils. How many of these animals are in the pet shelter in all?

6. The pet shelter bought 85 pounds of dog food, 50 pounds of cat food, and 15 pounds of gerbil food. How many pounds of animal food did the pet shelter buy?

_____

_____

7. **WRITE** ▸*Math* Give an example of an addition problem in which you would and would not group the addends differently to add.

_____

_____

Lesson Check (3.NBT.A.2)

1. At summer camp there are 52 boys, 47 girls, and 18 adults. How many people are at summer camp?

   _____

2. At camp, 32 children are swimming, 25 are fishing, and 28 are canoeing. How many children are swimming, fishing, or canoeing?

   _____

Spiral Review (Reviews 2.MD.A.3, 3.NBT.A.1)

3. Hank estimated the width of the door to his classroom in feet. What is a reasonable estimate?

   _____

   _____

4. Garth estimated the height of the door to his classroom in meters. What is a reasonable estimate?

   _____

   _____

5. Jeff's dog weighs 76 pounds. What is the dog's weight rounded to the nearest ten pounds?

   _____

   _____

6. Ms. Kirk drove 164 miles in the morning and 219 miles in the afternoon. Estimate the total number of miles she drove that day.

   _____

   _____

FOR MORE PRACTICE
GO TO THE
Personal Math Trainer

Name _____

Use the Break Apart Strategy to Add

Essential Question How can you use the break apart strategy to add 3-digit numbers?

Common Core — **Number and Operations in Base Ten—3.NBT.A.2** *Also 3.NBT.A.1, 3.OA.D.8*

MATHEMATICAL PRACTICES
MP2, MP5, MP6

? Unlock the Problem

There are more zoos in Germany than in any other country. At one time, there were 355 zoos in the United States and 414 zoos in Germany. How many zoos were there in the United States and Germany altogether?

You can use the break apart strategy to find sums.

Example 1 Add. 355 + 414

STEP 1 Estimate. 400 + 400 = _____

_____

STEP 2 Break apart the addends.
Start with the hundreds.
Then add each place value.

STEP 3 Add the sums.

    700 + 60 + 9 = _____

So, there were _____ zoos in the United States and Germany altogether.

Math Talk

MATHEMATICAL PRACTICES ②

Use Reasoning Do you think the sum will be greater than or less than 800? Explain.

$$355 \quad = \quad 300 + \boxed{} + 5$$
$$+\,414 \quad = \quad \boxed{} + 10 + 4$$
$$\overline{700 + 60 + 9}$$

Example 2 Add. 467 + 208

STEP 1 Estimate. 500 + 200 = _____

_____

STEP 2 Break apart the addends.
Start with the hundreds.
Then add each place value.

$$467 \quad = \quad 400 + \boxed{} + \boxed{}$$
$$+\,208 \quad = \quad \boxed{} + 0 + 8$$
$$\overline{600 + 60 + 15}$$

STEP 3 Add the sums.

    600 + 60 + 15 = _____

So, 467 + 208 = _____.

Try This! Use the break apart strategy to find 343 + 259.

Estimate. 300 + 300 = _____

$$343 = 300 + \boxed{} + \boxed{}$$
$$+\ 259 = \underline{\boxed{} + \boxed{} + \boxed{}}$$
$$\boxed{} + \boxed{} + \boxed{} = \boxed{}$$

1. **MATHEMATICAL PRACTICE ⑥** **Explain** why there is a zero in the tens place in the sum.

_____

_____

_____

2. How do you know your answer is reasonable?

_____

_____

 **Share and Show** MATH BOARD

1. Complete.
   Estimate: 400 + 400 = _____

$$425 = 400 + \boxed{} + 5$$
$$+\ 362 = \underline{\boxed{} + 60 + \boxed{}}$$
$$700 + \boxed{} + 7 = \boxed{}$$

So, 425 + 362 = _____.

2. Write the numbers the break apart strategy shows.

$$\boxed{} = 100 + 30 + 4$$
$$+\ \underline{\boxed{}} = \underline{200 + 40 + 9}$$
$$= 300 + 70 + 13$$

 Math Talk

MATHEMATICAL PRACTICES ②

Reason Abstractly
Explain how the break apart strategy uses expanded forms of numbers.

Estimate. Then use the break apart strategy to find the sum.

3. Estimate: _____

$142 =$
$+436 =$

4. Estimate: _____

$459 =$
$+213 =$

5. Estimate: _____

$291 =$
$+420 =$

6. Estimate: _____

$654 =$
$+243 =$

On Your Own

Estimate. Then use the break apart strategy to find the sum.

7. Estimate: _____

$435 =$
$+312 =$

8. Estimate: _____

$163 =$
$+205 =$

9. There are three baby giraffes at the zoo. One weighs 148 pounds, one weighs 125 pounds, and the other weighs 137 pounds. What is their combined weight?

_____

10. During one week, a bowling alley had 348 customers on Thursday night and 465 customers on Friday night. The following week, the bowling alley had 212 customers on Thursday and 318 customers on Friday. About how many customers did the bowling alley have during those 4 days?

_____

Practice: Copy and Solve **Estimate. Then solve.**

11. $163 + 205$ **12.** $543 + 215$ **13.** $213 + 328$ **14.** $372 + 431$

15. $152 + 304$ **16.** $268 + 351$ **17.** $413 + 257$ **18.** $495 + 312$

Problem Solving • Applications

Use the table for 19–20.

Number of Students	
School	**Number**
Harrison	304
Montgomery	290
Bryant	421

19. GO DEEPER Which two schools together have fewer than 600 students? Explain.

_____

_____

_____

_____

20. THINK SMARTER The number of students in Collins School is more than double the number of students in Montgomery School. What is the least number of students that could attend Collins School?

_____

21. **What's the Error?** Lexi used the break apart strategy to find 145 + 203. Describe her error. What is the correct sum?

$$100 + 40 + 5$$
$$+\ 200 + 30 + 0$$
$$\overline{300 + 70 + 5} = 375$$

_____

22. MATHEMATICAL PRACTICE ⑤ **Communicate** Is the sum of 425 and 390 less than or greater than 800? How do you know?

_____

_____

23. THINK SMARTER What is the sum of 421 and 332? Show your work.

_____

© Houghton Mifflin Harcourt Publishing Company

Name _____

Use the Break Apart Strategy to Add

COMMON CORE STANDARD—3.NBT.A.2
Use place value understanding and properties of operations to perform multi-digit arithmetic.

Estimate. Then use the break apart strategy to find the sum.

1. Estimate: __800__

$$
\begin{array}{rcl}
325 & = & 300 + 20 + 5 \\
+\ 494 & = & 400 + 90 + 4 \\
\hline
& & 700 + 110 + 9
\end{array}
$$

2. Estimate: _____

$$
\begin{array}{rcl}
518 & = & \\
+\ 372 & = &
\end{array}
$$

3. Estimate: _____

$$
\begin{array}{rcl}
731 & = & \\
+\ 207 & = &
\end{array}
$$

4. Estimate: _____

$$
\begin{array}{rcl}
495 & = & \\
+\ 254 & = &
\end{array}
$$

Problem Solving · Real World

Use the table for 5–6.

5. Laura is making a building using Set A and Set C. How many blocks can she use in her building?

_____

6. Clark is making a building using Set B and Set C. How many blocks can he use in his building?

_____

Build-It Blocks	
Set	Number of Blocks
A	165
B	188
C	245

7. **WRITE** ▸*Math* Explain how to use the break apart strategy to find 247 + 358.

_____

_____

Lesson Check (3.NBT.A.2)

1. Arthur read two books last week. One book has 216 pages. The other book has 327 pages. Altogether, how many pages are in the two books?

2. One skeleton in a museum has 189 bones. Another skeleton has 232 bones. How many bones are in the two skeletons?

Spiral Review (Reviews 2.MD.C.8, 3.OA.D.9, 3.NBT.A.2)

3. Culver has 1 quarter, 3 dimes, and 1 penny. How much money does he have?

4. Felicia has 34 quarters, 25 dimes, and 36 pennies. How many coins does Felicia have?

5. Jonas wrote $9 + 8 = 17$. What number sentence shows the Commutative Property of Addition?

6. At Kennedy School there are 37 girls and 36 boys in the third grade. How many students are in the third grade at Kennedy School?

FOR MORE PRACTICE
GO TO THE
Personal Math Trainer

Name _____

Use Place Value to Add

Essential Question How can you use place value to add 3-digit numbers?

Common Core
Number and Operations in Base Ten—3.NBT.A.2
MATHEMATICAL PRACTICES
MP1, MP2, MP6

Unlock the Problem Real World

Dante is planning a trip to Illinois. His airplane leaves from Dallas, Texas, and stops in Tulsa, Oklahoma. Then it flies from Tulsa to Chicago, Illinois. How many miles does Dante fly?

Chicago

585 miles

Tulsa

236 miles

Dallas

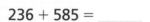 **Use place value to add two addends.**

Add. $236 + 585$

Estimate. $200 + 600 =$ _____

STEP 1

Add the ones. Regroup the ones as tens and ones.

$$\begin{array}{r} \overset{1}{2}\,3\,6 \\ +\ 5\,8\,5 \\ \hline \end{array}$$

STEP 2

Add the tens. Regroup the tens as hundreds and tens.

$$\begin{array}{r} \overset{1}{2}\,\overset{1}{3}\,6 \\ +\ 5\,8\,5 \\ \hline 1 \end{array}$$

STEP 3

Add the hundreds.

$$\begin{array}{r} \overset{1}{2}\,\overset{1}{3}\,6 \\ +\ 5\,8\,5 \\ \hline 2\,1 \end{array}$$

$236 + 585 =$ _____

So, Dante flies _____ miles.

Since _____ is close to the estimate of _____, the answer is reasonable.

! ERROR Alert

Remember to add the regrouped ten and hundred.

- You can also use the Commutative Property of Addition to check your work. Change the order of the addends and find the sum.

$$\begin{array}{r} 5\,8\,5 \\ +\,2\,3\,6 \\ \hline \end{array}$$

Try This! Find 563 + 48 in two ways.

Estimate. 550 + 50 = _____

A **Use the break apart strategy.**

563 =   500 + ▢ + ▢
+ 48 =   40 + ▢
_____

▢ + ▢ + ▢ = ▢

B **Use place value.**

563
+ 48
_____
▢

Use place value to add three addends.

A **Add.** 140 + 457 + 301

Estimate. 150 + 450 + 300 = _____

STEP 1 Add the ones.

   1 4 0
   4 5 7
+ 3 0 1
_____
     ▢

STEP 2 Add the tens.

   1 4 0
   4 5 7
+ 3 0 1
_____
   ▢ 8

STEP 3 Add the hundreds.

   1 4 0
   4 5 7
+ 3 0 1
_____
 ▢ 9 8

So, 140 + 457 + 301 = _____.

B **Add.** 173 + 102 + 328

Estimate. 200 + 100 + 300 = _____

STEP 1 Add the ones. Regroup the ones as tens and ones.

    1
  1 7 3
  1 0 2
+ 3 2 8
_____
     ▢

STEP 2 Add the tens. Regroup the tens as hundreds and tens.

  1 1
  1 7 3
  1 0 2
+ 3 2 8
_____
   ▢ 3

STEP 3 Add the hundreds.

  1 1
  1 7 3
  1 0 2
+ 3 2 8
_____
 ▢ 0 3

So, 173 + 102 + 328 = _____.

Name _____

1. **Circle the problem in which you need to regroup. Use the strategy that is easier to find the sum.**

   a. 496 + 284

   b. 482 + 506

Estimate. Then find the sum.

✓ 2. Estimate: _____

$$251 \\ +345$$

3. Estimate: _____

$$479 \\ +395$$

✓ 4. Estimate: _____

$$686 \\ +314$$

5. Estimate: _____

$$231 \\ 410 \\ +158$$

 Math Talk

MATHEMATICAL PRACTICES ①

Evaluate How can you compute 403 + 201 mentally?

On Your Own

Practice: Copy and Solve **Estimate. Then solve.**

6. 253 + 376

7. 654 + 263

8. 321 + 439 + 112

9. 182 + 321

10. 701 + 108

11. 543 + 372 + 280

MATHEMATICAL PRACTICE ② **Use Reasoning** **Algebra** **Find the unknown digits.**

12.
$$1\ \square\ 4 \\ +\ \square\ 3\ \square \\ \overline{2\ 5\ 7}$$

13.
$$\square\ 7\ \square \\ +6\ \square\ 4 \\ \overline{9\ 8\ 6}$$

14.
$$2\ \square\ \square \\ +\ \square\ 2\ 9 \\ \overline{6\ 8\ 2}$$

15.
$$3\ \square\ \square \\ +\ \square\ 1\ 7 \\ \overline{9\ 0\ 3}$$

16. **GO DEEPER** There are 431 crayons in a box and 204 crayons on the floor. About how many fewer than 1,000 crayons are there? Estimate. Then solve.

_____

🔑 Unlock the Problem

17. **THINK SMARTER** A plane flew 187 miles from New York City, New York, to Boston, Massachusetts. It then flew 273 miles from Boston to Philadelphia, Pennsylvania. The plane flew the same distance on the return trip. How many miles did the plane fly?

a. What do you need to find?

_____

b. What is an estimate of the total distance?

_____

c. Show the steps you used to solve the problem.

d. How do you know your answer is reasonable?

_____

_____

e. The total distance is _____ miles round trip.

---

18. **THINK SMARTER** Help Max find the sum of the problem.

```
    4 5 1
    2 4 6
  + 2 2 2
```

For numbers 18a–18d, choose Yes or No to tell if Max should regroup.

18a. Regroup the ones. ○ Yes ○ No

18b. Add the regrouped ten. ○ Yes ○ No

18c. Regroup the tens. ○ Yes ○ No

18d. Add the regrouped hundred. ○ Yes ○ No

Use Place Value to Add

Common Core   **COMMON CORE STANDARD—3.NBT.A.2**
*Use place value understanding and properties
of operations to perform multi-digit arithmetic.*

Estimate. Then find the sum.

1. Estimate: _____

$$\begin{array}{r} ^{1} \\ 324 \\ + \ 285 \\ \hline 609 \end{array}$$

2. Estimate: _____

$$\begin{array}{r} 519 \\ + \ 347 \\ \hline \end{array}$$

3. Estimate: _____

$$\begin{array}{r} 323 \\ + \ 151 \\ \hline \end{array}$$

4. Estimate: _____

$$\begin{array}{r} 169 \\ + \ 354 \\ \hline \end{array}$$

5. Estimate: _____

$$\begin{array}{r} 127 \\ + \ 290 \\ \hline \end{array}$$

6. Estimate: _____

$$\begin{array}{r} 258 \\ + \ 565 \\ \hline \end{array}$$

7. Estimate: _____

$$\begin{array}{r} 311 \\ + \ 298 \\ \hline \end{array}$$

8. Estimate: _____

$$\begin{array}{r} 534 \\ + \ 256 \\ \hline \end{array}$$

Problem Solving · Real World

9. Mark has 215 baseball cards. Emily has 454 baseball cards. How many baseball cards do Mark and Emily have altogether?

10. Jason has 330 pennies. Richie has 268 pennies. Rachel has 381 pennies. Which two students have more than 700 pennies combined?

_____

11. **WRITE** ▸*Math* Explain one way to add 3-digit numbers.

_____

_____

Lesson Check (3.NBT.A.2)

1. There are 167 students in the third grade. The same number of students is in the fourth grade. How many third graders and fourth graders are there?

2. Jamal read a book with 128 pages. Then he read a book with 179 pages. How many pages did Jamal read?

_____

_____

Spiral Review (3.NBT.A.1, 3.NBT.A.2)

3. Adam travels 248 miles on Monday. He travels 167 miles on Tuesday. Estimate the total number of miles Adam travels.

4. Wes made $14, $62, $40, and $36 mowing lawns. How much did he make mowing lawns?

_____

_____

_____

_____

5. There are 24 students in Mrs. Cole's class and 19 students in Mr. Garmen's class. How many students are in the two classes?

6. There were 475 children at the baseball game on Sunday. What is 475 rounded to the nearest ten?

_____

_____

FOR MORE PRACTICE
GO TO THE
Personal Math Trainer

Name _____

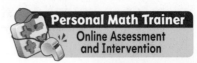
Vocabulary

Choose the best term from the box.

Vocabulary

Commutative Property
of Addition
compatible numbers
Identity Property of
Addition
pattern

1. A _____ is an ordered set of numbers or objects in which the order helps you predict what comes next. (p. 5)

2. The _____ states that when you add zero to any number, the sum is that number. (p. 5)

Concepts and Skills

Is the sum even or odd? Write *even* or *odd*. (3.OA.D.9)

3. $8 + 5$ _____

4. $9 + 7$ _____

5. $4 + 6$ _____

Use rounding or compatible numbers to estimate the sum. (3.NBT.A.1)

6.
$$
\begin{array}{r}
56 \\
+32 \\
\hline
\end{array}
$$
+ _____

7.
$$
\begin{array}{r}
271 \\
+425 \\
\hline
\end{array}
$$
+ _____

8.
$$
\begin{array}{r}
328 \\
+127 \\
\hline
\end{array}
$$
+ _____

Use mental math to find the sum. (3.NBT.A.2)

9. $46 + 14 =$ _____

10. $39 + 243 =$ _____

11. $326 + 402 =$ _____

Estimate. Then find the sum. (3.NBT.A.2)

12. Estimate: _____
$$
\begin{array}{r}
356 \\
+442 \\
\hline
\end{array}
$$

13. Estimate: _____
$$
\begin{array}{r}
164 \\
+230 \\
\hline
\end{array}
$$

14. Estimate: _____
$$
\begin{array}{r}
545 \\
+139 \\
\hline
\end{array}
$$

15. Estimate: _____
$$
\begin{array}{r}
437 \\
+184 \\
\hline
\end{array}
$$

16. Nancy planted 77 daisies, 48 roses, and 39 tulips. About how many roses and tulips did she plant? (3.NBT.A.1)

_____

17. Tomas collected 139 cans for recycling on Monday, and twice that number on Tuesday. How many cans did he collect on Tuesday? (3.NBT.A.2)

_____

18. There are 294 boys and 332 girls in the Hill School. How many students are in the school? (3.NBT.A.2)

_____

19. GO DEEPER Monday's art group made 25 paper models. Tuesday's group made 32 paper models. Wednesday's group made 15 paper models. How many paper models did the groups make? (3.NBT.A.2)

_____

Estimate Differences

Essential Question How can you use compatible numbers and rounding to estimate differences?

Common Core
Number and Operations in Base Ten—
3.NBT.A.1 *Also 3.NBT.A.2*
MATHEMATICAL PRACTICES
MP2, MP3, MP6

Unlock the Problem

The largest yellowfin tuna caught by fishers weighed 387 pounds. The largest grouper caught weighed 436 pounds. About how much more did the grouper weigh than the yellowfin tuna?

You can estimate to find *about* how much more.

One Way Use compatible numbers.

Think: Compatible numbers are numbers that are easy to compute mentally and are close to the real numbers.

$$
\begin{array}{rcr}
436 & \to & 425 \\
-387 & \to & -375 \\
\hline
& &
\end{array}
$$

So, the grouper weighed about

_____ pounds more than the yellowfin tuna.

- Does the question ask for an exact answer? How do you know?

_____

_____

- Circle the numbers you need to use.

Yellowfin tuna

Grouper

- What other compatible numbers could you have used?

_____

Try This! Estimate. Use compatible numbers.

Ⓐ
$$
\begin{array}{rcr}
73 & \to & 75 \\
-22 & \to & - \\
\hline
& &
\end{array}
$$

Ⓑ
$$
\begin{array}{rcr}
376 & \to & \\
-148 & \to & -150 \\
\hline
& &
\end{array}
$$

🔓 Another Way Use place value to round.

$436 - 387 = \blacksquare$

STEP 1 Round 436 to the nearest ten.

> **Think:** Find the place to which you want to round. Look at the digit to the right.

- Look at the digit in the ones place.
- Since 6 > 5, the digit 3 increases by one.
- Write a zero for the ones place.

$$
\begin{array}{ccc}
4\,3\,6 & 4\,3\,6 & \rightarrow \\
\uparrow & -\,3\,8\,7 & \overline{} \\
\end{array}
$$

STEP 2 Round 387 to the nearest ten.

- Look at the digit in the ones place.
- Since 7 > 5, the digit 8 increases by one.
- Write a zero for the ones place.

$$
\begin{array}{ccc}
 & 4\,3\,6 & \rightarrow \quad 4\,4\,0 \\
3\,8\,7 & -\,3\,8\,7 & \rightarrow \\
\uparrow & & \overline{-} \\
\end{array}
$$

STEP 3 Find the difference of the rounded numbers.

$$
\begin{array}{ccc}
4\,3\,6 & \rightarrow & 4\,4\,0 \\
-\,3\,8\,7 & \rightarrow & -\,3\,9\,0 \\
\hline
\end{array}
$$

So, $436 - 387$ is about _____ .

Try This! Estimate. Use place value to round.

A
$$
\begin{array}{ll}
761 & \rightarrow \quad 800 \\
-528 & \rightarrow \quad - \\
\hline
\end{array}
$$

> **Think:** Round both numbers to the same place value.

B
$$
\begin{array}{ll}
642 & \rightarrow \\
-287 & \rightarrow \quad -300 \\
\hline
\end{array}
$$

 Math Talk

Name _____

1. Use compatible numbers to complete the problem. Then estimate the difference.

$$546 \rightarrow \quad 550$$
$$-209 \rightarrow -\underline{\quad}$$

Math Talk

MATHEMATICAL PRACTICES ⑥

Explain a Method How does rounding help you to estimate?

Use rounding or compatible numbers to estimate the difference.

2.
$$57$$
$$-21$$
$$-\underline{\quad}$$

✓ 3.
$$642$$
$$-137$$
$$-\underline{\quad}$$

✓ 4.
$$374$$
$$-252$$
$$-\underline{\quad}$$

On Your Own

Use rounding or compatible numbers to estimate the difference.

5.
$$67$$
$$-24$$
$$-\underline{\quad}$$

6.
$$81$$
$$-39$$
$$-\underline{\quad}$$

7.
$$936$$
$$-421$$
$$-\underline{\quad}$$

8. There are 298 students in the third grade. If 227 students take the bus to school, about how many students do not take the bus?

_____

9. *GO DEEPER* A museum has 324 oil paintings, 227 watercolors paintings, and 158 statues. About how many more oil and watercolor paintings does the museum have than statues?

_____

10. *GO DEEPER* There are 262 students in the second grade and 298 students in the third grade. If 227 students ride their bikes to school, about how many students do not ride their bikes?

_____

Problem Solving • Applications

Use the table for 11–13.

11. **MATHEMATICAL PRACTICE ③** **Use Counterexamples** Melissa said the estimated difference between the weight of the Pacific halibut and the yellowfin tuna is zero. Do you agree or disagree? Explain.

_____

_____

_____

Largest Saltwater Fish Caught	
Type of Fish	**Weight in Pounds**
Pacific Halibut	459
Conger	133
Yellowfin Tuna	387

12. **What's the Question?** The answer is about 500 pounds.

_____

_____

WRITE ▸ *Math* • **Show Your Work**

13. **THINK SMARTER** About how much more is the total weight of the Pacific halibut and conger than the weight of the yellowfin tuna? Explain.

_____

_____

_____

_____

Personal Math Trainer

14. **THINK SMARTER ✛** A total of 907 people went to a fishing tournament. Of these people, 626 arrived before noon. Alina estimates that fewer than 300 people arrived in the afternoon. How did she estimate? Explain.

_____

_____

Estimate Differences

COMMON CORE STANDARD—3.NBT.A.1
Use place value understanding and properties of
operations to perform multi-digit arithmetic.

Use rounding or compatible numbers to estimate the difference.

1.
$$\begin{array}{r} 40 \\ -13 \\ \hline \end{array} \qquad \begin{array}{r} 40 \\ -10 \\ \hline 30 \end{array}$$

2.
$$\begin{array}{r} 762 \\ -332 \\ \hline \end{array} \qquad \begin{array}{r} \underline{\quad} \\ -\underline{\quad} \\ \hline \end{array}$$

3.
$$\begin{array}{r} 823 \\ -242 \\ \hline \end{array} \qquad \begin{array}{r} \underline{\quad} \\ -\underline{\quad} \\ \hline \end{array}$$

4.
$$\begin{array}{r} 98 \\ -49 \\ \hline \end{array} \qquad \begin{array}{r} \underline{\quad} \\ -\underline{\quad} \\ \hline \end{array}$$

5.
$$\begin{array}{r} 287 \\ -162 \\ \hline \end{array} \qquad \begin{array}{r} \underline{\quad} \\ -\underline{\quad} \\ \hline \end{array}$$

6.
$$\begin{array}{r} 359 \\ -224 \\ \hline \end{array} \qquad \begin{array}{r} \underline{\quad} \\ -\underline{\quad} \\ \hline \end{array}$$

7. $771 - 531$

___ − ___ = ___

8. $299 - 61$

___ − ___ = ___

Problem Solving ·Real· World

9. Ben has a collection of 812 stamps. He gives his brother 345 stamps. About how many stamps does Ben have left?

_____

_____

10. Savannah's bakery sold 284 loaves of bread in September. In October the bakery sold 89 loaves. About how many more loaves of bread did Savannah's bakery sell in September than in October?

_____

_____

11. **WRITE** ▸Math Explain how to estimate $586 - 321$ two different ways.

_____

_____

Lesson Check (3.NBT.A.1)

1. Jorge has 708 baseball cards and 394 basketball cards. About how many more baseball cards than basketball cards does Jorge have?

2. Danika is making necklaces. She has 512 silver beads and 278 blue beads. About how many more silver than blue beads does Danika have?

Spiral Review (3.NBT.A.1, 3.NBT.A.2)

3. A store manager ordered 402 baseball caps and 122 ski caps. Estimate the total number of caps the manager ordered.

4. Autumn collected 129 seashells at the beach. What is 129 rounded to the nearest ten?

5. Find the sum.

$$\begin{array}{r} 585 \\ + 346 \\ \hline \end{array}$$

6. Julie made $22, $55, $38, and $25 babysitting. How much did she make babysitting?

FOR MORE PRACTICE
GO TO THE
Personal Math Trainer

Name _____

Mental Math Strategies for Subtraction

Essential Question What mental math strategies can you use to find differences?

Common Core Number and Operations in Base Ten—
3.NBT.A.2
MATHEMATICAL PRACTICES
MP2, MP3, MP6

🔑 Unlock the Problem Real World

A sunflower can grow to be very tall. Dylan is 39 inches tall. She watered a sunflower that grew to be 62 inches tall. How many inches shorter was Dylan than the sunflower?

🔑 One Way Use a number line to find 62 − 39.

Ⓐ Count up by tens and then ones.

Think: Start at 39. Count up to 62.

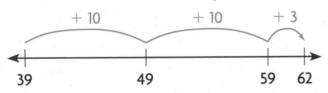

Add the lengths of the jumps to find the difference.

$$10 + 10 + 3 = \underline{\hspace{1cm}}$$

$$62 - 39 = \underline{\hspace{1cm}}$$

So, Dylan was _____ inches shorter than the sunflower.

Ⓑ Take away tens and ones.

Think: Start at 62. Count back 39.

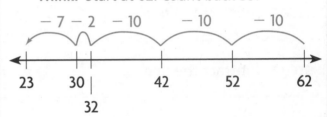

Take away lengths of jumps to end on the difference.

Math Talk

MATHEMATICAL PRACTICES ③

Compare Representations Compare the number lines. Explain where the answer is on each one.

🔑 Other Ways

Ⓐ Use friendly numbers and adjust to find 74 − 28.

STEP 1 Make the number you subtract a friendly number.

Think: Add to 28 to make a number with 0 ones.

$$28 + 2 = \underline{\hspace{1cm}}$$

STEP 2 Since you added 2 to 28, you have to add 2 to 74.

$$74 + 2 = \underline{\hspace{1cm}}$$

STEP 3 Find the difference.

$$\underline{\hspace{0.8cm}} - \underline{\hspace{0.8cm}} = \underline{\hspace{0.8cm}}$$

So, $74 - 28 = \underline{\hspace{1cm}}$.

Try This! **Use friendly numbers to subtract 9 and 99.**

- **Find 36 – 9.**

  Think: 9 is 1 less than 10.

  Subtract 10. $36 - 10 =$ _____

  Then add 1.   _____ $+ 1 =$ _____

  So, $36 - 9 =$ _____ .

- **Find 423 – 99.**

  Think: 99 is 1 less than 100.

  Subtract 100. $423 - 100 =$ _____

  Then add 1.   _____ $+ 1 =$ _____

  So, $423 - 99 =$ _____ .

Ⓑ **Use the break apart strategy to find 458 – 136.**

STEP 1 Subtract the hundreds. $400 - 100 =$ _____

_____

STEP 2 Subtract the tens. $50 - 30 =$ _____

_____

STEP 3 Subtract the ones. $8 - 6 =$ _____

_____

STEP 4 Add the differences.   _____ $+$ _____ $+$ _____ $=$ _____

So, $458 - 136 =$ _____ .

Share and Show

1. Find $61 - 24$. Draw jumps and label the number line to show your thinking.

   Think: Take away tens and ones.

   ⟵——————————————————————————|——⟶
                                                    61

   $61 - 24 =$ _____

2. Use friendly numbers to find the difference.

   $86 - 42 =$ _____   **Think:** $42 - 2 = 40$
                                          $86 - 2 = 84$

Math Talk

MATHEMATICAL PRACTICES ⑥

Describe the break apart strategy for subtracting numbers.

Name _____

Use mental math to find the difference.
Draw or describe the strategy you use.

3. $56 - 38 =$ _____

4. $435 - 121 =$ _____

Problem Solving • Applications (Real World)

5. **MATHEMATICAL PRACTICE ③ Make Arguments** Erica used friendly numbers to find $43 - 19$. She added 1 to 19 and subtracted 1 from 43. What is Erica's error? Explain.

_____

_____

6. **THINK SMARTER** The farm shop had 68 small bags of bird treats and 39 large bags of bird treats on a shelf. If Jill buys 5 small bags and 1 large bag, how many more small bags than large bags of bird treats are left on the shelf?

_____

_____

_____

7. **THINK SMARTER** There were 87 sunflowers at the flower shop in the morning. There were 56 sunflowers left at the end of the day. How many sunflowers were sold? Explain a way to solve the problem.

_____

_____

Compare and Contrast

Emus and ostriches are the world's largest birds. They are alike in many ways and different in others.

When you compare things, you decide how they are alike. When you contrast things, you decide how they are different.

The table shows some facts about emus and ostriches. Use the information on this page to compare and contrast the birds.

Facts About Emus and Ostriches		
	Emus	**Ostriches**
Can they fly?	No	No
Where do they live?	Australia	Africa
How much do they weigh?	About 120 pounds	About 300 pounds
How tall are they?	About 72 inches	About 108 inches
How fast can they run?	About 40 miles per hour	About 40 miles per hour

Ostrich

Emu

8. How are emus and ostriches alike? How are they different?

   Alike: 1. _____

            2. _____

   Different: 1. _____

              2. _____

              3. _____

9. **GO DEEPER** What if two emus weigh 117 pounds and 123 pounds, and an ostrich weighs 338 pounds. How much more does the ostrich weigh than the two emus?

   _____

Mental Math Strategies
for Subtraction

COMMON CORE STANDARD—3.NBT.A.2
Use place value understanding and properties of operations to perform multi-digit arithmetic.

**Use mental math to find the difference.
Draw or describe the strategy you use.**

1. $74 - 39 =$ ____35____

$$-5 \quad -4 \quad -10 \qquad -10 \qquad -10$$

35   40   44   54   64   74

2. $93 - 28 =$ _____

3. $51 - 12 =$ _____

4. $76 - 23 =$ _____

Problem Solving · Real World

5. Ruby has 78 books. Thirty-one of the books are on shelves. The rest are still packed in boxes. How many of Ruby's books are still in boxes?

6. Kyle has 130 pins in his collection. He has 76 of the pins displayed on his wall. The rest are in a drawer. How many of Kyle's pins are in a drawer?

7. **WRITE** ▸*Math* Give one example of when you would use the friendly numbers strategy to subtract. Explain why.

_____

_____

Lesson Check (3.NBT.A.2)

1. One day, a baker made 54 fruit pies. At the end of the day, only 9 of the pies were NOT sold. How many pies were sold that day?

_____

2. George's father bought a 50-pound bag of wild bird seed. At the end of two weeks, 36 pounds of seed were left in the bag. How many pounds of seed had been used?

_____

Spiral Review (3.NBT.A.1, 3.NBT.A.2)

3. For a party, Shaun blew up 36 red balloons, 28 white balloons, and 24 blue balloons. How many total balloons did he blow up?

_____

4. Tiffany has read 115 pages of her book. She has 152 pages left to read. How many pages are in the book?

_____

5. The flower shop had 568 flowers on Monday. By Tuesday, the shop had 159 flowers left. About how many flowers had been sold?

_____

6. There are 383 books in one section of the school library. Of the books, 165 are fiction books. Estimate the number of books in that section that are NOT fiction.

_____

FOR MORE PRACTICE
GO TO THE
Personal Math Trainer

Use Place Value to Subtract

Essential Question How can you use place value to subtract 3-digit numbers?

 Common Core **Number and Operations in Base Ten—3.NBT.A.2** *Also 3.NBT.A.1*
MATHEMATICAL PRACTICES
MP1, MP2, MP5

Unlock the Problem

Ava sold 473 tickets for the school play. Kim sold 294 tickets. How many more tickets did Ava sell than Kim?

 Use place value to subtract.

Subtract. 473 − 294

Estimate. 475 − 300 = _____

- Do you need to combine or compare the number of tickets sold?

  _____

- Circle the numbers you will need to use.

STEP 1

Subtract the ones.
3 < 4, so regroup.

7 tens 3 ones =

6 tens _____ ones

```
    6 13
  4 7 3
 − 2 9 4
  ▢
```

STEP 2

Subtract the tens.
6 < 9, so regroup.

4 hundreds 6 tens =

3 hundreds _____ tens

```
   3 6 13
   4 7 3
 − 2 9 4
       9
```

STEP 3

Subtract the hundreds.
Add to check your answer.

```
    16           1 1
   3 6 13        1 7 9
   4 7 3       + 2 9 4
 − 2 9 4         4 7 3
     7 9
```

So, Ava sold _____ more tickets than Kim.

Since _____ is close to the estimate of _____, the answer is reasonable.

Math Idea
Addition and subtraction undo each other. So you can use addition to check subtraction.

Try This! Use place value to subtract. Use addition to check your work.

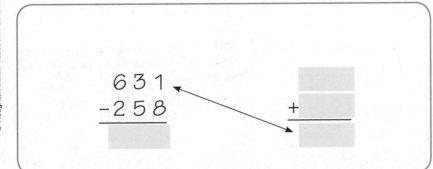

```
   6 3 1              ▢
 − 2 5 8          +   ▢
   ▢                  ▢
```

Example Use place value to find 890 − 765.

Estimate. 900 − 750 = _____

STEP 1	STEP 2	STEP 3
Subtract the ones. Regroup the tens as tens and ones.	Subtract the tens.	Subtract the hundreds. Add to check your answer.

STEP 1:
```
    8 10
  8 9̸ 0̸
 −7 6 5
```

STEP 2:
```
    8 10
  8 9̸ 0̸
 −7 6 5
        5
```

STEP 3:
```
    8 10
  8 9̸ 0̸        1 2 5
 −7 6 5       +7 6 5
    2 5
```

So, 890 − 765 = _____.

Math Talk

MATHEMATICAL PRACTICES ①

Describe Reasonableness How do you know your answer is reasonable?

Try This! Circle the problem in which you need to regroup. Find the difference.

Ⓐ
```
   8 9 4
  −5 8 3
```

Ⓑ
```
   5 2 1
  −3 0 1
```

Ⓒ
```
   9 1 8
  −4 2 7
```

Share and Show MATH BOARD

1. Estimate. Then use place value to find 627 − 384. Add to check your answer.

   Estimate. _____ − _____ = _____

```
  6 2 7            
 −3 8 4      +3 8 4
```

Math Talk

MATHEMATICAL PRACTICES ①

Evaluate Did you need to regroup to find the difference?

Since _____ is close to the estimate of _____, the answer is reasonable.

Name _____

Estimate. Then find the difference.

2. Estimate: _____

$$386$$
$$-123$$

3. Estimate: _____

$$519$$
$$-205$$

4. Estimate: _____

$$456$$
$$-217$$

5. Estimate: _____

$$642$$
$$-159$$

6. Estimate: _____

$$242$$
$$-220$$

7. Estimate: _____

$$870$$
$$-492$$

8. Estimate: _____

$$654$$
$$-263$$

9. Estimate: _____

$$937$$
$$-618$$

Math Talk

MATHEMATICAL PRACTICES ①

Make Sense of Problems Which exercises can you compute mentally? Explain why.

On Your Own

10. Darius has 127 photos. Jillian has 467 photos. How many more photos does Jillian have than Darius?

_____

11. Beth, Dan, and Yoshi collect stamps. Beth has 157 stamps. Dan has 265 stamps. Yoshi has 79 fewer stamps than Beth and Dan do combined. How many stamps does Yoshi have?

_____

Practice: Copy and Solve Estimate. Then solve.

12. $568 - 276$

13. $761 - 435$

14. $829 - 765$

15. $974 - 285$

MATHEMATICAL PRACTICE ② Use Reasoning **Algebra** Find the unknown number.

16.

$$86$$
$$-$$
$$\overline{62}$$

17.

$$372$$
$$-$$
$$\overline{240}$$

18.

$$537$$
$$-$$
$$\overline{172}$$

19.

$$629$$
$$-$$
$$\overline{335}$$

Problem Solving • Applications

Use the table for 20–21.

20. **THINK SMARTER** Alicia sold 59 fewer tickets than Jenna and Matt sold together. How many tickets did Alicia sell? Explain.

_____

_____

_____

School Play Tickets Sold	
Student	**Number of Tickets**
Jenna	282
Matt	178
Sonja	331

21. **GO DEEPER** How many more tickets would each student need to sell so that each student sells 350 tickets?

_____

_____

22. Nina says to check subtraction, add the difference to the number you subtracted from. Does this statement make sense? Explain.

_____

_____

_____

23. **MATHEMATICAL PRACTICE ⑤ Communicate** Do you have to regroup to find 523 − 141? Explain. Then solve.

_____

_____

Personal Math Trainer

24. **THINK SMARTER +** Students want to sell 400 tickets to the school talent show. They have sold 214 tickets. How many more tickets do they need to sell to reach their goal? Show your work.

_____

Use Place Value to Subtract

Common Core

COMMON CORE STANDARD—3.NBT.A.2
Use place value understanding and properties of operations to perform multi-digit arithmetic.

Estimate. Then find the difference.

1. Estimate: __500__

$$\begin{array}{r} \overset{7\ \ 15}{5\cancel{8}5} \\ -\ 119 \\ \hline \end{array}$$

2. Estimate: _____

$$\begin{array}{r} 738 \\ -\ 227 \\ \hline \end{array}$$

3. Estimate: _____

$$\begin{array}{r} 651 \\ -\ 376 \\ \hline \end{array}$$

4. Estimate: _____

$$\begin{array}{r} 815 \\ -\ 281 \\ \hline \end{array}$$

5. Estimate: _____

$$\begin{array}{r} 627 \\ -\ 253 \\ \hline \end{array}$$

6. Estimate: _____

$$\begin{array}{r} 862 \\ -\ 419 \\ \hline \end{array}$$

7. Estimate: _____

$$\begin{array}{r} 726 \\ -\ 148 \\ \hline \end{array}$$

8. Estimate: _____

$$\begin{array}{r} 543 \\ -\ 358 \\ \hline \end{array}$$

Problem Solving · Real World

9. Mrs. Cohen has 427 buttons. She uses 195 buttons to make puppets. How many buttons does Mrs. Cohen have left?

_____

10. There were 625 ears of corn and 247 tomatoes sold at a farm stand. How many more ears of corn were sold than tomatoes?

_____

11. **WRITE** ▸*Math* Explain how to subtract 247 from 538.

_____

_____

_____

Lesson Check (3.NBT.A.2)

1. On Saturday, 453 people go to a school play. On Sunday, 294 people go to the play. How many more people go to the play on Saturday?

_____

2. Corey has 510 marbles. He fills one jar with 165 marbles. How many of Corey's marbles are NOT in the jar?

_____

Spiral Review (3.NBT.A.1, 3.NBT.A.2)

3. Pattie brought 64 peppers to sell at the farmers' market. There were 12 peppers left at the end of the day. How many peppers did Pattie sell?

_____

_____

4. An airplane flies 617 miles in the morning. Then it flies 385 miles in the afternoon. About how many more miles does the airplane fly in the morning?

_____

_____

5. What is the unknown number?

$$(\blacksquare + 4) + 59 = 70$$

6. Dexter has 128 shells. He needs 283 more shells for his art project. How many shells will Dexter use for his art project?

_____

_____

FOR MORE PRACTICE,
GO TO THE
Personal Math Trainer

Name _____

Combine Place Values to Subtract

Essential Question How can you use the combine place values strategy to subtract 3-digit numbers?

 Common Core **Number and Operations in Base Ten—** **3.NBT.A.2** *Also 3.NBT.A.1, 3.OA.D.8*
MATHEMATICAL PRACTICES
MP1, MP5, MP8

Unlock the Problem Real World

Elena collected 431 bottles for recycling. Pete collected 227 fewer bottles than Elena. How many bottles did Pete collect?

- What do you need to find?

  _____

- Circle the numbers you need to use.

Combine place values to find the difference.

(A) Subtract. 431 − 227

Estimate. 400 − 200 = _____

STEP 1 Look at the ones place. Since 7 > 1, combine place values. Combine the tens and ones places. There are 31 ones and 27 ones. Subtract the ones. Write 0 for the tens.

4|3 1|
− 2|2 7|

Think: 31 − 27

STEP 2 Subtract the hundreds.

So, Pete collected _____ bottles.

Since _____ is close to the estimate

of _____, the answer is reasonable.

4 3 1
− 2 2 7
0 4

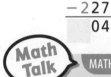
Math Talk

MATHEMATICAL PRACTICES ①

Analyze Explain why there is a zero in the tens place.

(B) Subtract. 513 − 482

Estimate. 510 − 480 = _____

STEP 1 Subtract the ones.

5 1 3
− 4 8 2

STEP 2 Look at the tens place. Since 8 > 1, combine place values. Combine the hundreds and tens places. There are 51 tens and 48 tens. Subtract the tens.

5 1|3
− 4 8|2
1

Think: 51 − 48

So, 513 − 482 = _____.

🔑 **Example** Combine place values to find 500 − 173.

Estimate. 500 − 175 = _____

STEP 1 Look at the ones and tens places. Since 3 > 0 and 7 > 0 , combine the hundreds and tens.

There are 50 tens. Regroup 50 tens as 49 tens 10 ones.

```
  4 9 10
  5 0 0
−   1 7 3
```

STEP 2 Subtract the ones.

Think: 10 − 3

```
  4 9 10
  5 0 0
−   1 7 3
```

STEP 3 Subtract the tens.

Think: 49 − 17

```
  4 9 10
  5 0 0
−   1 7 3
        7
```

So, 500 − 173 = _____ .

MATHEMATICAL PRACTICES ⑧

Use Repeated Reasoning Explain why you combined the hundreds and tens.

Try This! **Find 851 − 448 in two ways.**

Estimate. 850 − 450 = _____

Ⓐ Use place value.

```
  8 5 1
− 4 4 8
```

Ⓑ Combine place values.

```
  8 5 1
− 4 4 8
```

Think: Combine tens and ones.

1. When does the combine place values strategy make it easier to find the difference? Explain.

_____

_____

_____

2. Which strategy would you use to find 431 − 249? Explain.

_____

_____

Name _____

Math Talk MATHEMATICAL PRACTICES ⑧

Use Repeated Reasoning Explain how to combine place values.

1. Combine place values to find 406 − 274.

$$
\begin{array}{r}
406 \\
-274 \\
\hline
\end{array}
$$

Think: Subtract the ones. Then combine the hundreds and tens places.

Estimate. Then find the difference.

✓ 2. Estimate: _____

$$
\begin{array}{r}
595 \\
-286 \\
\hline
\end{array}
$$

3. Estimate: _____

$$
\begin{array}{r}
728 \\
-515 \\
\hline
\end{array}
$$

4. Estimate: _____

$$
\begin{array}{r}
543 \\
-307 \\
\hline
\end{array}
$$

✓ 5. Estimate: _____

$$
\begin{array}{r}
600 \\
-453 \\
\hline
\end{array}
$$

On Your Own

Estimate. Then find the difference.

6. Estimate: _____

$$
\begin{array}{r}
438 \\
-257 \\
\hline
\end{array}
$$

7. Estimate: _____

$$
\begin{array}{r}
706 \\
-681 \\
\hline
\end{array}
$$

8. Estimate: _____

$$
\begin{array}{r}
839 \\
-754 \\
\hline
\end{array}
$$

9. Estimate: _____

$$
\begin{array}{r}
916 \\
-558 \\
\hline
\end{array}
$$

10. GO DEEPER A train travels a distance of 872 miles. Then it travels another 342 miles. The train then travels another 403 miles. How many more miles does the train travel on the first part of the trip than on the second and third trips combined?

_____

11. Denzel wants to subtract 517 − 183. How can he combine the place values to find the difference?

_____

_____

_____

Practice: Copy and Solve Estimate. Then solve.

12. 457 − 364

13. 652 − 341

14. 700 − 648

15. 963 − 256

Problem Solving · Applications Real World

Use the table for 16–18.

16. **MATHEMATICAL PRACTICE 5 Use Appropriate Tools** The table shows the heights of some roller coasters in the United States. How much taller is Kingda Ka than Titan?

_____

17. **GO DEEPER** Jason rode two roller coasters with a difference in height of 115 feet. Which roller coasters did Jason ride?

_____

18. **THINK SMARTER** What if another roller coaster was 500 feet tall? Which roller coaster would be 195 feet shorter?

_____

19. **THINK SMARTER** Owen solves this problem. He says the difference is 127. Explain the mistake Owen made. What is the correct difference?

$$\begin{array}{r} 335 \\ -218 \\ \hline \end{array}$$

_____

_____

_____

_____

Roller Coaster Heights

Roller Coaster	State	Height in Feet
Titan	Texas	245
Kingda Ka	New Jersey	456
Intimidator 305	Virginia	305
Top Thrill Dragster	Ohio	420

WRITE *Math* · **Show Your Work**

Math on the Spot

Combine Place Values to Subtract

Common Core **COMMON CORE STANDARD—3.NBT.A.2**
Use place value understanding and properties of operations to perform multi-digit arithmetic.

Estimate. Then find the difference.

1. Estimate: ___200___

$$\begin{array}{r} 476 \\ -\ 269 \\ \hline \end{array}$$

2. Estimate: _____

$$\begin{array}{r} 615 \\ -\ 342 \\ \hline \end{array}$$

3. Estimate: _____

$$\begin{array}{r} 508 \\ -\ 113 \\ \hline \end{array}$$

4. Estimate: _____

$$\begin{array}{r} 716 \\ -\ 229 \\ \hline \end{array}$$

5. Estimate: _____

$$\begin{array}{r} 826 \\ -\ 617 \\ \hline \end{array}$$

6. Estimate: _____

$$\begin{array}{r} 900 \\ -\ 158 \\ \hline \end{array}$$

7. Estimate: _____

$$\begin{array}{r} 607 \\ -\ 568 \\ \hline \end{array}$$

8. Estimate: _____

$$\begin{array}{r} 973 \\ -\ 869 \\ \hline \end{array}$$

 Problem Solving Real World

9. Bev scored 540 points. This was 158 points more than Ike scored. How many points did Ike score?

10. A youth group earned $285 washing cars. The group's expenses were $79. How much profit did the group make washing cars?

_____

_____

11. **WRITE** ▸*Math* Explain how to use the combine place values strategy to find 223 − 119.

_____

_____

Lesson Check (3.NBT.A.2)

1. A television program lasts for 120 minutes. Of that time, 36 minutes are taken up by commercials. What is the length of the actual program without the commercials?

2. Syd spent 215 minutes at the library. Of that time, he spent 120 minutes on the computer. How much of his time at the library did Sid NOT spend on the computer?

Spiral Review (3.NBT.A.1, 3.NBT.A.2)

3. Xavier's older brother has 568 songs on his music player. To the nearest hundred, about how many songs are on the music player?

4. The students traveled to the zoo in 3 buses. One bus had 47 students. The second bus had 38 students. The third bus had 43 students. How many total students were on the three buses?

5. Callie has 83 postcards in her collection. Of the postcards, 24 are from Canada. The rest of the postcards are from the United States. How many of the postcards are from the United States?

6. There were 475 seats set up for the school play. At one performance, 189 of the seats were empty. How many seats were filled at that performance?

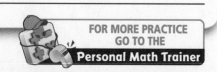
FOR MORE PRACTICE
GO TO THE
Personal Math Trainer

Name _____

Problem Solving •
Model Addition and Subtraction

Essential Question How can you use the strategy *draw a diagram* to solve one- and two-step addition and subtraction problems?

Operations and Algebraic Thinking—
3.OA.D.8 *Also 3.NBT.A.2*
MATHEMATICAL PRACTICES
MP2, MP4, MP6

Unlock the Problem Real World

Sami scored 84 points in the first round of a new computer game. He scored 21 more points in the second round than in the first round. What was Sami's total score?

Read the Problem

What do I need to find?	**What information do I need to use?**	**How will I use the information?**
I need to find _____ _____.	Sami scored _____ points in the first round. He scored _____ more points than that in the second round.	I will draw a bar model to show the number of points Sami scored in each round. Then I will use the bar model to decide which operation to use.

Solve the Problem

- Complete the bar model to show the number of points Sami scored in the second round.

_____ points

Round 1 | _____ points |

Round 2 | ▪ points |

_____ + _____ = ▪

_____ = ▪

- Complete another bar model to show Sami's total score.

| _____ points | _____ points |

▲ points

_____ + _____ = ▲

_____ = ▲

1. How many points did Sami score in the second round? _____

2. What was Sami's total score? _____

🔓 Try Another Problem

Anna scored 265 points in a computer game. Greg scored 142 points. How many more points did Anna score than Greg?

You can use a bar model to solve the problem.

Read the Problem

What do I need to find?	What information do I need to use?	How will I use the information?

Solve the Problem

Record the steps you used to solve the problem.

Anna
| _____ points |

Greg
| _____ points |
■ points

3. How many more points did Anna score than Greg?

_____

4. How do you know your answer is reasonable?

_____

_____

_____

5. How did your drawing help you solve the problem?

_____

_____

MATHEMATICAL PRACTICES ⑥

Make Connections Explain how the length of each bar in the model would change if Greg scored more points than Anna but the totals remained the same.

Name _____

Unlock the Problem

✓ Use the problem solving MathBoard.

✓ Choose a strategy you know.

✓ **1.** Sara received 73 votes in the school election. Ben received 25 fewer votes than Sara. How many students voted?

First, find how many students voted for Ben.

Think: 73 − 25 = ■

Write the numbers in the bar model.

So, Ben received _____ votes.

Next, find the total number of votes.

Think: 73 + 48 = ▲

Write the numbers in the bar model.

So, _____ students voted.

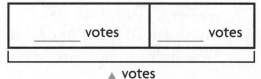

Sara | _____ votes

Ben | ■ votes

_____ votes

■ = _____ votes

_____ votes | _____ votes

▲ votes

▲ = _____ votes

✓ **2.** If Ben received 73 votes and Sara received 25 fewer votes than Ben, how would your bar models change? Would the total votes be the same? Explain.

_____

_____

_____

3. *THINK SMARTER* What if there were 3 students in another election and the total number of votes was the same? What would the bar model for the total number of votes look like? How many votes might each student get?

_____

_____

_____

4. Pose a Problem Use the bar model at the right. Write a problem to match it.

89	■

157

_____

_____

5. Solve your problem. Will you add or subtract?

_____

6. Tony's Tech Store had a big sale. The store had 142 computers in stock. During the sale, 91 computers were sold. How many computers were not sold?

_____

7. GO DEEPER There are 208 people in one movie theater. There are 78 fewer people in the next movie theater. How many people are in both movie theaters?

_____

8. GO DEEPER In one week, 128 cell phones were sold. The following week, 37 more cell phones were sold than the week before. How many cell phones were sold in those two weeks?

_____

9. MATHEMATICAL PRACTICE ⑥ On Monday, the number of customers in the store, rounded to the nearest hundred, was 400. What is the greatest number of customers that could have been in the store? **Explain**.

_____

_____

10. THINK SMARTER There are 306 people at the fair on Saturday. There are 124 fewer people on Sunday. How many people are at the fair during the two days?

_____

Problem Solving • Model Addition and Subtraction

Common Core **COMMON CORE STANDARD—3.OA.D.8**
Solve problems involving the four operations, and identify and explain patterns in arithmetic.

Use the bar model to solve the problem.

1. Elena went bowling. Elena's score in the first game was 127. She scored 16 more points in the second game than in the first game. What was her total score?

16 points

Game 1	**127** points

Game 2	▲ points

$$127 + 16 = ▲$$
$$143 = ▲$$
___270 points___

127 points	**143** points

■ points

$$127 + 143 = ■$$
$$270 = ■$$

---

2. Mike's Music sold 287 CDs on the first day of a 2-day sale. The store sold 96 more CDs on the second day than on the first day. How many CDs in all were sold during the 2-day sale?

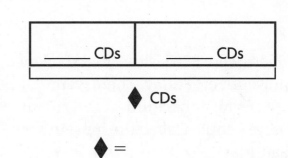

_____ CDs

Day 1	_____ CDs

Day 2	✦ CDs

✦ =

_____

_____ CDs	_____ CDs

◆ CDs

◆ =

---

3. **WRITE** ▸*Math* Write an addition or subtraction problem and draw a diagram to solve it.

_____

Lesson Check (3.OA.D.8)

1. Ms. Hinely picked 46 tomatoes from her garden on Friday. On Saturday, she picked 17 tomatoes. How many tomatoes did she pick?

2. Rosa read 57 pages of a book in the morning. She read 13 fewer pages in the afternoon. How many pages did Rosa read in the afternoon?

Spiral Review (3.NBT.A.1, 3.NBT.A.2)

3. Mike has 57 action figures. Alex has 186 action figures. Estimate the number of action figures Mike and Alex have altogether.

4. There are 500 sheets of paper in the pack Hannah bought. She has used 137 sheets already. How many sheets of paper does Hannah have left?

5. There were 378 visitors to the science museum on Friday. There were 409 visitors on Saturday. How many more people visited the museum on Saturday?

6. Ravi scores 247 points in a video game. How many more points does he need to score a total of 650?

FOR MORE PRACTICE
GO TO THE
Personal Math Trainer

☑ Chapter 1 Review/Test

Personal Math Trainer
Online Assessment
and Intervention

1. For numbers 1a–1d, choose Yes or No to tell whether the sum is even.

   1a. $5 + 8$ ○ Yes   ○ No

   1b. $9 + 3$ ○ Yes   ○ No

   1c. $6 + 7$ ○ Yes   ○ No

   1d. $9 + 5$ ○ Yes   ○ No

2. Select the number sentences that show the Commutative Property of Addition. Mark all that apply.

   Ⓐ $14 + 8 = 22$

   Ⓑ $8 + 14 = 14 + 8$

   Ⓒ $8 + (13 + 1) = (8 + 13) + 1$

   Ⓓ $(5 + 9) + 8 = (9 + 5) + 8$

3. Select the numbers that round to 300 when rounded to the nearest hundred. Mark all that apply.

   Ⓐ 238

   Ⓑ 250

   Ⓒ 283

   Ⓓ 342

   Ⓔ 359

4. There are 486 books in the classroom library. Complete the chart to show 486 rounded to the nearest 10.

Hundreds	Tens	Ones

 **Assessment Options**
Chapter Test

5. Write each number sentence in the box below the better estimate of the sum.

$393 + 225 = $ ▮ $481 + 215 = $ ▮

$352 + 328 = $ ▮ $309 + 335 = $ ▮

600	700

6. **GO DEEPER** Diana sold 336 muffins at the bake sale. Bob sold 287 muffins. Bob estimates that he sold 50 fewer muffins than Diana. How did he estimate? Explain.

7. The table shows how many books each class read.

Reading Contest

Class	Number of Books
Mr. Lopez	273
Ms. Martin	402
Mrs. Wang	247

For numbers 7a–7d, select True or False for each statement.

7a. Ms. Martin's class read about 100 more books than Mr. Lopez's class.   ○ True   ○ False

7b. The 3 classes read over 900 books altogether.   ○ True   ○ False

7c. Mrs. Wang's class read about 50 fewer books than Mr. Lopez's class.   ○ True   ○ False

7d. Ms. Martin's and Mrs. Wang's class read about 700 books.   ○ True   ○ False

8. Janna buys 2 bags of dog food for her dogs. One bag weighs 37 pounds. The other bag weighs 15 pounds. How many pounds do both bags weigh? Explain how you solved the problem.

_____

9. Choose the property that makes the statement true.

The | Identity / Commutative / Associative | Property of addition states that you can group addends in different ways and get the same sum.

Use the table for 10–12.

Susie's Sweater Shop	
Month	**Number of Sweaters Sold**
January	402
February	298
March	171

10. The table shows the number of sweaters sold online in three months. How many sweaters were sold in January and February?

_____ sweaters

11. How many more sweaters were sold in January than March?

_____ sweaters

12. How many more sweaters were sold in February and March than in January?

_____ sweaters

13. Help Dana find the sum.

$$346$$
$$421$$
$$+\ 152$$

For numbers 13a–13d, select Yes or No to tell Dana when to regroup.

13a. Regroup the ones.   ○ Yes   ○ No

13b. Add the regrouped
      ten.   ○ Yes   ○ No

13c. Regroup the tens.   ○ Yes   ○ No

13d. Add the regrouped
      hundred.   ○ Yes   ○ No

14. Alexandra has 78 emails in her inbox. She deletes 47 emails. How many emails are left in her inbox? Draw jumps and label the number line to show your thinking.

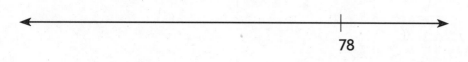

_____ emails

15. Daniel has 402 pieces in a building set. He uses 186 pieces to build a house. How many pieces does he have left? Show your work.

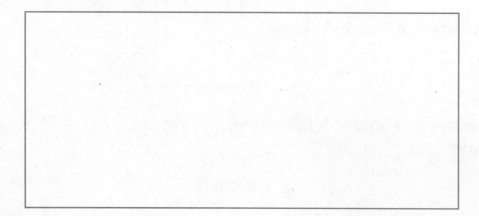

82

16. Luke solves this problem. He says the difference is 214. Explain the mistake Luke made. What is the correct difference?

```
   352
 − 148
```

17. Sunnyday Elementary School is having its annual Read-a-thon. The third graders have read 573 books so far. Their goal is to read more than 900 books. What is the least number of books they need to read to reach their goal? Explain.

Personal Math Trainer

18. THINK SMARTER + There are 318 fiction books in the class library. The number of nonfiction books is 47 less than the number of fiction books.

Part A

About how many nonfiction books are there in the class library? Explain.

Part B

How many fiction and nonfiction books are there in the class library altogether? Show your work.

19. **GO DEEPER** Alia used $67 + 38 = 105$ to check her subtraction. Which math problem could she be checking? Mark all that apply.

Ⓐ $67 - 38 = \blacksquare$

Ⓑ $105 - 67 = \blacksquare$

Ⓒ $105 + 38 = \blacksquare$

Ⓓ $105 - 38 = \blacksquare$

20. Alexa and Erika collect shells. The tables show the kinds of shells they collected.

Alexa's Shells	
Shell	Number of Shells
Scallop	36
Jingle	95
Clam	115

Erika's Shells	
Shell	Number of Shells
Scallop	82
Clam	108
Whelk	28

Part A

Who collected more shells? How many did she collect? About how many more is that? Explain how you solved the problem.

Part B

Alexa and Erika have the greatest number of what kind of shell? How many shells of that kind do they have? Show your work.

Chapter 2

Represent and Interpret Data

 **Show What You Know**

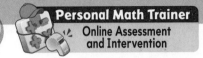 **Personal Math Trainer**
Online Assessment and Intervention

Check your understanding of important skills.

Name _____

▶ **Numbers to 20** Circle the number word. Write the number. (K.NBT.A.1)

1.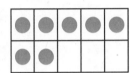

fourteen

fifteen

_____

2.

seventeen

eighteen

_____

▶ **Skip Count** Skip count to find the missing numbers. (2.NBT.A.2)

3. Count by twos. 2, 4, _____, _____, 10, _____, _____, 16

4. Count by fives. 5, 10, _____, _____, _____, 30, _____

▶ **Addition and Subtraction Facts** Find the sum or difference. (1.OA.C.6)

5. 12 − 4 = _____   6. 9 + 8 = _____   7. 11 − 7 = _____

Math in the Real World

Paige helps to sell supplies in the school store. Each month she totals all the sales and makes a bar graph. The graph shows sales through December. Help to find the month during which the hundredth sale was made.

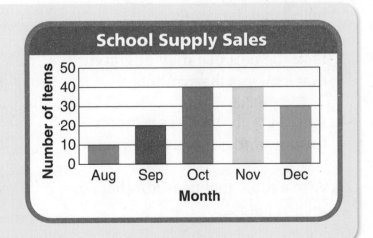

School Supply Sales

▶ **Visualize It** ••••••••••••••••••••••••••••••••

Complete the bubble map by using the words with a ✓.

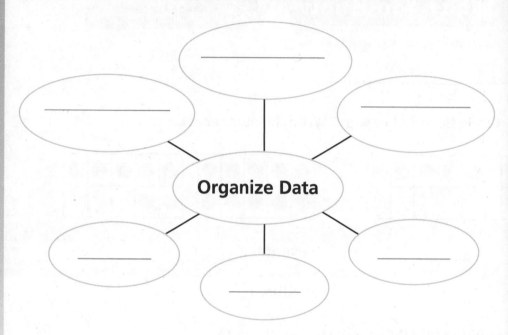

Organize Data

▶ **Understand Vocabulary** ••••••••••••••••••••••••

Write the review word or preview word that answers the riddle.

1. I am a graph that records each piece of data above a number line. _____

2. I am the numbers that are placed at fixed distances on a graph to help label the graph. _____

3. I am the part of a map or graph that explains the symbols. _____

4. I am a graph that uses pictures to show and compare information. _____

5. I am a table that uses numbers to record data. _____

GO DIGITAL
• **Interactive Student Edition**
• **Multimedia eGlossary**

Chapter 2 Vocabulary

Frequency Table

tabla de frecuencia

29

Horizontal Bar Graph

gráfica de barras horizontales

33

key

clave

38

line plot

diagrama de puntos

43

Picture Graph

gráfica con dibujos

61

Scale

escala

73

tally table

tabla de conteo

76

Vertical Bar Graph

gráfica de barras verticales

83

A bar graph in which the bars go across from left to right

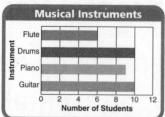

A table that uses numbers to record data

Favorite Color	
Color	Number
Blue	10
Green	8
Red	7
Yellow	4

A graph that records each piece of data on a number line

The part of a map or graph that explains the symbols

The numbers placed at fixed distances on a graph to help label the graph

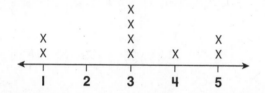

Scale

A graph that uses pictures to show and compare information

A bar graph in which the bars go up from bottom to top

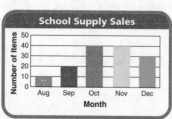

A table that uses tally marks to record data

Favorite Sport	
Sport	Tally
Soccer	卌 |||
Baseball	|||
Football	卌
Basketball	卌	

Picture It

Word Box
frequency table
horizontal bar
   graph
key
line plot
picture graph
scale
tally table
vertical bar graph

For 3 to 4 players

Materials
- timer
- sketch pad

How to Play
1. Take turns to play.
2. To take a turn, choose a math term but do not say it aloud.
3. Set the timer for 1 minute.
4. Draw pictures and numbers to give clues about the word.
5. The first player to guess the word before time runs out gets 1 point. If that player can use the word in a sentence, he or she gets 1 more point. Then that player gets a turn choosing a word.
6. The first player to score 10 points wins.

The Write Way

Reflect

Choose one idea. Write about it.

- Describe something you know about bar graphs.
- Write two questions you have about how to use a key or scale in graphs.
- Explain how to read a line plot.

Name _____

Problem Solving • Organize Data

Essential Question How can you use the strategy *make a table* to organize data and solve problems?

 Common Core — Measurement and Data—3.MD.B.3, 3.OA.D.8
MATHEMATICAL PRACTICES
MP1, MP2, MP5

Unlock the Problem

The students in Alicia's class voted for their favorite yogurt flavor. They organized the data in this tally table. How many more students chose chocolate than strawberry?

Another way to show the data is in a frequency table. A **frequency table** uses numbers to record data.

Favorite Yogurt Flavor	
Flavor	**Tally**
Vanilla	IIII II
Chocolate	IIII III
Strawberry	IIII

Read the Problem

What do I need to find?

How many more students chose

_____ than _____ yogurt
as their favorite?

What information do I need to use?

the data about favorite _____
in the tally table

How will I use the information?

I will count the _____. Then I will put the numbers in a frequency table and compare the number of students

who chose _____ to the number of

students who chose _____.

Solve the Problem

Favorite Yogurt Flavor	
Flavor	**Number**
Vanilla	

Count the tally marks. Record _____ for vanilla. Write the other flavors and record the number of tally marks.

To compare the number of students who chose strawberry and the number of students who chose chocolate, subtract.

_____ − _____ = _____

So, _____ more students chose chocolate as their favorite flavor.

 Math Talk

MATHEMATICAL PRACTICES ②

Reason Abstractly Why would you record data in a frequency table?

Try Another Problem

Two classes in Carter's school grew bean plants for a science project. The heights of the plants after six weeks are shown in the tally table. The plants were measured to the nearest inch. How many fewer bean plants were 9 inches tall than 7 inches and 8 inches combined?

Bean Plant Heights	
Height in Inches	Tally
7	卌 IIII
8	卌 III
9	卌 卌 II
10	卌 IIII

Read the Problem

What do I need to find?

What information do I need to use?

How will I use the information?

Solve the Problem

Record the steps you used to solve the problem.

- Suppose the number of 3-inch plants was half the number of 8-inch plants. How many 3-inch bean plants were there?

_____

MATHEMATICAL PRACTICES ①

Explain a Method What is another strategy you could use to solve the problem?

Name _____

Use the Shoe Lengths table for 1–3.

1. The students in three third-grade classes recorded the lengths of their shoes to the nearest centimeter. The data are in the tally table. How many more shoes were 18 or 22 centimeters long combined than 20 centimeters long?

   First, count the tally marks and record the data in a frequency table.

   To find the number of shoes that were 18 or 22 centimeters long, add

   6 + ____ + ____ + ____ = ____.

   To find the number of shoes that were

   20 centimeters long, add ____ + ____ = ____.

   To find the difference between the shoes that were 18 or 22 centimeters long and the shoes that were 20 centimeters long, subtract the sums.

   ____ − ____ = ____.

   So, ____ more shoes were 18 or 22 centimeters long than 20 centimeters long.

Shoe Lengths		
Length in Centimeters	Tally	
	Boys	Girls
18	JHT I	IIII
19	JHT	IIII
20	JHT III	JHT IIII
21	JHT II	JHT
22	JHT IIII	JHT II

Shoe Lengths		
Length in Centimeters	Number	
	Boys	Girls
18		
19		
20		
21		
22		

2. How many fewer boys' shoes were 19 cm long than 22 cm long?

   _____

3. *THINK SMARTER* What if the length of 5 more boys' shoes measured 21 centimeters? Explain how the table would change.

   _____

   _____

Math on the Spot

4. **MATHEMATICAL PRACTICE 1** **Analyze** Raj asked his classmates to choose their favorite outdoor game. His results are shown in the frequency table at the right. How many more students chose hide-and-seek than scavenger hunt?

Favorite Outdoor Game	
Game Type	**Number**
Hide-and-Seek	14
Jump Rope	9
Scavenger Hunt	6
Tag	16

_____

5. **GO DEEPER** How many students in all chose tag, jump rope, or hide-and-seek?

_____

6. **THINK SMARTER** Andrew has 10 more goldfish than Todd. Together, they have 50 goldfish. How many goldfish does each boy have?

_____

7. **THINK SMARTER** Jade made this tally table to record how many students have different types of pets.

Students' Pets	
Type of Pet	**Tally**
Dog	卌 卌 IIII
Rabbit	III
Hamster	卌
Cat	卌 II

For numbers 7a–7d, select True or False for each statement.

7a. Nine fewer students have hamsters than have dogs.   ○ True   ○ False

7b. Seven students have cats.   ○ True   ○ False

7c. Fewer students have cats than hamsters.   ○ True   ○ False

7d. More students have dogs than all other animals combined.   ○ True   ○ False

Problem Solving • Organize Data

Common Core   COMMON CORE STANDARD—3.MD.B.3,
3.OA.D.8 *Represent and interpret data.
Solve problems involving the four operations,
and identify and explain patterns in arithmetic.*

Use the Favorite School Subject tables for 1–3.

1. The students in two third-grade classes recorded their favorite school subject. The data are in the tally table. How many fewer students chose science than chose social studies as their favorite school subject?

   Think: Use the data in the tally table to record the data in the frequency table. Then solve the problem.

   social studies: __12__ students

   science: __5__ students

   $12 - 5 =$ __7__

   So, __7__ fewer students chose science.

2. What subject did the least number of students choose?

   _____

3. How many more students chose math than language arts as their favorite subject?

   _____ more students

Favorite School Subject	
Subject	Tally
Math	ЖЖ ЖЖ I
Science	ЖЖ
Language Arts	ЖЖ II
Reading	ЖЖ IIII
Social Studies	ЖЖ ЖЖ II

Favorite School Subject	
Subject	Number
Math	
Science	5
Language Arts	
Reading	
Social Studies	12

4. **WRITE** ▸*Math* Give one example of when you would make a frequency table to solve a problem.

_____

_____

Lesson Check (3.MD.B.3)

The tally table shows the cards in Kyle's sports card collection.

1. How many hockey and football cards does Kyle have combined?

Kyle's Sports Cards	
Sport	Tally
Baseball	$\cancel{||||}$ ||||
Hockey	$\cancel{||||}$
Basketball	|||
Football	$\cancel{||||}$ |||

_____

Spiral Review (3.OA.D.8, 3.NBT.A.1, 3.NBT.A.2)

2. There are 472 people in the concert hall. What is 472 rounded to the nearest hundred?

_____

3. Max and Anna played a video game as a team. Max scored 463 points and Anna scored 329 points. How many points did they score?

_____

4. Judy has 573 baseball cards in her collection. Todd has 489 baseball cards in his collection. How many fewer cards does Todd have than Judy?

_____

5. Ms. Westin drove 542 miles last week and 378 miles this week on business. How many miles did she drive on business during the two weeks?

_____

© Houghton Mifflin Harcourt Publishing Company

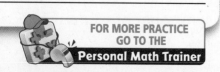

FOR MORE PRACTICE
GO TO THE
Personal Math Trainer

Name _____

Use Picture Graphs

Essential Question How can you read and interpret data in a picture graph?

Common Core Measurement and Data—3.MD.B.3, 3.NBT.A.2
MATHEMATICAL PRACTICES
MP4, MP6, MP8

⚷ Unlock the Problem

A **picture graph** uses small pictures or symbols to show and compare information.

Nick has a picture graph that shows how some students get to school. How many students ride the bus?

- Underline the words that tell you where to find the information to answer the question.
- How many ☺ are shown for Bus?

_____

| Each row has a label that names one way students get to school. |

How We Get to School

Walk	☺ ☺ ☺
Bike	☺ ☺ ☺ ☺
Bus	☺ ☺ ☺ ☺ ☺ ☺ ☺ ☺
Car	☺ ☺ ☺ ☺ ☺ ☺

Key: Each ☺ = 10 students.

The title says that the picture graph is about how some students get to school.

The **key** tells that each picture or symbol stands for the way 10 students get to school.

🔒 To find the number of students who ride the bus, count each ☺ as 10 students.

10, 20, _____, _____, _____, _____, _____, _____

So, _____ students ride the bus to school.

---

1. How many fewer students walk than ride the bus? _____

2. How many students were surveyed? _____

3. What if the symbol stands for 5 students? How many symbols will you need to show the number of students who walk to school? _____

Use a Half Symbol

How many students chose an orange as their favorite fruit?

Math Idea
Half of the picture stands for half the value of the whole picture.

☺ = 2 students

◖ = 1 student

Our Favorite Fruit	
Banana	☺ ☺ ☺ ☺ ☺
Apple	☺ ☺ ☺
Pear	☺ ☺
Orange	☺ ☺ ☺ ☺ ◖

Key: Each ☺ = 2 students.

Count the ☺ in the orange row by twos. Then add 1 for the half symbol.

2, 4, _____ , _____   _____ + _____ = _____

So, _____ students chose an orange as their favorite fruit.

Share and Show

Use the Number of Books Students Read picture graph for 1–3.

Number of Books Students Read	
September	📖 📖 📖 📖 ▯
October	📖 📖 📖 📖 📖 📖
November	📖 📖 📖 📖

Key: Each 📖 = 2 books.

1. What does ▮ stand for?
   Think: Half of 2 is 1.

   _____

2. How many books did the students read in September?

   _____

3. How many more books did the students read in October than in November?

   _____

Math Talk MATHEMATICAL PRACTICES ④

Use Graphs How does the graph change if 6 fewer books were read in October and 3 more books were read in September?

Name _____

On Your Own

Use the Favorite Game picture graph for 4–10.

Favorite Game	
Puzzles	♟♟♟♟♟
Card Games	♟♟♟♟
Board Games	♟♟♟♟♟♟

Key: Each ♟ = 4 students.

4. How many students chose puzzles?

_____

5. **GO DEEPER** If 6 more students voted for card games and 4 more students voted for board games, how many more students voted for puzzles and card games than board games?

_____

6. **MATHEMATICAL PRACTICE ⑧ Draw Conclusions** Which two types of games did a total of 34 students choose?

_____

7. **GO DEEPER** How many students were surveyed?

_____

8. How many students did not choose card games?

_____

9. **WRITE ▸ Math What's the Error?** Jacob said one more student chose board games than puzzles. Explain his error.

_____

_____

_____

10. **GO DEEPER** What if computer games were added as a choice and more students chose it than puzzles, but fewer students chose it than board games? How many students would choose computer games?

_____

🔑 Unlock the Problem (Real World)

Use the picture graph for 11–12.

11. **THINK SMARTER** The students who went to summer camp voted for their favorite activity. Which two activities received a total of 39 votes?

Favorite Camp Activity	
Biking	☀ ☀ ☀ ☼
Hiking	☀ ☀ ☀ ☀
Boating	☀ ☀ ☀
Fishing	☀ ☼
Key: Each ☀ = 6 students.	

a. What do you need to find?

_____

b. What steps will you use to solve the problem?

_____

c. Show the steps you used to solve the problem.

d. Complete the sentences.

Each ☀ = _____ students.

Each ☼ = _____ students.

votes for biking + hiking = _____

votes for hiking + boating = _____

votes for biking + boating = _____

votes for fishing + hiking = _____

So, _____ received a total of 39 votes.

---

12. **THINK SMARTER +** Choose the word from each box that makes the sentence true.

Personal Math Trainer

Fifteen fewer students voted for

| hiking |
| boating |
| fishing |

than for

| hiking |
| boating |
| fishing |

.

Use Picture Graphs

Common Core
COMMON CORE STANDARD—3.MD.B.3
3.NBT.A.2 *Represent and interpret data.*
Use place value understanding and properties
of operations to perform multi-digit arithmetic.

Use the Math Test Scores picture graph for 1–5.

Mrs. Perez made a picture graph of her students' scores on a math test.

Math Test Scores	
100	★★★★★
95	★★★
90	★★★⬎
85	★

Key: Each ★ = 4 students.

1. How many students scored 100? How can you find the answer?

   To find the number of students who

   scored 100, count each star as

   4 students. So, 20 students scored 100.

   _____

2. What does ◤ stand for?

   _____

3. How many students in all scored 100 or 95?

   _____

Problem Solving (Real World)

4. Suppose the students who scored 85 and 90 on the math test take the test again and score 95. How many stars would you have to add to the picture graph next to 95?

   _____

5. If 2 more students took the math test and both made a score of 80, what would the picture graph look like?

   _____

   _____

6. **WRITE** ▸*Math* Explain what you can tell just by comparing the symbols in a picture graph.

   _____

   _____

Lesson Check (3.MD.B.3)

1. Karen asked her friends to name their favorite type of dog.

Favorite Dog	
Retriever	🦴 🦴 🦴 🦴 🦴 🦴
Poodle	🦴 🦴 🦴
Terrier	🦴 🦴

Key: Each 🦴 = 2 people.

How many people chose poodles?

_____

2. Henry made a picture graph to show what topping people like on their pizza. This is his key.

Each 🍕 = 6 people.

What does 🍕 🍕 stand for?

_____

Spiral Review (3.NBT.A.1)

3. Estimate the sum.

$$523 + 295$$

_____

_____

4. Estimate the difference.

$$610 - 187$$

_____

_____

5. What is 871 rounded to the nearest ten?

_____

6. What is 473 rounded to the nearest hundred?

_____

© Houghton Mifflin Harcourt Publishing Company

FOR MORE PRACTICE
GO TO THE
Personal Math Trainer

Name _____

Make Picture Graphs

Essential Question How can you draw a picture graph to show data in a table?

 Measurement and Data—3.MD.B.3, 3.NBT.A.2
MATHEMATICAL PRACTICES
MP2, MP4

Unlock the Problem

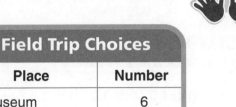

Delia made the table at the right. She used it to record the places the third grade classes would like to go during a field trip. How can you show the data in a picture graph?

Field Trip Choices	
Place	**Number**
Museum	6
Science Center	15
Aquarium	12
Zoo	9

🔑 **Make a picture graph.**

STEP 1

Write the title at the top of the picture graph. Write the name of a place in each row.

STEP 2

Look at the numbers in the table. Choose a picture for the key, and tell how many students each picture represents. Write the key at the bottom of the graph.

STEP 3

Draw the correct number of pictures for each field trip choice.

Museum	

Key: Each ____ = ____ students.

• How did you decide how many pictures to draw for the Science Center?

_____

_____

Try This! Make a picture graph from data you collect. Take a survey or observe a subject that interests you. Collect and record the data in a frequency table. Then make a picture graph. Decide on a symbol and a key. Include a title and labels.

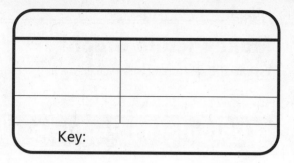

Key:

Jeremy pulled marbles from a bag one at a time, recorded their color, and then put them back. Make a picture graph of the data. Use this key:

Each ⬭ = 2 marbles.

Jeremy's Marble Experiment	
Color	Number
Blue	4
Green	11
Red	8

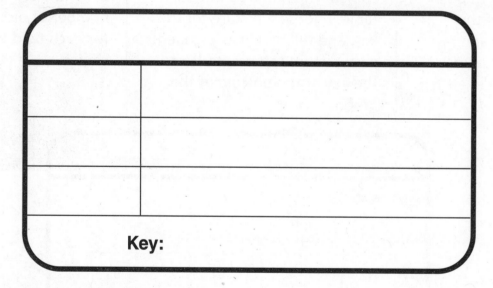

Key:

Use your picture graph above for 1–2.

1. How many more times did Jeremy pull out a red marble than a blue marble?

_____

2. How many fewer times did Jeremy pull out green marbles than blue and red marbles combined?

_____

Math Talk

MATHEMATICAL PRACTICES 2

Connect Symbols and Words How did you know how many pictures to draw for green?

Name _____

3. Two classes from Delia's school visited the
Science Center. They recorded their favorite
exhibit in the tally table. Use the data in the
table to make a picture graph. Use this key:

Each ☼ = 4 votes.

Favorite Exhibit	
Exhibit	**Tally**
Nature	卌 I
Solar System	卌 III
Light and Sound	卌 卌 IIII
Human Body	卌 III

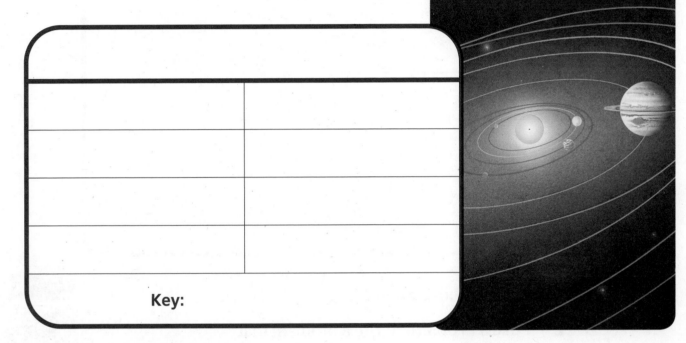

Key:

Use your picture graph above for 4–6.

4. Which exhibits received the same number of votes?

_____

5. (MATHEMATICAL PRACTICE ④) **Model Mathematics** What if a weather
exhibit received 22 votes? Explain how many pictures
you would draw.

_____

6. *THINK SMARTER* What if the Solar System exhibit received
15 votes? Would it make sense to use the key
Each ☼ = 4 votes to represent 15 votes? Explain.

_____

Problem Solving • Applications

Teeth in Mammals	
Animal	**Number**
Hamster	16
Cat	30
Dog	42
Cow	32

7. While at the Science Center, Delia's classmates learned how many teeth some mammals have. Use the data in the table to make a picture graph. Use this key:

Each △ = 4 teeth.

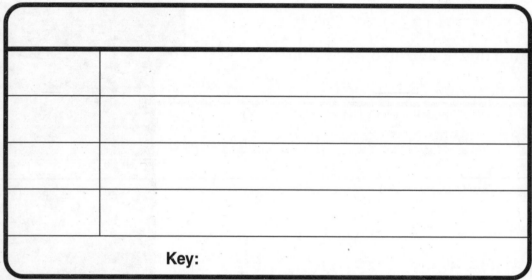

Key:

Use your picture graph above for 8–10.

8. **THINK SMARTER** **Pose a Problem** Write a problem that can be solved by using the data in your picture graph. Then solve the problem.

_____

9. **GO DEEPER** How many fewer teeth do cats and hamsters have combined than dogs and cows combined?

_____

10. **THINK SMARTER** How many pictures would you draw for Cat if each △ = 5 teeth? Explain your reasoning.

_____

_____

Make Picture Graphs

Common Core COMMON CORE STANDARD—3.MD.B.3,
3.NBT.A.2 *Represent and interpret data.*

Ben asked his classmates about their favorite kind of TV show. He recorded their responses in a frequency table. Use the data in the table to make a picture graph.

Favorite TV Show	
Type	Number
Cartoons	9
Sports	6
Movies	3

Follow the steps to make a picture graph.

Step 1 Write the title at the top of the graph

Step 2 Look at the numbers in the table. Tell how many students each picture represents for the key

Step 3 Draw the correct number of pictures for each type of show.

Cartoons	■ ■ ■
Sports	
Movies	

Key: Each ■ =

Use your picture graph for 1–4.

1. What title did you give the graph?

_____

2. What key did you use?

_____

Problem Solving (Real World)

3. How many pictures would you draw if 12 students chose game shows as their favorite kind of TV show?

_____

4. What key would you use if 10 students chose cartoons?

_____

5. **WRITE** ▸*Math* Describe why it might not be a good idea to use a key where each symbol stands for 1 in a picture graph.

_____

_____

Lesson Check (3.MD.B.3)

1. Sandy made a picture graph to show the sports her classmates like to play. How many fewer students chose baseball than chose soccer?

Favorite Sport

Basketball	○○○○○○○
Soccer	○○○○○○○○○○
Baseball	○○○○○○

Key: Each ○ = 2 students.

_____

2. Tommy is making a picture graph to show his friends' favorite kind of music. He plans to use one musical note to represent 2 people. How many notes will he use to represent that 4 people chose country music?

_____

Spiral Review (3.OA.D.9, 3.NBT.A.1, 3.NBT.A.2)

3. Find the sum.

$$490$$
$$+\ 234$$

_____

_____

4. Sophie wrote odd numbers on her paper. What is a number Sophie did NOT write?

_____

_____

5. Miles ordered 126 books to give away at the store opening. What is 126 rounded to the nearest hundred?

_____

_____

6. Estimate the difference.

$$422$$
$$-\ 284$$

_____

_____

FOR MORE PRACTICE
GO TO THE
Personal Math Trainer

Name _____

✓ Mid-Chapter Checkpoint

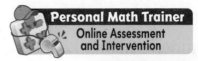

Personal Math Trainer
Online Assessment
and Intervention

Vocabulary

Choose the best term from the box.

Vocabulary
frequency table
key
picture graph

1. A _____ uses numbers to record data. (p. 87)

2. A _____ uses small pictures or symbols to show and compare information. (p. 93)

Concepts and Skills

Use the Favorite Season table for 3–6. (3.MD.B.3)

Favorite Season	
Season	**Number**
Spring	19
Summer	28
Fall	14
Winter	22

3. Which season got the most votes?

_____

4. Which season got 3 fewer votes than winter?

_____

5. How many more students chose summer than fall?

_____

6. How many students chose a favorite season?

_____

Use the Our Pets picture graph for 7–9. (3.MD.B.3)

7. How many students have cats as pets?

_____

8. Five more students have dogs than which other pet? _____

9. How many pets in all do students have?

_____

Our Pets	
Bird	🐾 🐾 🐾 🐾
Cat	🐾 🐾 🐾 🐾 🐾
Dog	🐾 🐾 🐾 🐾 🐾 🐾 🐾
Fish	🐾 🐾 🐾
Key: Each 🐾 = 2 students.	

Use the **Favorite Summer Activity** picture graph for 10–14.

Favorite Summer Activity

Camping	☀ ☀ ☀ ☀ ☀
Biking	☀ ☀ ☀ ☀
Swimming	☀ ☀ ☀ ☀ ☀ ☀
Canoeing	☀ ☀ ☀

Key: Each ☀ = 10 students.

10. Some students in Brooke's school chose their favorite summer activity. The results are in the picture graph at the right. How many students chose camping? (3.MD.B.3)

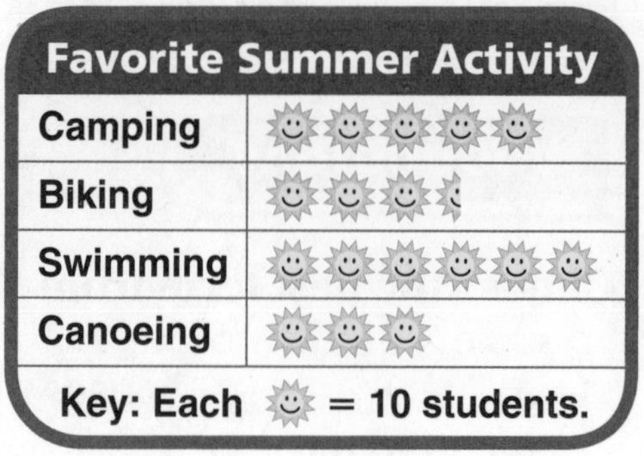

_____

11. How many more students chose swimming than canoeing? (3.MD.B.3)

_____

12. Which activity did 15 fewer students choose than camping? (3.MD.B.3)

_____

13. How many pictures would you draw for biking if each ☀ = 5 students? (3.MD.B.3)

_____

14. **GO DEEPER** How many more students choose swimming and camping combined than biking and canoeing? (3.MD.B.3)

_____

Name _____

Use Bar Graphs

Essential Question How can you read and interpret data in a bar graph?

Common Core Measurement and Data—3.MD.B.3, 3.NBT.A.2
MATHEMATICAL PRACTICES
MP1, MP2, MP4

Unlock the Problem Real World

A **bar graph** uses bars to show data. A **scale** of equally spaced numbers helps you read the number each bar shows.

The students in the reading group made a bar graph to record the number of books they read in October. How many books did Seth read?

• Underline the words that tell you where to find the information to answer the question.

The title tells what the bar graph is about.

Books Read in October

Student: Max, Amy, Seth, Kate
Number of Books: 0 2 4 6 8 10 12 14 16

The length of a bar tells how many books each student read.

The scale is 0–16 by twos.

Each bar is labeled with a student's name.

Math Talk

MATHEMATICAL PRACTICES ②

Connect Symbols and Words Explain how to read the bar that tells how many books Amy read.

Find the bar for Seth. It ends at _____.

So, Seth read _____ books in October.

1. How many books did Max read? _____

2. Who read 4 fewer books than Kate? _____

3. What if Amy read 5 more books? How many books did Amy read? _____ Shade the graph to show how many she read.

More Examples   These bar graphs show the same data.

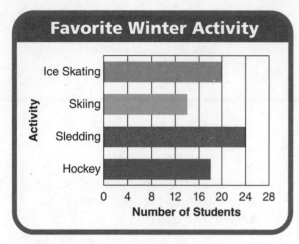

Favorite Winter Activity

In a **horizontal bar graph**, the bars go across from left to right. The length of the bar shows the number.

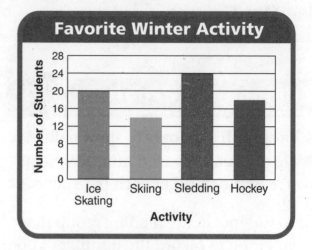

Favorite Winter Activity

In a **vertical bar graph**, the bars go up from the bottom. The height of the bar shows the number.

4. What does each space between two numbers represent?

_____

5. Why do you think the scale in the graphs is 0 to 28 by fours instead of 0 to 28 by ones? What other scale could you use?

_____

_____

Share and Show

Use the Favorite Way to Exercise bar graph for 1–3.

1. Which activity did the most students choose?

   Think: Which bar is the longest?

   _____

☑ **2.** How many students answered the survey? _____

☑ **3.** Which activity received 7 fewer votes than soccer? _____

Favorite Way to Exercise

Biking
Walking
Soccer
Karate

0 2 4 6 8 10 12 14 16
Number of Students

Activity

Math Talk   MATHEMATICAL PRACTICES ②

Reason Quantitatively
What can you tell just by comparing the lengths of the bars in the graph?

Name _____

Use the Favorite Kind of Book bar graph for 4–8.

4. Which kind of book was chosen by half the number of students as books about animals?

_____

5. **GO DEEPER** Which two kinds of books combined were chosen as often as books about sports?

_____

6. **MATHEMATICAL PRACTICE 4 Use Graphs** Write and solve a problem that matches the data in the graph.

_____

_____

7. **THINK SMARTER** What if 10 more students were asked and they chose books about animals? Describe what the bar graph would look like.

_____

_____

Favorite Kind of Book

8. **THINK SMARTER** For numbers 8a–8d, select True or False for each statement.

8a.	More students chose books about sports than any other kind of book.	○ True	○ False
8b.	Five more students chose books about puzzles than books about space.	○ True	○ False
8c.	Thirty more students chose books about animals than books about nature.	○ True	○ False
8d.	Fifteen fewer students chose books about puzzles than books about sports.	○ True	○ False

...

Sense or Nonsense?

9. **THINK SMARTER** The table shows data about some students' favorite amusement park rides. Four students graphed the data. Which student's bar graph makes sense?

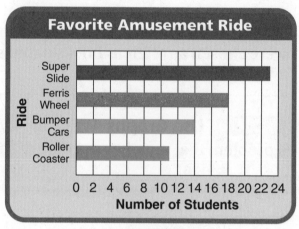

Favorite Amusement Ride	
Ride	Number of Students
Super Slide	11
Ferris Wheel	14
Bumper Cars	18
Roller Coaster	23

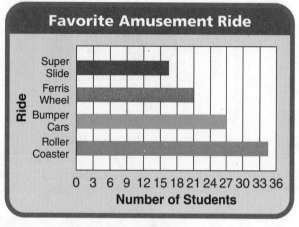

Alicia

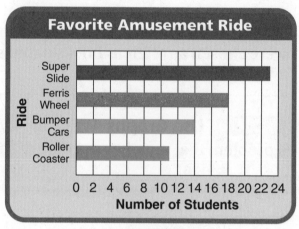

Spencer

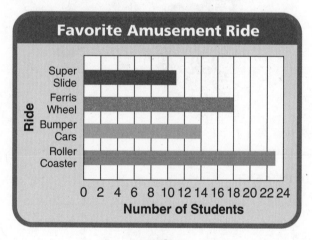

Tyler

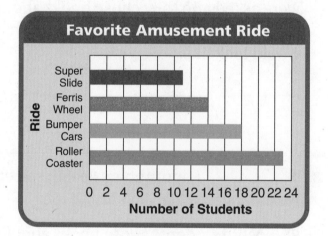

Kate

- Explain why the other bar graphs do not make sense.

_____

_____

_____

Name _____

Use Bar Graphs

COMMON CORE STANDARD—3.MD.B.3, 3.NBT.A.2
Represent and interpret data.

Use the After-Dinner Activities bar graph for 1–6.

The third-grade students at Case Elementary School were asked what they spent the most time doing last week after dinner. The results are shown in the bar graph at the right.

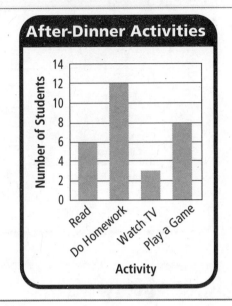

1. How many students spent the most time watching TV after dinner?

   _____3 students_____

2. How many students in all answered the survey?

   _____

3. How many students in all played a game or read?

   _____

4. How many fewer students read than did homework?

   _____

Problem Solving · Real World

5. Suppose 3 students changed their answers to reading instead of doing homework. Where would the bar for reading end?

   _____

6. **WRITE** ▸*Math* Use After-Dinner Activites bar graph to describe what the bar for Do Homework means.

   _____

   _____

Lesson Check (3.MD.B.3)

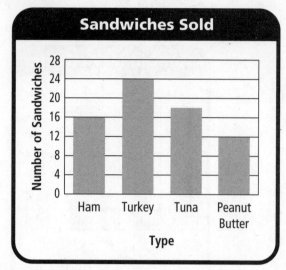

Sandwiches Sold

Number of Sandwiches
28
24
20
16
12
8
4
0

Ham   Turkey   Tuna   Peanut Butter

Type

1. The bar graph shows the number of sandwiches sold at Lisa's sandwich cart yesterday. How many tuna sandwiches were sold?

_____

Spiral Review (3.NBT.A.1)

2. What is 582 rounded to the nearest ten?

_____

3. Savannah read 178 minutes last week. What is 178 rounded to the nearest hundred?

_____

4. Estimate the difference.

$$\begin{array}{r} 371 \\ -\ 99 \\ \hline \end{array}$$

5. Estimate the difference.

$$\begin{array}{r} 625 \\ -\ 248 \\ \hline \end{array}$$

FOR MORE PRACTICE
GO TO THE
Personal Math Trainer

Make Bar Graphs

Essential Question How can you draw a bar graph to show data in a table or picture graph?

Common Core Measurement and Data—3.MD.B.3, 3.NBT.A.2
MATHEMATICAL PRACTICES
MP3, MP4, MP6

🔑 Unlock the Problem

Jordan took a survey of his classmates' favorite team sports. He recorded the results in the table at the right. How can he show the results in a bar graph?

Favorite Team Sport	
Sport	**Tally**
Soccer ⚽	~~IIII~~ ~~IIII~~ II
Basketball 🏀	IIII
Baseball ⚾	~~IIII~~ ~~IIII~~ IIII
Football 🏈	~~IIII~~ IIII

🔒 **Make a bar graph.**

STEP 1

Write a title at the top to tell what the graph is about. Label the side of the graph to tell about the bars. Label the bottom of the graph to explain what the numbers tell.

STEP 2

Choose numbers for the bottom of the graph so that most of the bars will end on a line. Since the least number is 4 and the greatest number is 14, make the scale 0–16. Mark the scale by twos.

STEP 3

Draw and shade a bar to show the number for each sport.

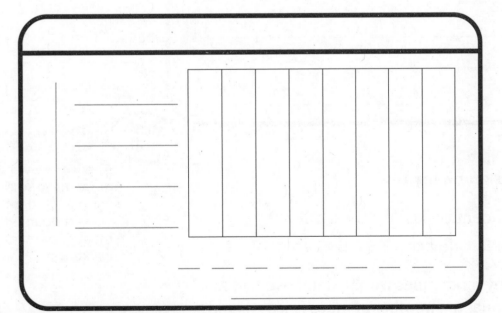

Math Talk

MATHEMATICAL PRACTICES ⑥

Make Connections How did you know how long to draw the bar for all of the sports?

School Walk-a-Thon					
Sam	👕	👕	👕	👕	👕
Matt	👕	👕	🏳		
Ben	👕				
Erica	👕	👕	👕	👕	

Key: Each 👕 = 2 miles.

Matt's school is having a walk-a-thon to raise money for the school library. Matt made a picture graph to show the number of miles some students walked. Make a bar graph of Matt's data. Use a scale of 0–_____, and mark the scale by _____.

Math Talk MATHEMATICAL PRACTICES ❸

Apply How would the graph have to change if another student, Daniel, walked double the number of miles Erica walked?

Use your bar graph for 1–4.

1. Which student walked the most miles? _____

   Think: Which student's bar is the tallest?

2. How many more miles would Matt have had to walk to equal the number of miles Erica walked? _____

3. How many miles did the students walk? _____

4. Write the number of miles the students walked in order from greatest to least. _____

114

Name _____

5. Lydia and Joey did an experiment with a spinner. Lydia recorded the result of each spin in the table at the right. Use the data in the table to make a bar graph. Choose numbers and a scale and decide how to mark your graph.

Spinner Results	
Color	**Tally**
Red	卌 卌 卌 l
Yellow	卌 lll
Blue	卌 卌 ll
Green	卌 卌

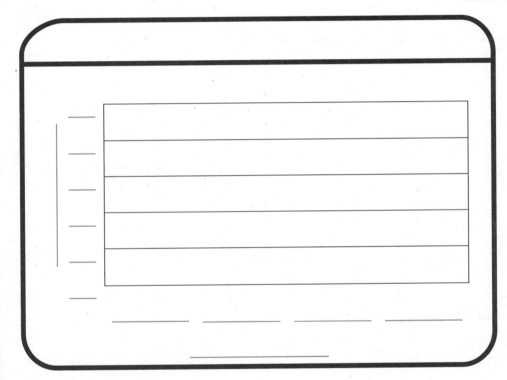

> **! ERROR Alert**
>
> Be sure to draw the bars correctly when you transfer data from a table.

Use your bar graph for 6–8.

6. The pointer stopped on _____ half the number

   of times that it stopped on _____.

7. GO DEEPER The pointer stopped on green _____ fewer times than it stopped on blue and yellow combined.

8. MATHEMATICAL PRACTICE ⑥ **Explain** why you chose the scale you did.

_____

_____

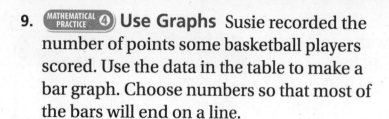

Problem Solving • Applications

9. **MATHEMATICAL PRACTICE 4** **Use Graphs** Susie recorded the number of points some basketball players scored. Use the data in the table to make a bar graph. Choose numbers so that most of the bars will end on a line.

Points Scored	
Player	**Number of Points**
Billy	10
Dwight	30
James	15
Raul	25
Sean	10

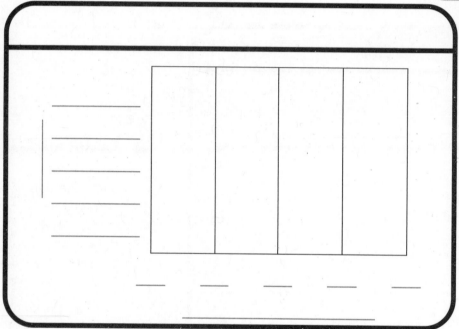

Use your bar graph for 10–12.

10. **GO DEEPER** Which player scored more points than James but fewer points than Dwight? _____

11. **THINK SMARTER** Write and solve a new question that matches the data in your bar graph.

_____

_____

12. **THINK SMARTER** Which player scored 10 more points than James?

_____

Make Bar Graphs

Common Core
COMMON CORE STANDARD—3.MD.B.3,
3.NBT.A.2 *Represent and interpret data.*

Ben asked some friends to name their favorite breakfast food. He recorded their choices in the frequency table at the right.

1. Complete the bar graph by using Ben's data.

Favorite Breakfast Food	
Food	Number of Votes
Waffles	8
Cereal	14
Pancakes	12
Oatmeal	4

Favorite Breakfast Food

Use your bar graph for 2–4.

2. Which food did the most people choose as their favorite breakfast food?

_____

3. How many people chose waffles as their favorite breakfast food?

_____

4. Suppose 6 people chose oatmeal as their favorite breakfast food. How would you change the bar graph?

_____

_____

_____

_____

5. **WRITE** ▶*Math* Have students use the data on page 116 and explain how to draw a bar for a player named Eric who scored 20 points.

_____

_____

© Houghton Mifflin Harcourt Publishing Company

Lesson Check (3.MD.B.3)

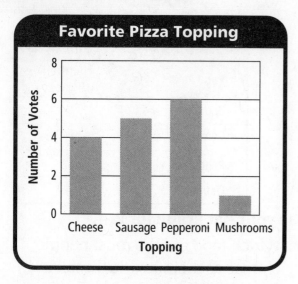

Favorite Pizza Topping

Number of Votes / Topping

Cheese, Sausage, Pepperoni, Mushrooms

1. Gary asked his friends to name their favorite pizza topping. He recorded the results in a bar graph. How many people chose pepperoni?

_____

2. Suppose 3 more friends chose mushrooms. Where would the bar for mushrooms end?

_____

Spiral Review (3.OA.D.9, 3.NBT.A.1)

3. Estimate the sum.

$$458$$
$$+\,214$$

_____

4. Matt added 14 + 0. What is this sum?

_____

5. There are 682 runners registered for an upcoming race. What is 682 rounded to the nearest hundred?

_____

6. There are 187 new students this year at Maple Elementary. What is 187 rounded to the nearest ten?

_____

FOR MORE PRACTICE
GO TO THE
Personal Math Trainer

Name _____

Solve Problems Using Data

Essential Question How can you solve problems using data represented in bar graphs?

Common Core Measurement and Data—3.MD.B.3, 3.OA.D.8
MATHEMATICAL PRACTICES
MP1, MP2, MP6

Unlock the Problem (Real World)

CONNECT Answering questions about data helps you better understand the information.

Derek's class voted on a topic for the school bulletin board. The bar graph shows the results. How many more votes did computers receive than space?

One Way Use a model.

Count back along the scale to find the difference between the bars.

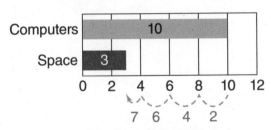

Count back from 10 to 3.
Skip count by twos.

The difference is _____ votes.

Another Way Write a number sentence.

Think: There are 10 votes for computers. There are 3 votes for space. Subtract to compare the number of votes.

_____

So, computers received _____ more votes than space.

• How do you know you need to subtract?

_____

_____

Votes for School Bulletin Board Topic

(bar graph: Topic vs Number of Votes, scale 0 2 4 6 8 10 12; bars for Books, Health, Computers, Space)

Math Talk MATHEMATICAL PRACTICES ⑥

Explain another way you can skip count to find the difference.

🔑 Example

Brooke's school collected cans of food. The bar graph at the right shows the number of cans. How many fewer cans were collected on Tuesday than on Thursday and Friday combined?

Cans of Food Collected

STEP 1 Find the total for Thursday and Friday.

_____

_____

STEP 2 Subtract to compare the total for Thursday and Friday to Tuesday and to find the difference.

_____

So, _____ fewer cans were collected on Tuesday than on Thursday and Friday combined.

- What if 4 fewer cans were collected on Monday than on Tuesday? How many cans were collected on Monday? Explain.

_____

Share and Show MATH BOARD

Use the Spinner Results bar graph for 1–3.

1. How many more times did the pointer stop on green than on purple?

   _____ more times

☑ 2. How many fewer times did the pointer stop on blue than on red and green combined?

   _____ fewer times

☑ 3. What if there were 15 more spins and the pointer stopped 10 more times on green and 5 more times on blue? How many more total times did the pointer stop on green than blue?

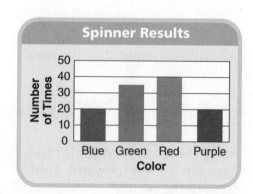

Spinner Results

Math Talk

MATHEMATICAL PRACTICES ②

Use Reasoning What can you tell just by comparing the lengths of the bars in the graphs?

Name _____

On Your Own

Use the Diego's DVDs bar graph for 4–6.

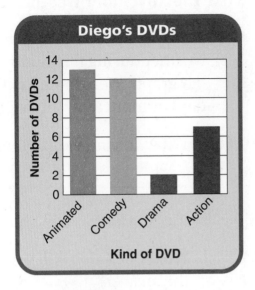

Diego's DVDs

4. Diego has 5 fewer of this kind of DVD than comedy. Which kind of DVD is this?

   _____

5. **GO DEEPER** Is the number of comedy and action DVDs greater than or less than the number of animated and drama DVDs? Explain.

   _____

   _____

6. **THINK SMARTER** How many DVDs does Diego have that are NOT comedy DVDs?

   _____

   _____

Problem Solving • Applications Real World

Use the Science Fair Projects bar graph for 7–9.

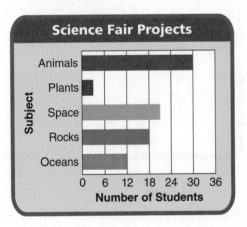

Science Fair Projects

7. How many more students would have to do a project on plants to equal the number of projects on space?

   _____

8. **WRITE** ▸*Math* **What's the Question?** The answer is animals, space, rocks, oceans, and plants.

   _____

   _____

9. **MATHEMATICAL PRACTICE ①** What if 3 fewer students did a project on weather than did a project on rocks? **Describe** what the bar graph would look like.

   _____

   _____

Unlock the Problem (Real World)

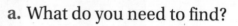

Use the November Weather bar graph for 10–12.

10. **GO DEEPER** Lacey's class recorded the kinds of weather during the month of November in a bar graph. Were there more cloudy and sunny days or more rainy and snowy days?

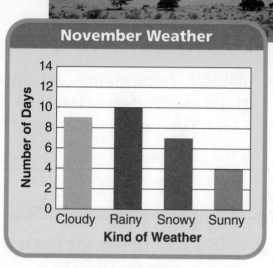

November Weather

a. What do you need to find?

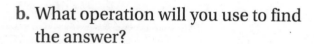

b. What operation will you use to find the answer?

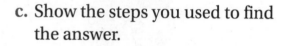

c. Show the steps you used to find the answer.

d. Complete the sentences.

_____ cloudy days +

_____ sunny days = _____ days

_____ rainy days +

_____ snowy days = _____ days

_____ > _____

So, there were more _____ days.

11. **GO DEEPER** How many days in November were NOT cloudy?

Think: There are 30 days in November.

_____

Personal Math Trainer

12. **THINK SMARTER +** Is the number of cloudy and snowy days greater than or less than the number of rainy and sunny days? Explain.

_____

_____

Name _____

Solve Problems Using Data

Common Core   COMMON CORE STANDARD—3.MD.B.3,
3.OA.D.8 *Represent and interpret data.*
Solve problems involving the four operations,
and identify and explain patterns in arithmetic.

Use the Favorite Hot Lunch bar graph for 1–2.

1. How many more students chose pizza than chose grilled cheese?

   Think: Subtract the number of students who chose grilled cheese, 2, from the number of students who chose pizza, 11.

   $11 - 2 = 9$ _____ more students

2. How many students did not choose chicken patty? _____ students

Use the Ways to Get to School bar graph for 3–5.

3. How many more students walk than ride in a car to get to school?

   _____ more students

 Problem Solving *Real World*

4. Is the number of students who get to school by car and bus greater than or less than the number of students who get to school by walking and biking? **Explain**.

   _____

   _____

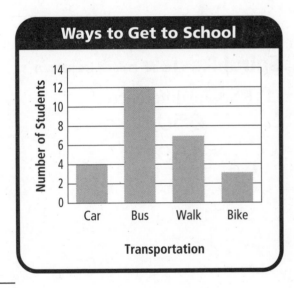

5. What if 5 more students respond that they get to school by biking? Would more students walk or ride a bike to school? **Explain**.

   _____

6. **WRITE** ▸*Math* Write a word problem that can be solved by using the November Weather bar graph on page 122.

   _____

   _____

Lesson Check (3.MD.B.3)

1. How many fewer votes were for bench repair than for food drive?

_____

2. How many votes were there in all?

Community Project

_____

Spiral Review (3.NBT.A.1, 3.NBT.A.2)

3. Find the difference.

$$650$$
$$-\ 189$$

4. Greyson has 75 basketball cards. What is 75 rounded to the nearest ten?

_____ _____

5. Sue spent $18 on a shirt, $39 on a jacket, and $12 on a hat. How much did she spend?

6. There are 219 adults and 174 children at a ballet. How many people are at the ballet?

_____ _____

FOR MORE PRACTICE
GO TO THE
Personal Math Trainer

Name _____

Use and Make Line Plots

Essential Question How can you read and interpret data in a line plot and use data to make a line plot?

Common Core Measurement and Data—3.MD.B.4, 3.NBT.A.2
MATHEMATICAL PRACTICES
MP1, MP5, MP8

⚷ Unlock the Problem

A **line plot** uses marks to record each piece of data above a number line. It helps you see groups in the data.

Some students took a survey of the number of letters in their first names. Then they recorded the data in a line plot.

How many students have 6 letters in their first names?

> Each **✗** stands for 1 student.
→

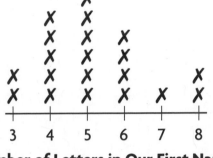

Number of Letters in Our First Names

> The numbers show the number of letters in a name. ←

🔑 Find 6 on the number line. The 6 stands for 6 _____.

There are _____ **✗**s above the 6.

So, _____ students have 6 letters in their first names.

---

1. Which number of letters was found most often? _____

2. Write a sentence to describe the data. _____

   _____

3. How many letters are in your first name? _____

4. Put an **✗** above the number of letters in your first name.

 Math Talk

MATHEMATICAL PRACTICES ⑧

Generalize What information can the shape of a graph tell you about the data used to create the graph?

Activity Make a line plot.

Materials ■ ruler ■ measuring tape

Measure the height of four classmates to the nearest inch. Combine your data with other groups. Make a line plot to show the data you collected.

STEP 1 Record the heights in the table.
_____

STEP 2 Write a title below the number line to describe your line plot.
_____

STEP 3 Write the number of inches in order from left to right above the title.
_____

STEP 4 Draw *X*s above the number line to show each student's height.

Heights in Inches	
Number of Inches	Tally

5. Which height appears most often? _____

   Think: Which height has the most *X*s?

6. Which height appears least often? _____

7. Complete the sentence. Most of the students in the

   class are _____ inches tall or taller.

8. *THINK SMARTER* Is there any height for which there are no data? Explain.

_____

_____

Name _____

1. Measure the length of three drawing tools from your desk to the nearest inch. Combine your data with several other classmates. Record the lengths in the table.

✓ 2. Make a line plot to show the data you collected.

Lengths in Inches	
Number of Inches	Tally

✓ 3. Which length appears most often? _____

Problem Solving • Applications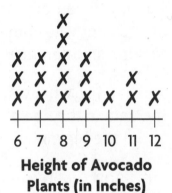

Use the line plot at the right for 4–6.

4. **MATHEMATICAL PRACTICE ⑤ Use Appropriate Tools** Garden club members recorded the height of their avocado plants to the nearest inch in a line plot. Write a sentence to describe what the line plot shows.

_____

_____

Height of Avocado Plants (in Inches)

5. **THINK SMARTER** How many more plants are 8 or 9 inches tall than are 6 or 7 inches tall? Explain.

_____

_____

6. **THINK SMARTER** How many plants are taller than 8 inches?

_____ plants

GO DEEPER **Make an Inference**

Addison made the line plot below to show the high temperature every day for one month. What *inference* can you make about what season this is?

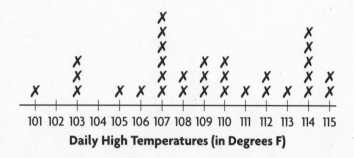

Daily High Temperatures (in Degrees F)

When you combine what you see with what you already know to come up with an idea, you are making an inference.

You can use what you know about weather and the data in the line plot to make an inference about the season.

You know that the numbers in the line plot are the high temperatures recorded during the month.

The highest temperature recorded was _____.

The lowest temperature recorded was _____.

The temperature recorded most often was _____.

Since all the high temperatures are greater than 100, you know the days were hot. This will help you make an inference about the season.

So, you can infer that the season is _____.

Remember

The Four Seasons

spring

summer

fall

winter

COMMON CORE STANDARD—3.MD.B.4,
3.NBT.A.2 *Represent and interpret data.*
Use place value understanding and properties
of operations to perform multi-digit arithmetic.

Use the data in the table to make a line plot.

How Many Shirts Were Sold at Each Price?	
Price	Number Sold
$11	1
$12	4
$13	6
$14	4
$15	0
$16	2

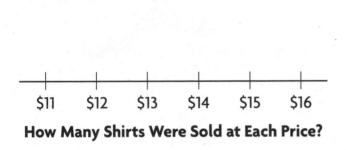

$11 $12 $13 $14 $15 $16

How Many Shirts Were Sold at Each Price?

1. How many shirts sold for $12?

   _____ 4 shirts _____

2. How many shirts were sold for $13 or more?

   _____

Problem Solving Real World

Use the line plot above for 3–4.

3. Were more shirts sold for less than $13 or more than $13? **Explain.**

   _____

4. Is there any price for which there are no data? **Explain.**

   _____

   _____

5. **WRITE** ▸*Math* Have students write and solve another problem using the data in the Daily High Temperatures line plot on page 128.

   _____

   _____

Lesson Check (3.MD.B.4)

1. Pedro made a line plot to show the heights of the plants in his garden. How many plants are less than 3 inches tall?

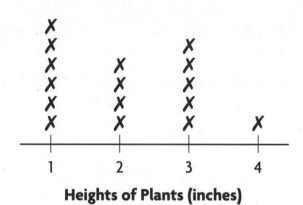

Heights of Plants (inches)

_____

Spiral Review (3.NBT.A.1, 3.NBT.A.2)

2. Find the sum.

$$642$$
$$+ \ 259$$

_____

3. Find the difference.

$$460$$
$$- \ 309$$

_____

4. There were 262 hamburgers cooked for the school fair. What is 262 rounded to the nearest hundred?

_____

5. Makenzie has 517 stickers in her collection. What is 517 rounded to the nearest ten?

_____

FOR MORE PRACTICE
GO TO THE
Personal Math Trainer

✓ Chapter 2 Review/Test

Personal Math Trainer
Online Assessment and Intervention

1. Mia made a tally table to record the different types of birds she saw at the bird feeder in the garden.

Birds at the Feeder	
Name	**Tally**
Jay	llll
Sparrow	llll llll ll
Finch	llll lll
Blackbird	llll l

For numbers 1a–1c, select True or False for each statement.

1a. Mia saw twice as many sparrows as blackbirds. ○ True ○ False

1b. Mia saw 8 finches. ○ True ○ False

1c. Mia saw 4 fewer jays than blackbirds. ○ True ○ False

2. Jake asked 25 students in his class how close they live to school. The frequency table shows the results.

Miles to School		
	Boys	**Girls**
about 1 mile	4	5
about 2 miles		4
about 3 miles	3	2

Part A

Complete the table and explain how you found the answer.

Part B

How many more students live about 2 miles or less from school than students who live about 3 miles from school? Show your work.

GO DIGITAL Assessment Options
Chapter Test

Use the picture graph for 3–6.

Students at Barnes School are performing in a play. The picture graph shows the number of tickets each class has sold so far.

3. How many tickets were sold altogether?
Explain how you found the total.

Number of Tickets Sold	
Ms. Brown's Class	✓ ✓ ✓ ✓ ✓ ✓ ✓ ✓
Mrs. Gold's Class	✓ ✓ ✓ ✓
Mr. Castro's Class	✓ ✓ ✓ ✓ ✓

Key: Each ✓ = 5 tickets.

4. Choose the name from each box that makes the sentence true.

Five fewer tickets were sold by
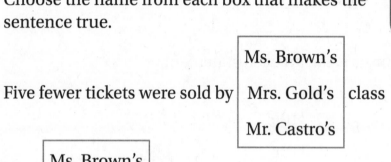
Ms. Brown's
Mrs. Gold's   class
Mr. Castro's

than
Ms. Brown's
Mrs. Gold's   class.
Mr. Castro's

5. How many more tickets were sold by Ms. Brown's class than Mr. Castro's class?

_____ tickets

6. What if Mrs. Gold's class sold 20 more tickets? Draw a picture to show how the graph would change.

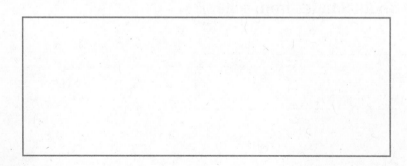

Name _____

Use the frequency table for 7–8.

7. **GO DEEPER** The Pet Shop keeps track of the number of fish it has for sale. The frequency table shows how many fish are in three tanks.

Fish in Tanks	
Tank	Number of Fish
Tank 1	16
Tank 2	9
Tank 3	12

Part A

Use the data in the table to complete the picture graph.

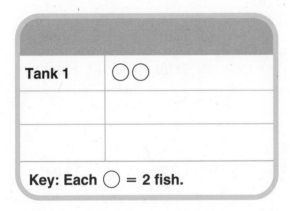

Part B

How many pictures did you draw for Tank 2? Explain.

8. Each tank can hold up to 20 fish. How many more fish can the Pet Shop put in the three tanks?

(A) 60 fish   (C) 20 fish

(B) 23 fish   (D) 33 fish

Use the bar graph for 9–12.

9. Three more students play piano than which other instrument?

    _____

10. The same number of students play which two instruments?

    _____

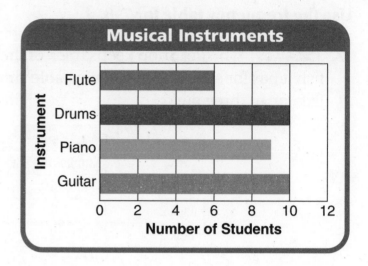

Musical Instruments

11. For numbers 11a–11d, select True or False for each statement.

    11a. Ten more students play guitar than play flute.   ○ True   ○ False

    11b. Nine students play piano.   ○ True   ○ False

    11c. Six fewer students play flute and piano combined than play drums and guitar combined.   ○ True   ○ False

    11d. Nine more students play piano and guitar combined than play drums.   ○ True   ○ False

12. There are more students who play the trumpet than play the flute, but fewer students than play the guitar. Explain how you would change the bar graph to show the number of students who play the trumpet.

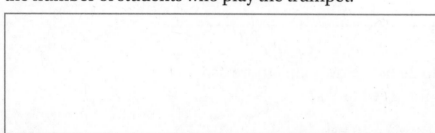

Name _____

Use the frequency table for 13–14.

13. **THINK SMARTER +** Karen asks students what vegetables they would like to have in the school cafeteria. The table shows the results of her survey.

Favorite Vegetables	
Vegetable	**Number of Votes**
broccoli	15
carrots	40
corn	20
green beans	10

Part A

Use the data in the table to complete the bar graph.

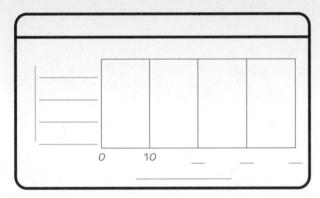

0   10   __   __   __

Part B

How do you know how long to make the bars on your graph? How did you show 15 votes for broccoli? Explain.

14. How many more votes did the two most popular vegetables get than the two least popular vegetables? Explain how you solved the problem.

_____

_____

_____

Use the line plot for 15–16.

The line plot shows the number of goals the players on Scot's team scored.

15. For numbers 15a–15d, select True or False for each statement.

15a. Three players scored 2 goals. ○ True ○ False

15b. Six players scored fewer than 2 goals. ○ True ○ False

15c. There are 8 players on the team. ○ True ○ False

15d. Five players scored more than 1 goal. ○ True ○ False

16. What if two more people played and each scored 3 goals? Describe what the line plot would look like.

Use the line plot for 17–18.

Robin collected shells during her vacation. She measured the length of each shell to the nearest inch and recorded the data in a line plot.

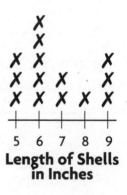

17. How many shells were 6 inches long or longer?

_____ shells

18. How many more shells did Robin collect that were 5 inches long than 8 inches long?

_____ shells

Chapter 3

Understand Multiplication

Show What You Know

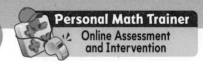

Personal Math Trainer
Online Assessment and Intervention

Check your understanding of important skills.

Name _____

▶ **Count On to Add** Use the number line. Write the sum. (1.OA.C.5)

0 1 2 3 4 5 6 7 8 9 10

1. $6 + 2 =$ _____

2. $3 + 7 =$ _____

▶ **Skip Count by Twos and Fives** Skip count. Write the missing numbers. (2.NBT.A.2)

3. 2, 4, 6, _____, _____, _____

4. 5, 10, 15, _____, _____, _____

▶ **Model with Arrays** Use the array. Complete. (2.OA.C.4)

5.

_____ + _____ + _____ = _____

6.

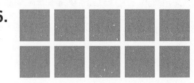

_____ + _____ = _____

Math in the Real World

Ryan's class went on a field trip to a farm. They saw 5 cows and 6 chickens. Help to find how many legs were on all the animals they saw.

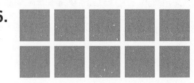

© Houghton Mifflin Harcourt Publishing Company • Image Credits: ©David Frazier/Corbis

Vocabulary Builder

▶ **Visualize It** ⋯⋯⋯⋯⋯⋯⋯⋯⋯⋯⋯⋯⋯

Complete the tree map by using the review words.

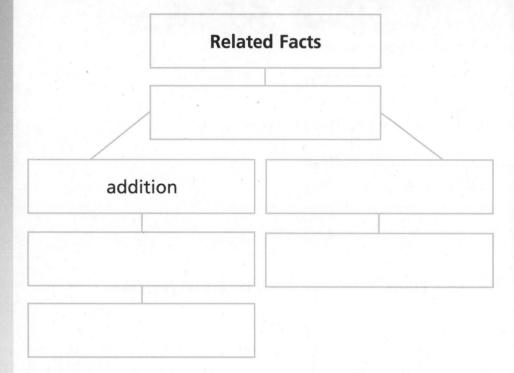

Related Facts

addition

▶ **Understand Vocabulary** ⋯⋯⋯⋯⋯⋯⋯⋯⋯

Read the definition. Write the preview word that matches it.

1. A set of objects arranged in rows and columns _____

2. The answer in a multiplication problem _____

3. When you combine equal groups to find how many in all _____

4. A number that is multiplied by another number to find a product _____

138

• **Interactive Student Edition**
• **Multimedia eGlossary**

© Houghton Mifflin Harcourt Publishing Company

Chapter 3 Vocabulary

array

matriz

4

Commutative Property of Multiplication

Propiedad conmutativa de la multiplicación

9

equal groups

grupos iguales

20

factor

factor

25

Identity Property of Multiplication

Propiedad de identidad de la multiplicación

35

multiply

multiplicar

51

product

producto

65

Zero Property of Multiplication

Propiedad del cero de la multiplicación

85

The property that states that you can multiply two factors in any order and get the same product

Example: $4 \times 3 = 3 \times 4$

A set of objects arranged in rows and columns

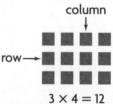

$3 \times 4 = 12$

A number that is multiplied by another number to find a product

Example: $4 \times 5 = 20$

factor   factor

Groups that have the same number of objects

To combine equal groups to find how many in all; the opposite operation of division

2   ×   2   =   4

factor   factor   product

The property that states that the product of any number and 1 is that number

Example: $17 \times 1 = 17$

The property that states that the product of zero and any number is zero

Example: $34 \times 0 = 0$

The answer in a multiplication problem

Example: $4 \times 5 = 20$

product

Matchup

For 2–3 players

Materials
1 set of word cards

How to Play

1. Put the cards face-down in rows. Take turns to play.
2. Choose two cards and turn them face-up.
   - If the cards show a word and its meaning, it's a match. Keep the pair and take another turn.
   - If the cards do not match, turn them back over.
3. The game is over when all cards have been matched. The players count their pairs. The player with the most pairs wins.

Word Box
array
equal groups
factors
multiply
product
Commutative Property of Multiplication
Identity Property of Multiplication
Zero Property of Multiplication

The Write Way

Reflect

Choose one idea. Write about it.

- Do $4 + 4 + 4$ and 4×3 represent equal groups? Explain why or why not.
- Explain how to use an array to find a product.
- Summarize how to solve 5×0, including any "false starts" or "dead ends" you might take.

Name _____

Count Equal Groups

Essential Question How can you use equal groups to find how many in all?

Common Core Operations and Algebraic Thinking— 3.OA.A.1 *Also 3.OA.A.3*
MATHEMATICAL PRACTICES
MP2, MP3, MP4

？Unlock the Problem *Real World*

Equal groups have the same number of objects in each group.

Tim has 6 toy cars. Each car has 4 wheels. How many wheels are there in all?

- How many wheels are on each car?

  _____

- How many equal groups of wheels are there?

  _____

- How can you find how many wheels in all?

  _____

🔑 Activity Use counters to model the equal groups.

Materials ▪ counters

STEP 1 Draw 4 counters in each group.

_____

STEP 2 Skip count to find how many wheels in all.
Skip count by 4s until you say 6 numbers.

number of
equal groups → 1   2   3   4   5   6

4, _____, 12, _____, _____, _____

There are _____ groups with _____ wheels in each group.

So, there are _____ wheels in all.

 Math Talk

MATHEMATICAL PRACTICES ②

Reason Quantitatively
What if Tim had 8 cars? How could you find the total number of wheels?

🔒 **Example** Count equal groups to find the total.

Sam, Kyla, and Tia each have 5 pennies.
How many pennies do they have in all?

How many pennies does each person have? _____

How many equal groups of pennies are there? _____

Draw 5 counters in each group.

Think: There are _____ groups of 5 pennies.

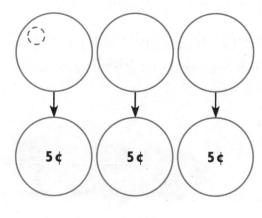

Think: There are _____ fives.

Skip count to find how many pennies.   _____, _____, _____

So, they have _____ pennies.

- **THINK SMARTER** Explain why you can skip count by 5s to find how many.

_____

 **Share and Show** MATH BOARD

1. Complete. Use the picture. Skip count to find
   how many wheels in all.

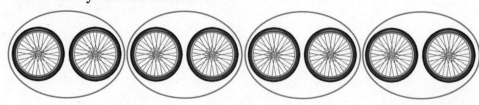

_____ groups of 2

_____ twos

Skip count by 2s.   2, 4, _____, _____

So, there are _____ wheels.

Math Talk MATHEMATICAL PRACTICES ③

Apply How would your
answer change if 2
more groups of wheels
were added?

© Houghton Mifflin Harcourt Publishing Company

140

Name _____

Draw equal groups. Skip count to find how many.

2. 2 groups of 6 _____

3. 3 groups of 2 _____

Count equal groups to find how many.

4.

_____ groups of _____

_____ in all

5.

_____ groups of _____

_____ in all

On Your Own

Draw equal groups. Skip count to find how many.

6. 3 groups of 3 _____

7. 2 groups of 9 _____

8. **GO DEEPER** A toy car costs $3. A toy truck costs $4. Which costs more—4 cars or 3 trucks? Explain.

_____

_____

9. **MATHEMATICAL PRACTICE ③ Make Arguments** Elliott has a collection of 20 toy cars. Will he be able to put an equal number of toy cars on 3 shelves? Explain your answer.

_____

_____

🔑 Unlock the Problem

10. **THINK SMARTER** Tina, Charlie, and Amber have toy cars. Each car has 4 wheels. How many wheels do their cars have altogether?

Toy Cars

a. What do you need to find?

_____

b. What information will you use from the graph to solve the problem?

_____

c. Show the steps you used to solve the problem.

d. So, the cars have _____ wheels.

11. **THINK SMARTER** A bookcase has 4 shelves. Each shelf holds 5 books. How many books are in the bookcase?

Draw counters to model the problem. Then explain how you solved the problem.

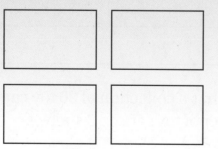

_____

_____

Count Equal Groups

  COMMON CORE STANDARD—3.OA.A.1
*Represent and solve problems involving
multiplication and division.*

Draw equal groups. Skip count to find how many.

1. 2 groups of 2 ___4___

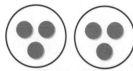

2. 3 groups of 6 _____

Count equal groups to find how many.

3.

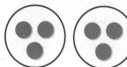

_____ groups of _____

_____ in all

4.

_____ groups of _____

_____ in all

 Problem Solving *Real World*

5. Marcia puts 2 slices of cheese on
each sandwich. She makes 4 cheese
sandwiches. How many slices of
cheese does Marcia use in all?

_____

6. Tomas works in a cafeteria kitchen.
He puts 3 cherry tomatoes on each
of 5 salads. How many tomatoes does
he use?

_____

7. **WRITE** *Math* Write a problem that can be solved by using equal groups.

_____

_____

Lesson Check (3.OA.A.1)

1. Jen makes 3 bracelets. Each bracelet has 3 beads. How many beads does Jen use?

2. Ian has 5 cards to mail. Each card needs 2 stamps. How many stamps does Ian need?

Spiral Review (3.NBT.A.1, 3.NBT.A.2)

3. There were 384 people at a play on Friday night. There were 512 people at the play on Saturday night. Estimate the total number of people who attended the play on both nights.

4. Walking the Dog Pet Store has 438 leashes in stock. They sell 79 leashes during a one-day sale. How many leashes are left in stock after the sale?

5. The Lakeside Tour bus traveled 490 miles on Saturday and 225 miles on Sunday. About how many more miles did it travel on Saturday?

6. During one week at Jackson School, 210 students buy milk and 196 students buy juice. How many drinks are sold that week?

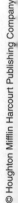

FOR MORE PRACTICE
GO TO THE
Personal Math Trainer

Relate Addition and Multiplication

Essential Question How is multiplication like addition?
How is it different?

Common Core Operations and Algebraic Thinking—
3.OA.A.1 Also 3.OA.A.3, 3.OA.C.7,
3.NBT.A.2
MATHEMATICAL PRACTICES
MP3, MP4, MP6

⚷ Unlock the Problem

Tomeka needs 3 apples to make one loaf of apple bread. Each loaf has the same number of apples. How many apples does Tomeka need to make 4 loaves?

- How many loaves is Tomeka making?
  _____

- How many apples are in each loaf?
  _____

- How can you solve the problem?
  _____

🔓 **One Way** Add equal groups.

Use the 4 circles to show the 4 loaves.

Draw 3 counters in each circle to show the apples Tomeka needs for each loaf.

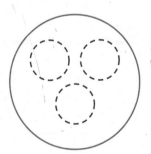 

Find the number of counters.
Complete the addition sentence.

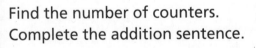
3 + _____ + _____ + _____ = _____

So, Tomeka needs _____ apples to

make _____ loaves of apple bread.

Math Talk

MATHEMATICAL PRACTICES ④

Use Diagrams How can drawing a picture help you to solve a multiplication problem?

① **Another Way** Multiply.

When you combine equal groups, you can **multiply** to find how many in all.

Think: 4 groups of 3

Draw 3 counters in each circle.

Since there are the same number of counters in each circle, you can multiply to find how many in all.

Multiplication is another way to find how many there are altogether in equal groups.

Write: 4   ×   3   =   12   **or**   4 ← factor
        ↑   ↑   ↑   × 3 ← factor
    factor   factor   product   12 ← product

Read: Four times three equals twelve.

The **factors** are the numbers multiplied.

The **product** is the answer to a multiplication problem.

Share and Show

1. Write related addition and multiplication sentences for the model.

_____ + _____ + _____ + _____ = _____

_____ × _____ = _____

MATHEMATICAL PRACTICES ④

Use Models How would you change this model so you could write a multiplication sentence to match it?

Name _____

**Draw a quick picture to show the equal groups. Then
write related addition and multiplication sentences.**

2. 3 groups of 6

___ + ___ + ___ = ___

___ × ___ = ___

3. 2 groups of 3

___ + ___ = ___

___ × ___ = ___

On Your Own

**Draw a quick picture to show the equal groups. Then
write related addition and multiplication sentences.**

4. 4 groups of 2

___ + ___ + ___ + ___ = ___

___ × ___ = ___

5. 5 groups of 4

___ + ___ + ___ + ___ + ___ = ____

___ × ___ = ____

Complete. Write a multiplication sentence.

6. Zach buys 4 packs of pens. Each pack
has 4 pens. Write a multiplication
sentence to show how many pens
Zach buys.

___ × ___ = ___

7. Ada has 3 vases. She puts 5 flowers
in each vase. Write a multiplication
sentence to show how many flowers
Ada puts in the vases.

___ × ___ = ___

8. **GO DEEPER** Mrs. Tomar buys 2 packs of
vanilla yogurt and 3 packs of strawberry
yogurt. Each pack has 4 yogurts. How
many yogurts does Mrs. Tomar buy?

_____

9. **GO DEEPER** Murray buys 3 packs of red
peppers and 4 packs of green peppers.
Each pack has 4 peppers. How many
peppers does Murray buy?

_____

Problem Solving • Applications

Use the table for 10–11.

Average Weight of Fruits	
Fruit	**Weight in Ounces**
Apple	6
Orange	5
Peach	3
Banana	4

10. Morris bought 4 peaches. How much do the peaches weigh? Write a multiplication sentence to find the weight of the peaches.

_____ × _____ = _____ ounces

11. **THINK SMARTER** Thomas bought 2 apples. Sydney bought 4 bananas. Which weighed more—the 2 apples or the 4 bananas? How much more? Explain how you know.

_____

_____

_____

12. **MATHEMATICAL PRACTICE ③ Make Arguments** Shane said that he could write related multiplication and addition sentences for 6 + 4 + 3. Does Shane's statement make sense? Explain.

_____

_____

13. **GO DEEPER** Write a word problem that can be solved using 3 × 4. Solve the problem.

_____

_____

14. **THINK SMARTER** Select the number sentences that represent the model at the right. Mark all that apply.

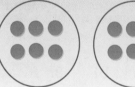

Ⓐ 3 + 6 = 9   Ⓒ 3 × 6 = 18

Ⓑ 6 + 6 + 6 = 18   Ⓓ 6 + 3 = 9

Name _____

Relate Addition and Multiplication

COMMON CORE STANDARD—3.OA.A.1
Represent and solve problems involving multiplication and division.

Draw a quick picture to show the equal groups. Then write related addition and multiplication sentences.

1. 3 groups of 5

   __5__ + __5__ + __5__ = __15__

   __3__ × __5__ = __15__

2. 3 groups of 4

   ___ + ___ + ___ = ___

   ___ × ___ = ___

3. 5 groups of 2

   ___ + ___ + ___ + ___ + ___ = ___

   ___ × ___ = ___

Complete. Write a multiplication sentence.

4. 7 + 7 + 7 = ___

   ___ × ___ = ___

5. 3 + 3 + 3 = ___

   ___ × ___ = ___

 Problem Solving Real World

6. There are 6 jars of pickles in a box. Ed has 3 boxes of pickles. How many jars of pickles does he have? Write a multiplication sentence to find the answer.

   ___ × ___ = ___ jars

7. Each day, Jani rides her bike 5 miles. How many miles does Jani ride in 4 days? Write a multiplication sentence to find the answer.

   ___ × ___ = ___ miles

8. **WRITE** ▸*Math* Write a word problem that involves combining three equal groups.

   _____

   _____

Lesson Check (3.OA.A.1)

1. What is another way to show

$3 + 3 + 3 + 3 + 3 + 3$?

2. Use the model. How many counters are there?

_____

Spiral Review (3.NBT.A.1, 3.NBT.A.2, 3.MD.B.4)

3. A school gave 884 pencils to students on the first day of school. What is 884 rounded to the nearest hundred?

4. Find the difference.

$$632$$
$$-\ 274$$

_____

5. The line plot below shows how many points Trevor scored in 20 games.

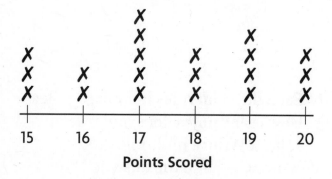

Points Scored

In how many games did Trevor score 18 points or fewer?

6. Darrien read 97 pages last week. Evan read 84 pages last week. How many pages did the boys read?

_____

FOR MORE PRACTICE
GO TO THE
Personal Math Trainer

Skip Count on a Number Line

Essential Question How can you use a number line to skip count and find how many in all?

**Operations and Algebraic Thinking—
3.OA.A.3** *Also 3.OA.A.1*
MATHEMATICAL PRACTICES
MP3, MP4, MP7

？Unlock the Problem · Real World

Caleb wants to make 3 balls of yarn for his cat to play with. He uses 6 feet of yarn to make each ball. How many feet of yarn does Caleb need in all?

- How many equal groups of yarn will Caleb make?

  _____

- How many feet of yarn will be in each group?

  _____

- What do you need to find?

  _____

Use a number line to count equal groups.

How many feet of yarn does Caleb

need for each ball? _____

How many equal lengths of yarn does he need? _____

Begin at 0. Skip count by 6s by drawing jumps on the number line.

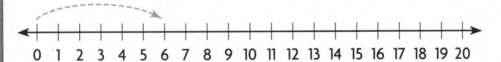

How many jumps did you make? _____

How long is each jump? _____

Multiply. $3 \times 6 =$ _____

So, Caleb needs _____ feet of yarn in all.

Math Talk   MATHEMATICAL PRACTICES ③

Compare Representations How would what you draw on the number line change if instead of 3 balls of yarn made with 6 feet of yarn there were 4 balls of yarn made with 5 feet of yarn?

- **MATHEMATICAL PRACTICE ①** **Analyze** Why did you jump by 6s on the number line?

_____

1. Skip count by drawing jumps on the number line. Find how many in 5 jumps of 4. Then write the product.

Think: 1 jump of 4 shows 1 group of 4.

$5 \times 4 =$ _____

Draw jumps on the number line to show equal groups. Find the product.

2. 3 groups of 8

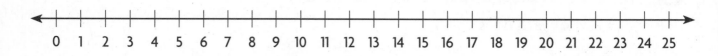

$3 \times 8 =$ _____

3. 8 groups of 3

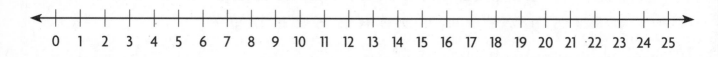

$8 \times 3 =$ _____

Write the multiplication sentence shown by the number line.

4.

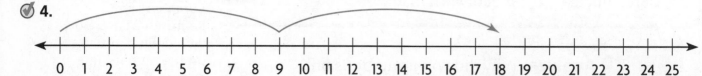

_____ $\times$ _____ $=$ _____

Math Talk

MATHEMATICAL PRACTICES ④

Model Mathematics
How do equal jumps on the number line show equal groups?

On Your Own

Draw jumps on the number line to show equal groups. Find the product.

5. 6 groups of 4

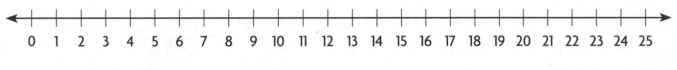

$6 \times 4 =$ _____

6. 7 groups of 3

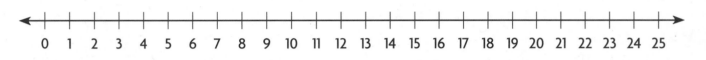

$7 \times 3 =$ _____

7. Sam, Kyra, Tia, and Abigail each have 10 pennies. How many pennies do they have in all?

_____

8. Eddie bought snacks for a picnic. He has 3 bags of snacks. Each bag has 4 snacks. How many snacks does Eddie have in all?

_____

9. Ashley digs 7 holes. She puts 2 seeds in each hole. She has 3 seeds left over. How many seeds are there in all?

_____

10. GO DEEPER Carla puts 8 pictures on each page of a photo album. She fills 3 pages. She has 5 pictures left. How many pictures does she have?

_____

11. GO DEEPER A band marches in rows of 5. Each row has 6 people. There are 4 people who carry flags. How many people are in the marching band?

_____

12. GO DEEPER In Mr. Gupta's classroom, there are 4 rows of desks. Each row has 6 desks. Mrs. Loew's classroom has 3 rows of 9 desks. How many desks are in Mr. Gupta's and Mrs. Loew's classrooms?

_____

Problem Solving • Applications

13. **GO DEEPER** Erin displays her toy cat collection on
3 shelves. She puts 8 cats on each shelf. If she collects
3 more cats, how many cats will she have?

_____

14. **THINK SMARTER** Write two multiplication sentences that
have a product of 12. Draw jumps on the number line to
show the multiplication.

____ × ____ = ____

0 1 2 3 4 5 6 7 8 9 10 11 12

____ × ____ = ____

15. **MATHEMATICAL PRACTICE 7 Identify Relationships** Write a problem
that can be solved by finding 8 groups of 5. Write a
multiplication sentence to solve the problem. Then solve.

_____

_____

Personal Math Trainer

16. **THINK SMARTER +** Rebecca practices piano for 3 hours each week.
How many hours does she practice in 4 weeks?

Draw jumps and label the number line to show your thinking.

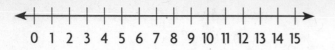

0 1 2 3 4 5 6 7 8 9 10 11 12 13 14 15

_____

Skip Count on a Number Line

Draw jumps on the number line to show equal groups. Find the product.

Common Core **COMMON CORE STANDARD—3.OA.A.3**
Represent and solve problems involving multiplication and division.

1. 6 groups of 3

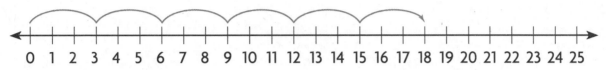

$6 \times 3 =$ ___18___

Write the multiplication sentence the number line shows.

2. 2 groups of 6

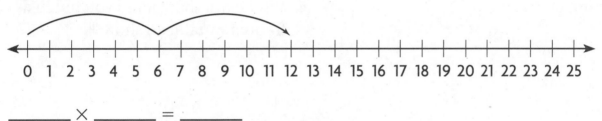

_____ × _____ = _____

Problem Solving Real World

3. Allie is baking muffins for students in her class. There are 6 muffins in each baking tray. She bakes 5 trays of muffins. How many muffins is she baking?

_____

4. A snack package has 4 cheese sticks. How many cheese sticks are in 4 packages?

_____

5. **WRITE** ▸*Math* Write a problem that can be solved by skip counting on a number line.

_____

_____

Lesson Check (3.OA.A.3)

1. Louise skip counts by 4 on a number line to find 5 × 4. How many jumps should she draw on the number line?

2. Theo needs 4 boards that are each 3 feet long to make bookshelves. How many feet of boards does he need altogether?

Spiral Review (3.NBT.A.1, 3.MD.B.3)

3. Estimate the sum.

$$518$$
$$+251$$

4. Which number would you put in a frequency table to show |||| |||?

5. A manager at a shoe store received an order for 346 pairs of shoes. What is 346 rounded to the nearest hundred?

6. Toby is making a picture graph. Each picture of a book is equal to 2 books he has read. The row for Month 1 has 3 pictures of books. How many books did Toby read during Month 1?

FOR MORE PRACTICE
GO TO THE
Personal Math Trainer

Name _____

Vocabulary

Choose the best term from the box.

Vocabulary
equal groups
factors
multiply
product

1. When you combine equal groups, you can

   _____ to find how many in all. (p. 146)

2. The answer in a multiplication problem is called the

   _____. (p. 146)

3. The numbers you multiply are called the _____. (p. 146)

Concepts and Skills

Count equal groups to find how many. (3.OA.A.1)

4.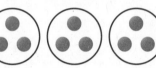

   ___ groups of ___

   ___ in all

5.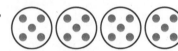

   ___ groups of ___

   ___ in all

6.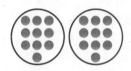

   ___ groups of ___

   ___ in all

Write related addition and multiplication sentences. (3.OA.A.1)

7. 3 groups of 9

   ___ + ___ + ___ = ___

   ___ × ___ = ___

8. 5 groups of 7

   ___ + ___ + ___ + ___ + ___ = ___

   ___ × ___ = ___

Draw jumps on the number line to show equal groups.
Find the product. (3.OA.A.3)

9. 6 groups of 3

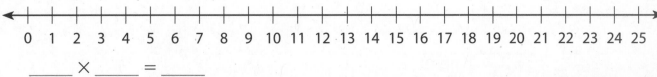

   _____ × _____ = _____

10. Beth's mother cut some melons into equal slices. She put 4 slices each on 8 plates. Write a multiplication sentence to show the total number of melon slices she put on the plates. (3.0A.A.1)

_____

11. Avery had 125 animal stickers. She gave 5 animal stickers to each of her 10 friends. How many animal stickers did she have left? What number sentences did you use to solve? (3.0A.A.3)

_____

12. Matt made 2 equal groups of marbles. Write a multiplication sentence to show the total number of marbles. (3.0A.A.1)

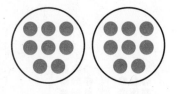

_____

13. [GO DEEPER] Lindsey has 10 inches of ribbon. She buys another 3 lengths of ribbon, each 5 inches long. How much ribbon does she have now? (3.0A.A.3)

_____

14. Jack's birthday is in 4 weeks. How many days is it until Jack's birthday? Describe how you could use a number line to solve. (3.0A.A.3)

_____

_____

Name _____

Problem Solving • Model Multiplication

Essential Question How can you use the strategy *draw a diagram* to solve one- and two-step problems?

Common Core Operations and Algebraic Thinking—
3.OA.D.8 *Also 3.OA.A.1, 3.OA.A.3*
MATHEMATICAL PRACTICES
MP1, MP3, MP4, MP8

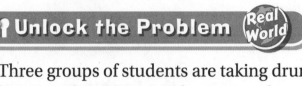 **Unlock the Problem**

Three groups of students are taking drum lessons. There are 8 students in each group. How many students are taking drum lessons?

Read the Problem

What do I need to find?

I need to find how many _____

are taking drum lessons.

What information do I need to use?

There are _____ groups of students

taking drum lessons. There are

_____ students in each group.

How will I use the information?

I will draw a bar model to help me see

_____

_____ .

Solve the Problem

Complete the bar model to show the drummers.

Write 8 in each box to show the 8 students in each of the 3 groups.

8	_____	_____

▨ students

Since there are equal groups, I can multiply to find the number of students taking drum lessons.

_____ × _____ = ▨

_____ = ▨

So, there are _____ students in all.

Math Talk MATHEMATICAL PRACTICES ④

Use Models How would the bar model change if there were 6 groups of 4 students?

1 Try Another Problem

Twelve students in Mrs. Taylor's class want to start a band. Seven students each made a drum. The rest of the students made 2 shakers each. How many shakers were made?

Read the Problem	Solve the Problem
What do I need to find?	**Record the steps you used to solve the problem.**
What information do I need to use?	
How will I use the information?	

Record the steps you used to solve the problem.

7	_____

12 students

1. How many shakers in all did the students make? _____

2. How do you know your answer is reasonable? _____

Math Talk

Evaluate Why wouldn't you draw 2 boxes and write 5 in each box?

Name _____

1. There are 6 groups of 4 students who play the trumpet in the marching band. How many students play the trumpet in the band?

First, draw a bar model to show each group of students.

Draw _____ boxes and write _____ in each box.

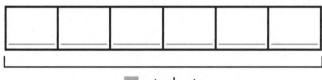

 students

Then, multiply to find the total number of trumpet players.

_____ × _____ = ▇

_____ = ▇

So, _____ students play the trumpet in the marching band.

2. What if there are 4 groups of 7 students who play the saxophone? How many students play the saxophone or trumpet?

_____

3. *THINK SMARTER* Suppose there are 5 groups of 4 trumpet players. In front of the trumpet players are 18 saxophone players. How many students play the trumpet or saxophone?

_____

4. *GO DEEPER* In a garden there are 3 rows of plants. There are 5 plants in each row. Six of the plants are pumpkin plants and the rest are corn. How many corn plants are in the garden?

_____

Use the picture graph for 5–7.

Favorite Instrument Survey	
Flute	☺☺
Trumpet	☺☺☺
Guitar	☺☺☺☺☺
Drum	☺☺☺☺

Key: Each ☺ = 2 votes.

5. The picture graph shows how students in Jillian's class voted for their favorite instrument. How many students voted for the guitar?

_____

6. **GO DEEPER** On the day of the survey, two students were absent. The picture graph shows the votes of all the other students in the class, including Jillian. How many students are in the class? Explain your answer.

_____

_____

_____

7. **THINK SMARTER** Jillian added the number of votes for two instruments and got a total of 12 votes. For which two instruments did she add the votes?

_____ and _____

8. **MATHEMATICAL PRACTICE ⑧ Use Repeated Reasoning** The flute was invented 26 years after the harmonica. The electric guitar was invented 84 years after the flute. How many years was the electric guitar invented after the harmonica?

_____

9. **THINK SMARTER +** Raul buys 4 packages of apple juice and 3 packages of grape juice. There are 6 drink boxes in each package. How many drink boxes does Raul buy? Show your work.

Personal Math Trainer

_____

Problem Solving • Model Multiplication
Draw a diagram to solve each problem.

 Common Core

COMMON CORE STANDARD—3.OA.D.8
Solve problems involving the four operations,
and identify and explain patterns in
arithmetic.

1. Robert put some toy blocks into 3 rows.
   There are 5 blocks in each row. How many
   blocks are there?

   _____ **15 blocks**

2. Mr. Fernandez is putting tiles on his
   kitchen floor. There are 2 rows with
   9 tiles in each row. How many tiles are
   there?

   _____

3. In Jillian's garden, there are 3 rows of carrots,
   2 rows of string beans, and 1 row of peas.
   There are 8 plants in each row. How many
   plants are there in the garden?

   _____

4. Maya visits the movie rental store. On one
   wall, there are 6 DVDs on each of 5 shelves.
   On another wall, there are 4 DVDs on each of
   4 shelves. How many DVDs are there on the shelves?

   _____

5. The media center at Josh's school has a
   computer area. The first 4 rows have
   6 computers each. The fifth row has 4 computers.
   How many computers are there?

   _____

6. **WRITE** ▸Math Describe one kind of diagram you might draw
   to help you solve a problem.

   _____

   _____

Lesson Check (3.OA.D.8)

1. There are 5 shelves of video games in a video store. There are 6 video games on each shelf. How many video games are there on the shelves?

   _____

   _____

2. Ken watches a marching band. He sees 2 rows of flute players. Six people are in each row. He sees 8 trombone players. How many flute players and trombone players does Ken see?

   _____

   _____

Spiral Review (3.NBT.1, 3.NBT.2, 3.MD.3)

3. What is the sum of 438 and 382?

   _____

   _____

4. Estimate the sum.

   $$\begin{array}{r} 622 \\ +\ \ 84 \\ \hline \end{array}$$

   _____

   _____

5. Francine uses 167 silver balloons and 182 gold balloons for her store party. How many silver and gold balloons does Francine use?

   _____

   _____

6. Yoshi is making a picture graph. Each picture of a soccer ball stands for two goals he scored for his team. The row for January has 9 soccer balls. How many goals did Yoshi score during January?

   _____

   _____

© Houghton Mifflin Harcourt Publishing Company

FOR MORE PRACTICE
GO TO THE
Personal Math Trainer

Name _____

Model with Arrays

Essential Question How can you use arrays to model multiplication and find factors?

Common Core **Operations and Algebraic Thinking—**
3.OA.A.3 Also 3.OA.A.1
MATHEMATICAL PRACTICES
MP2, MP4, MP5

Unlock the Problem (Real World)

Many people grow tomatoes in their gardens. Lee plants 3 rows of tomato plants with 6 plants in each row. How many tomato plants are there?

Activity 1

Materials ■ square tiles ■ MathBoard

- You make an **array** by placing the same number of tiles in each row. Make an array with 3 rows of 6 tiles to show the tomato plants.

- Now draw the array you made.

▲ Tomatoes are a great source of vitamins.

- Find the total number of tiles.

   Multiply.   3   ×   6 = _____
                    ↑   ↑
                 number   number
                 of rows   in each row

So, there are _____ tomato plants.

Math Talk

MATHEMATICAL PRACTICES ②

Reason Abstractly Does the number of tiles change if you turn the array to show 6 rows of 3?

 Activity 2 Materials ■ square tiles ■ MathBoard

Use 8 tiles. Make as many different arrays as you can, using all 8 tiles. Draw the arrays. The first one is done for you.

A □ □ □ □ □ □ □ □

1 row of 8

$1 \times 8 = 8$

B

8 rows of _____

$8 \times$ _____ $= 8$

C

_____ rows of _____

_____ $\times$ _____ $= 8$

D

_____ rows of _____

_____ $\times$ _____ $= 8$

You can make _____ different arrays using 8 tiles.

1. Complete. Use the array.

_____ rows of _____ = _____

_____ $\times$ _____ = _____

■■■■■■■■■
■■■■■■■■■

Write a multiplication sentence for the array.

 2. ■■■■■
   ■■■■■
   ■■■■■

_____

 3. ■■■■■■
   ■■■■■■

_____

Name _____

Write a multiplication sentence for the array.

4.

_____

5.

_____

Draw an array to find the product.

6. $3 \times 6 =$ _____

7. $4 \times 7 =$ _____

8. GO DEEPER   DeShawn makes an array using 3 rows of 5 tiles. How many tiles does Deshawn have if he adds 2 more rows to the array?

_____

9. GO DEEPER   Ming makes an array using 2 rows of 7 tiles. She adds 3 more rows to the array. Write a multiplication sentence that shows Ming's array.

_____

10. GO DEEPER   Use 6 tiles. Make as many different arrays as you can using all the tiles. Draw the arrays. Then write a multiplication sentence for each array.

_____

_____

Problem Solving • Applications Real World

Use the table to solve 11–12.

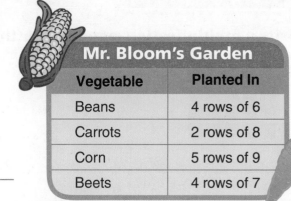

Mr. Bloom's Garden	
Vegetable	**Planted In**
Beans	4 rows of 6
Carrots	2 rows of 8
Corn	5 rows of 9
Beets	4 rows of 7

11. **MATHEMATICAL PRACTICE ④** **Use Models** Mr. Bloom grows vegetables in his garden. Draw an array and write the multiplication sentence to show how many corn plants Mr. Bloom has in his garden.

_____

12. **THINK SMARTER** Could Mr. Bloom have planted his carrots in equal rows of 4? If so, how many rows could he have planted? Explain.

_____

_____

_____

13. **MATHEMATICAL PRACTICE ⑤** **Communicate** Mr. Bloom has 12 strawberry plants. Describe all of the different arrays that Mr. Bloom could make using all of his strawberry plants. The first one is done for you.

2 rows of 6;

_____

14. **THINK SMARTER** Elizabeth planted 5 rows of pansies with 3 pansies in each row. How many pansies did she plant in all? Draw the rest of the squares to make an array to represent the problem. Then solve.

_____

Model with Arrays

  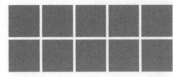

Common Core COMMON CORE STANDARD—3.OA.A.3
*Represent and solve problems involving
multiplication and division.*

Write a multiplication sentence for the array.

1.

$3 \times 7 = \underline{\ 21\ }$

2.

$2 \times 5 = \underline{\quad}$

Draw an array to find the product.

3. $4 \times 2 = \underline{\quad}$

4. $2 \times 8 = \underline{\quad}$

Problem Solving · Real World

5. Lenny is moving tables in the school cafeteria. He places all the tables in a 7×4 array. How many tables are in the cafeteria?

_____

6. Ms. DiMeo directs the school choir. She has the singers stand in 3 rows. There are 8 singers in each row. How many singers are there?

_____

7. **WRITE** ▸*Math* Write a word problem that can be solved by drawing an array. Then draw the array and solve the problem.

_____

_____

Lesson Check (3.OA.A.3)

1. What multiplication sentence does this array show?

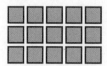

_____

2. What multiplication sentence does this array show?

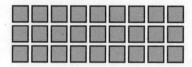

_____

Spiral Review (3.NBT.A.1, 3.NBT.A.2, 3.MD.B.3)

3. Use the table to find who traveled 700 miles farther than Paul during summer vacation.

Summer Vacations	
Name	Distance in Miles
Paul	233
Andrew	380
Bonnie	790
Tara	933
Susan	853

_____

4. Use the bar graph to find what hair color most students have.

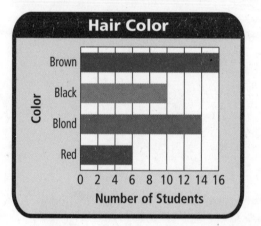

_____

5. Spencer orders 235 cans of tomatoes to make salsa for the festival. What is 235 rounded to the nearest ten?

_____

6. Which bar would be the longest on a bar graph of the data?

Favorite Pizza Topping	
Topping	Votes
Cheese	5
Pepperoni	4
Vegetable	1
Sausage	3

_____

FOR MORE PRACTICE
GO TO THE
Personal Math Trainer

Commutative Property of Multiplication

Name _____

Essential Question How can you use the Commutative Property of Multiplication to find products?

 Common Core

Operations and Algebraic Thinking—
3.OA.B.5 *Also 3.OA.A.1,*
3.OA.A.3, 3.OA.C.7

MATHEMATICAL PRACTICES
MP1, MP2, MP6, MP7

 **Unlock the Problem** *Real World*

Dave works at the Bird Store. He arranges 15 boxes of birdseed in rows on the shelf. What are two ways he can arrange the boxes in equal rows?

• Circle the number that is the product.

Activity Make an array.

Materials ■ square tiles ■ MathBoard

Arrange 15 tiles in 5 equal rows.
Draw a quick picture of your array.

How many tiles are in each row? _____

What multiplication sentence does your array show? _____

Suppose Dave arranges the boxes in 3 equal rows.
Draw a quick picture of your array.

How many tiles are in each row? _____

What multiplication sentence does your array show?

_____

So, two ways Dave can arrange the 15 boxes are

in _____ rows of 3 or in 3 rows of _____.

 Math Talk   MATHEMATICAL PRACTICES ⑦

Identify Relationships When using an array to help solve a multiplication problem, why does the answer stay the same when the array is turned?

Multiplication Property The **Commutative Property of Multiplication** states that when you change the order of the factors, the product stays the same. You can think of it as the Order Property of Multiplication.

 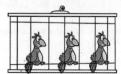     

2 × _____ = _____   3 × _____ = _____

> **Math Idea**
> Facts that show the Commutative Property of Multiplication have the same factors in a different order.
>
> 2 × 3 = 6 and 3 × 2 = 6

So, 2 × _____ = 3 × _____.

- Explain how the models are alike and how they are different.

_____

_____

Try This! Draw a quick picture on the right that shows the Commutative Property of Multiplication. Then complete the multiplication sentences.

Ⓐ

_____ × 4 = _____   _____ × 3 = _____

Ⓑ

2 × _____ = _____   5 × _____ = _____

Name _____

1. Write a multiplication sentence for the array.

MATHEMATICAL PRACTICES ①

Make Sense of Problems Explain what the factor 2 means in each multiplication sentence.

_____   _____

Write a multiplication sentence for the model. Then use the Commutative Property of Multiplication to write a related multiplication sentence.

2.

◯3.

◯4.

____ × ____ = ____

____ × ____ = ____

____ × ____ = ____

____ × ____ = ____

____ × ____ = ____

____ × ____ = ____

Write a multiplication sentence for the model. Then use the Commutative Property of Multiplication to write a related multiplication sentence.

5.

6.

7.

____ × ____ = ____

____ × ____ = ____

____ × ____ = ____

____ × ____ = ____

____ × ____ = ____

____ × ____ = ____

MATHEMATICAL PRACTICE ② **Use Reasoning Algebra** Write the unknown factor.

8. $3 \times 7 =$ _____ $\times 3$

9. $4 \times 5 = 10 \times$ _____

10. $3 \times 6 =$ _____ $\times 9$

11. $6 \times$ _____ $= 4 \times 9$

12. _____ $\times 8 = 4 \times 6$

13. $5 \times 8 = 8 \times$ _____

Problem Solving • Applications

14. Jenna used pinecones to make 18 peanut butter bird feeders. She hung the same number of feeders in 6 trees. Draw an array to show how many feeders she put in each tree.

She put _____ bird feeders in each tree.

15. GODEEPER Mr. Diaz sets out 6 rows of glasses with 3 glasses in each row. Mrs. Diaz sets out 3 rows of glasses with 6 glasses in each row. How many glasses do Mr. and Mrs. Diaz set out in all?

_____

16. GODEEPER Write two different word problems about 12 birds to show 2×6 and 6×2. Solve each problem.

_____

_____

_____

17. THINKSMARTER There are 4 rows of 6 bird stickers in Don's sticker album. There are 7 rows of 5 bird stickers in Lindsey's album. How many bird stickers do they have?

_____

18. THINKSMARTER Write the letter for each multiplication sentence on the left next to the multiplication sentence on the right that has the same value.

Ⓐ $5 \times 7 = \blacksquare$ ☐ $6 \times 3 = \blacksquare$

Ⓑ $8 \times 2 = \blacksquare$ ☐ $2 \times 8 = \blacksquare$

Ⓒ $3 \times 6 = \blacksquare$ ☐ $4 \times 9 = \blacksquare$

Ⓓ $9 \times 4 = \blacksquare$ ☐ $7 \times 5 = \blacksquare$

Commutative Property of Multiplication

COMMON CORE STANDARD—3.OA.B.5
Understand properties of multiplication and the relationship between multiplication and division.

Write a multiplication sentence for the model. Then use the Commutative Property of Multiplication to write a related multiplication sentence.

1.

$\underline{5} \times \underline{2} = \underline{10}$

$\underline{2} \times \underline{5} = \underline{10}$

2.

$\underline{} \times \underline{} = \underline{}$

$\underline{} \times \underline{} = \underline{}$

3.

$\underline{} \times \underline{} = \underline{}$

$\underline{} \times \underline{} = \underline{}$

4.

$\underline{} \times \underline{} = \underline{}$

$\underline{} \times \underline{} = \underline{}$

Problem Solving

5. A garden store sells trays of plants. Each tray holds 2 rows of 8 plants. How many plants are in one tray?

6. Jeff collects toy cars. They are displayed in a case that has 4 rows. There are 6 cars in each row. How many cars does Jeff have?

_____

7. **WRITE** *Math* How are the Commutative Property of Addition and the Commutative Property of Multiplication alike?

_____

_____

Lesson Check (3.OA.B.5)

1. Write a sentence that shows the Commutative Property of Multiplication.

_____

_____

_____

2. What factor makes the number sentence true?

$7 \times 4 = \blacksquare \times 7$

_____

_____

Spiral Review (3.NBT.A.1, 3.NBT.A.2, 3.MD.B.3)

3. Ms. Williams drove 149 miles on Thursday and 159 miles on Friday. About how many miles did she drive altogether?

_____

_____

4. Inez has 699 pennies and 198 nickels. Estimate how many more pennies than nickels she has.

_____

_____

5. This year, the parade had 127 floats. That was 34 fewer floats than last year. How many floats were in the parade last year?

_____

6. Jeremy made a tally table to record how his friends voted for their favorite pet. His table shows IIII IIII II next to Dog. How many friends voted for dog?

_____

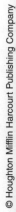

FOR MORE PRACTICE
GO TO THE
Personal Math Trainer

Name _____

Multiply with 1 and 0

Essential Question What happens when you multiply a number by 0 or 1?

 Common Core Operations and Algebraic Thinking—
3.OA.B.5 Also 3.OA.A.1, 3.OA.A.3, 3.OA.C.7
MATHEMATICAL PRACTICES
MP1, MP2, MP3, MP6

 Unlock the Problem Real World

Luke sees 4 birdbaths. Each birdbath has 2 birds in it. What multiplication sentence tells how many birds there are?

 Draw a quick picture to show the birds in the birdbaths.

- How many birdbaths are there?

  _____

- How many birds does Luke see in

  each birdbath? _____

_____ × _____ = _____

One bird flies away from each birdbath. Cross out 1 bird in each birdbath above. What multiplication sentence shows the total number of birds now?

_____ × _____ = _____
↑   ↑   ↑
birdbaths   bird in each   total number
      birdbath now   of birds

Now cross out another bird in each birdbath. What multiplication sentence shows the total number of birds in the birdbaths now?

_____ × _____ = _____
↑   ↑   ↑
birdbaths   birds in each   total number
      birdbath now   of birds

- How do the birdbaths look now? _____

Math Talk MATHEMATICAL PRACTICES ①

Analyze What if there were 5 birdbaths with 0 birds in each of them? What would be the product? Explain.

🔒 Example

Jenny has 2 pages of bird stickers. There are 4 stickers on each page. How many stickers does she have in all?

$2 \times 4 =$ _____   **Think:** 2 groups of 4

So, Jenny has _____ stickers in all.

Suppose Jenny uses 1 page of the stickers. What fact shows how many stickers she has now?

_____ $\times$ _____ = _____   **Think:** 1 group of 4

So, Jenny has _____ stickers now.

Then, Jenny uses the rest of the stickers. What fact shows how many stickers Jenny has now?

_____ $\times$ _____ = _____   **Think:** 0 groups of 4

So, Jenny has _____ stickers now.

> **! ERROR Alert**
>
> A 0 in a multiplication sentence means 0 groups or 0 things in a group, so the product is always 0.

- What does each number in $0 \times 4 = 0$ tell you?

_____

_____

---

1. What pattern do you see when you multiply numbers with 1 as a factor?

Think: $1 \times 2 = 2$ $1 \times 3 = 3$ $1 \times 4 = 4$

_____

_____

> The **Identity Property of Multiplication** states that the product of any number and 1 is that number.
>
> $7 \times 1 = 7$ $6 \times 1 = 6$
> $1 \times 7 = 7$ $1 \times 6 = 6$

2. What pattern do you see when you multiply numbers with 0 as a factor?

Think: $0 \times 1 = 0$ $0 \times 2 = 0$ $0 \times 5 = 0$

_____

_____

> The **Zero Property of Multiplication** states that the product of zero and any number is zero.
>
> $0 \times 5 = 0$ $0 \times 8 = 0$
> $5 \times 0 = 0$ $8 \times 0 = 0$

Name _____

1. What multiplication sentence matches this picture? Find the product.

_____

Find the product.

2. $5 \times 1 =$ _____

3. $0 \times 2 =$ _____

✓ 4. $4 \times 0 =$ _____

✓ 5. $1 \times 6 =$ _____

6. $3 \times 0 =$ _____

7. $1 \times 2 =$ _____

8. $0 \times 6 =$ _____

9. $8 \times 1 =$ _____

Math Talk MATHEMATICAL PRACTICES ⑥

Compare Explain how 3×1 and $3 + 1$ are different.

On Your Own

Find the product.

10. $3 \times 1 =$ _____

11. $8 \times 0 =$ _____

12. $1 \times 9 =$ _____

13. $0 \times 7 =$ _____

MATHEMATICAL PRACTICE ② **Use Reasoning** **Algebra** **Complete the multiplication sentence.**

14. _____ $\times 1 = 15$

15. $1 \times 28 =$ _____

16. $0 \times 46 =$ _____

17. $36 \times 0 =$ _____

18. _____ $\times 5 = 5$

19. $19 \times$ _____ $= 0$

20. _____ $\times 0 = 0$

21. $7 \times$ _____ $= 7$

22. Noah sets out 7 baskets at the Farmers' Market. Each basket holds 1 watermelon. How many watermelons does Noah set out?

_____

23. **Go DEEPER** Mason and Alexis each have 1 bag of marbles. There are 9 marbles in each bag. How many marbles do they have altogether?

_____

24. **Go DEEPER** Each box holds 6 black markers and 4 red markers. Derek has 0 boxes of markers. Write a number sentence that shows how many markers Derek has. Explain how you found your answer.

_____

_____

Problem Solving • Applications

Use the table for 25–27.

25. At the circus Jon saw 5 unicycles. How many wheels are on the 5 unicycles? Write a multiplication sentence.

    _____ × _____ = _____

26. **What's the Question?** Julia used multiplication with 1 and the information in the table. The answer is 3.

    _____

    _____

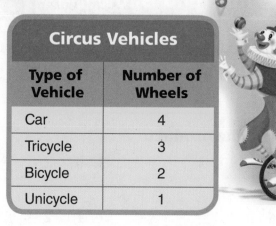

Circus Vehicles

Type of Vehicle	Number of Wheels
Car	4
Tricycle	3
Bicycle	2
Unicycle	1

27. THINK SMARTER   Brian saw some circus vehicles. He saw 17 wheels in all. If 2 of the vehicles are cars, how many vehicles are bicycles and tricycles?

    _____

28. WRITE ▸ Math   Write a word problem that uses multiplying with 1 or 0. Show how to solve your problem.

    _____

    _____

29. THINK SMARTER   For numbers 29a–29d, select True or False for each multiplication sentence.

    29a. $6 \times 0 = 0$ ○ True   ○ False

    29b. $0 \times 9 = 9 \times 0$ ○ True   ○ False

    29c. $1 \times 0 = 1$ ○ True   ○ False

    29d. $3 \times 1 = 3$ ○ True   ○ False

Multiply with 1 and 0

Common Core

COMMON CORE STANDARD—3.OA.B.5
Understand properties of multiplication and the relationship between multiplication and division.

Find the product.

1. $1 \times 4 = \underline{\ 4\ }$　　**2.** $0 \times 8 = \underline{\quad}$　　**3.** $0 \times 4 = \underline{\quad}$　　**4.** $1 \times 6 = \underline{\quad}$

5. $3 \times 0 = \underline{\quad}$　　**6.** $0 \times 9 = \underline{\quad}$　　**7.** $8 \times 1 = \underline{\quad}$　　**8.** $1 \times 2 = \underline{\quad}$

9. $10 \times 1 = \underline{\quad}$　　**10.** $2 \times 0 = \underline{\quad}$　　**11.** $5 \times 1 = \underline{\quad}$　　**12.** $1 \times 0 = \underline{\quad}$

13. $0 \times 0 = \underline{\quad}$　　**14.** $1 \times 3 = \underline{\quad}$　　**15.** $9 \times 0 = \underline{\quad}$　　**16.** $1 \times 1 = \underline{\quad}$

Problem Solving

17. Peter is in the school play. His teacher gave 1 copy of the play to each of 6 students. How many copies of the play did the teacher hand out?

18. There are 4 egg cartons on the table. There are 0 eggs in each carton. How many eggs are there in all?

_____

_____

19. **WRITE** ▸*Math* One group has 5 people, and each person has 1 granola bar. Another group has 5 people, and each person has 0 granola bars. Which group has more granola bars? Explain.

_____

_____

Lesson Check (3.OA.B.5)

1. There are 0 bicycles in each bicycle rack. If there are 8 bicycle racks, how many bicycles are there in the rack?

2. What is the product?

   $1 \times 0 = \underline{\hspace{1cm}}$

Spiral Review (3.NBT.A.2, 3.OA.A.3, 3.MD.B.3)

3. Mr. Ellis drove 197 miles on Monday and 168 miles on Tuesday. How many miles did he drive?

4. What multiplication sentence does the array show?

Use the bar graph for 5–6.

5. How many cars were washed on Friday and Saturday combined?

6. How many more cars were washed on Saturday than on Sunday?

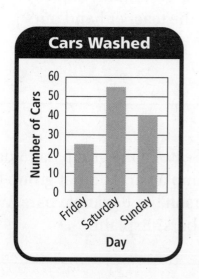

FOR MORE PRACTICE
GO TO THE
Personal Math Trainer

Name _____

1. There are 3 boats on the lake. Six people ride in each boat. How many people ride in the boats? Draw equal groups to model the problem and explain how to solve it.

_____ people

2. Nadia has 4 sheets of stickers. There are 8 stickers on each sheet. She wrote this number sentence to represent the total number of stickers.

$$4 \times 8 = 32$$

What is a related number sentence that also represents the total number of stickers she has?

Ⓐ $8 + 4 = \blacksquare$

Ⓑ $4 + 4 + 4 + 4 = \blacksquare$

Ⓒ $8 \times 8 = \blacksquare$

Ⓓ $8 \times 4 = \blacksquare$

3. Lindsay went hiking for two days in Yellowstone National Park. The first jump on the number line shows how many birds she saw the first day. She saw the same number of birds the next day.

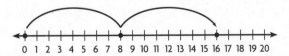

Write the multiplication sentence that is shown on the number line.

_____ × _____ = _____

4. Paco drew an array to show the number of desks in his classroom.

Write a multiplication sentence for the array.

_____

5. Alondra makes 4 necklaces. She uses 5 beads on each necklace.

For numbers 5a–5d, choose Yes or No to tell if the number sentence could be used to find the number of beads Alondra uses.

5a. $4 \times 5 = \blacksquare$ ○ Yes   ○ No

5b. $4 + 4 + 4 + 4 = \blacksquare$ ○ Yes   ○ No

5c. $5 + 5 + 5 + 5 = \blacksquare$ ○ Yes   ○ No

5d. $5 + 4 = \blacksquare$ ○ Yes   ○ No

6. John sold 3 baskets of apples at the market. Each basket contained 9 apples. How many apples did John sell? Make a bar model to solve the problem.

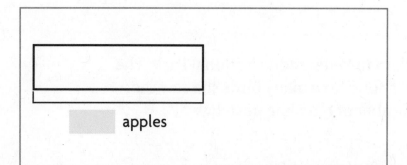

apples

7. Select the number sentences that show the Commutative Property of Multiplication. Mark all that apply.

Ⓐ $3 \times 2 = 2 \times 3$

Ⓑ $4 \times 9 = 4 \times 9$

Ⓒ $5 \times 0 = 0$

Ⓓ $6 \times 1 = 1 \times 6$

Ⓔ $7 \times 2 = 14 \times 1$

8. A waiter carried 6 baskets with 5 dinner rolls in each basket. How many dinner rolls did he carry? Show your work.

_____ dinner rolls

9. Sonya needs 3 equal lengths of wire to make 3 bracelets. The jump on the number line shows the length of one wire in inches. How many inches of wire will Sonya need to make the 3 bracelets?

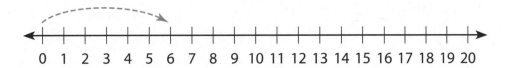

_____ inches

10. Josh has 4 dogs. Each dog gets 2 dog biscuits every day. How many biscuits will Josh need for all of his dogs for Saturday and Sunday?

_____ biscuits

11. **GO DEEPER** Jorge displayed 28 cans of paint on a shelf in his store.

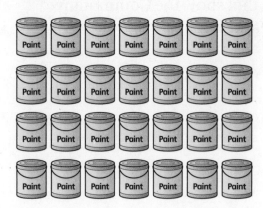

Select other ways Jorge could arrange the same number of cans.
Mark all that apply.

(A) 2 rows of 14   (D) 8 rows of 3

(B) 1 row of 28   (E) 7 rows of 4

(C) 6 rows of 5

12. Choose the number that makes the statement true.

The product of any number and $\begin{array}{|c|} \hline 0 \\ 1 \\ 10 \\ \hline \end{array}$ is zero.

13. James made this array to show that $3 \times 5 = 15$.

Part A

James says that $5 \times 3 = 15$. Is James correct? Draw an array to
explain your answer.

_____

Part B

Which number property supports your answer?

_____

_____

Name _____

14. Julio has a collection of coins. He puts the coins in 2 equal groups. There are 6 coins in each group. How many coins does Julio have? Use the number line to show your work.

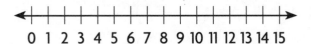

_____ coins

15. GO DEEPER Landon collects trading cards.

Part A

Yesterday, Landon sorted his trading cards into 4 groups. Each group had 7 cards. Draw a bar model to show Landon's cards. How many cards does he have?

_____ trading cards

Part B

Landon buys 3 more packs of trading cards today. Each pack has 8 cards. Write a multiplication sentence to show how many cards Landon buys today. Then find how many cards Landon has now. Show your work.

_____

16. A unicycle has only 1 wheel. Write a multiplication sentence to show how many wheels there are on 9 unicycles.

_____ $\times$ _____ = _____

17. Carlos spent 5 minutes working on each of 8 math problems. He can use 8×5 to find the total amount of time he spent on the problems.

For numbers 17a–17d, choose Yes or No to show which are equal to 8×5.

17a. $8 + 5$ ○ Yes   ○ No

17b. $5 + 5 + 5 + 5 + 5$ ○ Yes   ○ No

17c. $8 + 8 + 8 + 8 + 8$ ○ Yes   ○ No

17d. $5 + 5 + 5 + 5 + 5 + 5 + 5 + 5$ ○ Yes   ○ No

18. Lucy and her mother made tacos. They put 2 tacos on each of 7 plates.

Select the number sentences that show all the tacos Lucy and her mother made. Mark all that apply.

Ⓐ $2 + 2 + 2 + 2 + 2 + 2 + 2 = 14$

Ⓑ $2 + 7 = 9$

Ⓒ $7 + 7 = 14$

Ⓓ $8 + 6 = 14$

Ⓔ $2 \times 7 = 14$

19. **THINK SMARTER+** Jayson is making 5 sock puppets. He glues 2 buttons on each puppet for its eyes. He glues 1 pompom on each puppet for its nose.

Personal Math Trainer

Part A

Write the total number of buttons and pompoms he uses. Write a multiplication sentence for each.

Eyes

_____ buttons

_____ × _____ = _____

Noses

_____ pompoms

_____ × _____ = _____

Part B

After making 5 puppets, Jayson has 4 buttons and 3 pompoms left. What is the greatest number of puppets he can make with those items if he wants all his puppets to look the same? Draw models and use them to explain.

At most, he can make _____ more puppets.

_____

_____

_____

_____

Chapter 4 Multiplication Facts and Strategies

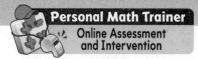
Personal Math Trainer
Online Assessment and Intervention

✓ Show What You Know

Check your understanding of important skills.

Name _____

▶ **Doubles and Doubles Plus One** Write the doubles and doubles plus one facts. (1.0A.C.6)

1.

___ + ___ = ___   ___ + ___ = ___

2.

___ + ___ = ___   ___ + ___ = ___

▶ **Equal Groups** Complete. (2.0A.C.4)

3. ⊙ ⊙ ⊙ ⊙

___ groups of ___

___ in all

4. ⊙ ⊙ ⊙ ⊙ ⊙

___ groups of ___

___ in all

Math in the Real World

Stephen needs to use these clues to find a buried time capsule.
• Start with a number that is the product of 3 and 4.
• Double the product and go to that number.
• Add 2 tens and find the number that is 1 less than the sum.
Help Stephen find the time capsule. At what number is the time capsule buried?

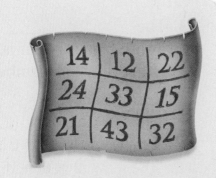

▶ **Visualize It** •••

Complete the tree map by using the words with a ✓.

Multiplication Properties

_____ Property of Multiplication	_____ Property of Multiplication	_____ Property of Multiplication
$1 \times 4 = 4$ 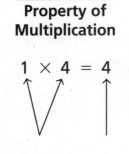 _____ _____	$(4 \times 2) \times 3 =$ $4 \times (2 \times 3)$	$3 \times 2 = 2 \times 3$ ⠿ ⠿ _____

Review Words

✓ arrays

✓ Commutative Property
   of Multiplication

even

✓ factors

✓ Identity Property
   of Multiplication

odd

✓ product

Preview Words

✓ Associative Property
   of Multiplication

Distributive Property

multiple

▶ **Understand Vocabulary** ••••••••••••••••••••••••••••••••

Complete the sentences by using the preview words.

1. The _____ Property of Multiplication states
   that when the grouping of factors is changed, the
   product is the same.

2. A _____ of 5 is any product that has
   5 as one of its factors.

3. The _____ Property states that multiplying
   a sum by a number is the same as multiplying each
   addend by the number and then adding the products.

   Example: $2 \times 8 = 2 \times (4 + 4)$
   $2 \times 8 = (2 \times 4) + (2 \times 4)$
   $2 \times 8 = 8 + 8$
   $2 \times 8 = 16$

GO DIGITAL • Interactive Student Edition
 • Multimedia eGlossary

Chapter 4 Vocabulary

array

matriz

4

Associative Property of Multiplication

Propiedad asociativa de la multiplicación

6

Commutative Property of Multiplication

Propiedad conmutativa de la multiplicación

9

Distributive Property

Propiedad distributiva

13

---

factor

factor

25

Identity Property of Multiplication

Propiedad de identidad de la multiplicación

35

---

multiple

múltiplo

50

---

product

producto

65

The property that states that when the grouping of factors is changed, the product remains the same

Example: $(5 \times 4) \times 3 = 5 \times (4 \times 3)$

A set of objects arranged in rows and columns

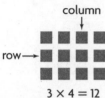

$3 \times 4 = 12$

The property that states that multiplying a sum by a number is the same as multiplying each addend by the number and then adding the products

Example: $5 \times 8 = 5 \times (4 + 4)$
$5 \times 8 = (5 \times 4) + (5 \times 4)$
$5 \times 8 = 20 + 20$
$5 \times 8 = 40$

The property that states that you can multiply two factors in any order and get the same product

Example: $4 \times 3 = 3 \times 4$

The property that states that the product of any number and 1 is that number

Example: $17 \times 1 = 17$

A number that is multiplied by another number to find a product

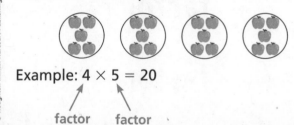

Example: $4 \times 5 = 20$

factor   factor

The answer in a multiplication problem

Example: $4 \times 5 = 20$

product

A number that is the product of two counting numbers

6	6	6	6	counting
$\times\ 1$	$\times\ 2$	$\times\ 3$	$\times\ 4$	← numbers
6	12	18	24	← multiples of 6

Guess the Word

Word Box

arrays

Associative
   Property of
   Multiplication

Commutative
   Property of
   Multiplication

Distributive
   Property

Identity Property
   of Multiplication

factors

multiple

product

For 3 to 4 players

Materials

- timer

How to Play

1. Take turns to play.

2. Choose a math term, but do not say it aloud.

3. Set the timer for 1 minute.

4. Give a one-word clue about your term. Give each player one chance to guess the term.

5. If nobody guesses correctly, repeat Step 4 with a different clue. Repeat until a player guesses the term or time runs out.

6. The player who guesses the term gets 1 point. If the player can use the word in a sentence, he or she gets 1 more point. Then that player gets a turn choosing a word.

7. The first player to score 10 points wins.

The Write Way

Reflect

Choose one idea. Write about it.

- Tell how to solve this problem: $4 \times 6 =$ _____.
- Explain the Distributive Property.
- Write about a topic in Chapter 4 that was hard to learn. Tell how you figured out how to learn it.

Name _____

Multiply with 2 and 4

Essential Question How can you multiply with 2 and 4?

 Common Core **Operations and Algebraic Thinking—3.OA.A.3**
Also 3.OA.A.1, 3.OA.C.7

MATHEMATICAL PRACTICES
MP1, MP2, MP4, MP7

Unlock the Problem Real World

Two students are in a play. Each of the students has 3 costumes. How many costumes do they have in all?

Multiplying when there are two equal groups is like adding doubles.

 Find 2 × 3.

- What does the word "each" tell you?

_____

- How can you find the number of costumes the 2 students have?

_____

MODEL	THINK	RECORD
Draw counters to show the costumes. 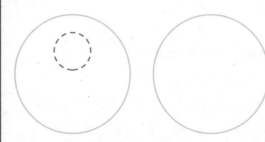	2 groups of 3 3 + 3 6	2 × 3 = 6 ↑ ↑ ↑ how many groups / how many in each group / how many in all

So, the 2 students have ____ costumes in all.

Try This!

$2 \times 1 = 1 + 1 = 2$

$2 \times 2 = 2 + 2 = 4$

$2 \times \underline{\quad} = 3 + \underline{\quad} = 6$

$2 \times \underline{\quad} = 4 + \underline{\quad} = 8$

$2 \times \underline{\quad} = 5 + \underline{\quad} = \underline{\quad}$

$2 \times \underline{\quad} = 6 + \underline{\quad} = \underline{\quad}$

$2 \times \underline{\quad} = 7 + \underline{\quad} = \underline{\quad}$

$2 \times \underline{\quad} = 8 + \underline{\quad} = \underline{\quad}$

$2 \times \underline{\quad} = 9 + \underline{\quad} = \underline{\quad}$

Math Talk MATHEMATICAL PRACTICES ②

Reason Abstractly What do you notice about the product when you multiply by 2?

Count by 2s.

When there are 2 in each group, you can count by 2s to find how many there are in all.

There are 4 students with 2 costumes each. How many costumes do they have in all?

Skip count by drawing the jumps on the number line.

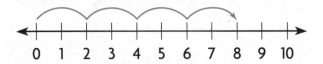

So, the 4 students have _____ in all.

- How can you decide whether to count by 2s or double?

_____

Example Use doubles to find 4×5.

When you multiply with 4, you can multiply with 2 and then double the product.

	MULTIPLY WITH 2	**DOUBLE THE PRODUCT**
4×5	$2 \times 5 = 10$	$10 + 10 = 20$

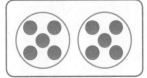 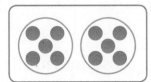 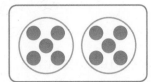

So, $4 \times 5 =$ ____.

Share and Show MATH BOARD

1. Double 2×7 to find 4×7.

Multiply with 2. $2 \times 7 =$ ____

Double the product. $14 + 14 =$ ____

So, $4 \times 7 =$ ____.

Math Talk MATHEMATICAL PRACTICES ⑦

Identify Relationships Explain how knowing the product for 2×8 helps you find the product for 4×8.

Name _____

Write a multiplication sentence for the model.

2.

____ × ____ = ____

3.

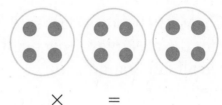

____ × ____ = ____

Find the product.

4. 6 ×2	**5.** 9 ×4	**6.** 2 ×7	**7.** 8 ×4	**8.** 5 ×2

On Your Own

Find the product. Use your MathBoard.

9. 10 × 4	**10.** 2 ×9	**11.** 4 ×6	**12.** 7 ×2	**13.** 2 ×0

14. 4 ×3	**15.** 2 ×8	**16.** 4 ×4	**17.** 10 × 2	**18.** 4 ×5

MATHEMATICAL PRACTICE ⑦ **Look for Structure Algebra** Complete the table for the factors 2 and 4.

×	1	2	3	4	5	6	7	8	9	10
19. 2										
20. 4										

MATHEMATICAL PRACTICE ② **Reason Quantitatively Algebra** Write the unknown number.

21. $4 \times 8 = 16 + $ ____

22. $20 = 2 \times $ ____

23. $8 \times 2 = 10 + $ ____

24. **THINK SMARTER** Lindsey, Louis, Sally, and Matt each bring 5 guests to the school play. How many guests in all did they bring to the school play? Explain.

_____

Unlock the Problem

25. GO DEEPER Ms. Peterson's class sold tickets for the class play. How many tickets in all did Brandon and Haylie sell?

Play Tickets	
Brandon	🎟🎟🎟🎟
Haylie	🎟🎟🎟🎟🎟🎟🎟
Elizabeth	🎟🎟🎟🎟🎟🎟🎟

Key: Each 🎟 = 2 tickets sold.

a. What do you need to find?

_____

_____

b. Why should you multiply to find the number of tickets shown? Explain.

_____

_____

c. Show the steps you used to solve the problem.

d. Complete the sentences.

Brandon sold _____ tickets. Haylie sold

_____ tickets. So, Brandon and Haylie

sold _____ tickets.

26. MATHEMATICAL PRACTICE ➊ **Analyze** Suppose Sam sold 20 tickets to the school play. How many pictures of tickets should be on the picture graph above to show his sales? Explain.

_____

_____

27. THINK SMARTER Alex exchanges some dollar bills for quarters at the bank. He receives 4 quarters for each dollar bill. Select the numbers of quarters that Alex could receive. Mark all that apply.

(A) 16   (D) 32

(B) 18   (E) 50

(C) 24

Name _____

Multiply with 2 and 4

 COMMON CORE STANDARD—3.OA.A.3
Represent and solve problems involving multiplication and division.

Write a multiplication sentence for the model.

1.

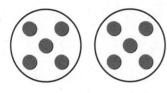

Think: There are 2 groups of 5 counters.

$\underline{\ 2\ } \times \underline{\ 5\ } = \underline{\ 10\ }$

2.

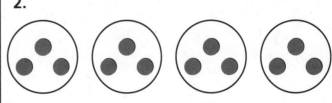

$\underline{\ \ \ } \times \underline{\ \ \ } = \underline{\ \ \ }$

Find the product.

3.   2
   $\times\ 6$

4.   4
   $\times\ 8$

5.   2
   $\times\ 3$

6.   4
   $\times\ 6$

 Problem Solving *Real World*

7. On Monday, Steven read 9 pages of his new book. To finish the first chapter on Tuesday, he needs to read double the number of pages he read on Monday. How many pages does he need to read on Tuesday?

_____

8. Courtney's school is having a family game night. Each table has 4 players. There are 7 tables in all. How many players are at the game night?

_____

9. **WRITE** *Math* Explain how you can use doubles when multiplying with 4 to find 4×8.

_____

_____

Lesson Check (3.OA.A.3)

1. What multiplication sentence matches the model?

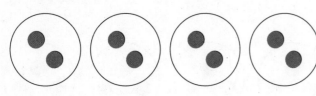

_____

_____

2. Find the product.

$$\begin{array}{r} 2 \\ \times\ 8 \\ \hline \end{array}$$

Spiral Review (3.NBT.A.2, 3.MD.B.3)

3. Sean made a picture graph to show his friends' favorite colors.

This is the key for the graph.
Each ⬤ = 2 friends.

How many friends does
⬤⬤⬤⬤ stand for?

_____

4. The table shows the lengths of some walking trails.

Walking Trails	
Name	**Length (in feet)**
Mountain Trail	844
Lake Trail	792
Harmony Trail	528

How many feet longer is Mountain Trail than Harmony Trail?

_____

5. Find the sum.

$$\begin{array}{r} 527 \\ +\ 154 \\ \hline \end{array}$$

6. A bar graph shows that sports books received 9 votes. If the scale is 0 to 20 by twos, where should the bar end for the sports books?

_____

© Houghton Mifflin Harcourt Publishing Company

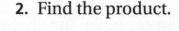

FOR MORE PRACTICE
GO TO THE
Personal Math Trainer

Multiply with 5 and 10

Essential Question How can you multiply with 5 and 10?

 Common Core **Operations and Algebraic Thinking—3.OA.A.3**
Also 3.OA.A.1, 3.OA.C.7

MATHEMATICAL PRACTICES
MP1, MP3, MP4, MP7

Unlock the Problem Real World

Marcel is making 6 toy banjos. He needs 5 strings for each banjo. How many strings does he need in all?

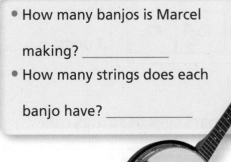

- How many banjos is Marcel making? _____
- How many strings does each banjo have? _____

Use skip counting.

Skip count by 5s until you say 6 numbers.

5, _____, _____, _____, _____, _____

6 × 5 = _____

So, Marcel needs _____ strings in all.

Example 1 Use a number line.

Each string is 10 inches long. How many inches of string will Marcel use for each banjo?

Think: 1 jump = 10 inches

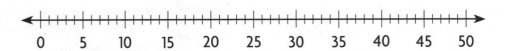

| | | | | | | | | | | |
|0|5|10|15|20|25|30|35|40|45|50|

- Draw 5 jumps for the 5 strings. Jump 10 spaces at a time for the length of each string.

- You land on 10, _____, _____, _____, and _____.   5 × 10 = _____

The numbers 10, 20, 30, 40, and 50 are multiples of 10.

So, Marcel will use _____ inches of string for each banjo.

A **multiple** of 10 is any product that has 10 as one of its factors.

 Math Talk

MATHEMATICAL PRACTICES ①

Analyze What do you notice about the multiples of 10?

Example 2 Use a bar model.

Marcel bought 3 packages of strings. Each package cost 10¢. How much did the packages cost in all?

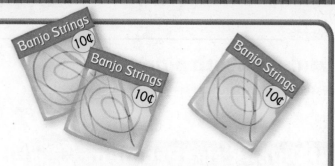

MODEL	THINK	RECORD
10¢ 10¢ 10¢	1 unit → 10¢ 3 units → _____ × _____	_____ × _____ = _____

So, the packages of strings cost _____ in all.

 **Share and Show** MATH BOARD

1. How can you use this number line to find 8×5?

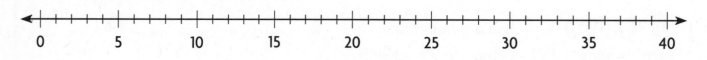

0   5   10   15   20   25   30   35   40

_____

_____

Math Talk MATHEMATICAL PRACTICES ❸

Apply How can knowing 4×5 help you find 4×10?

Find the product.

2. $2 \times 5 =$ _____

3. _____ $= 6 \times 10$

4. _____ $= 5 \times 5$

5. $10 \times 7 =$ _____

6. $\begin{array}{r} 10 \\ \times\ 4 \\ \hline \end{array}$

7. $\begin{array}{r} 5 \\ \times 6 \\ \hline \end{array}$

8. $\begin{array}{r} 10 \\ \times\ 0 \\ \hline \end{array}$

9. $\begin{array}{r} 5 \\ \times 3 \\ \hline \end{array}$

10. $\begin{array}{r} 7 \\ \times 5 \\ \hline \end{array}$

11. $\begin{array}{r} 5 \\ \times 10 \\ \hline \end{array}$

12. $\begin{array}{r} 4 \\ \times 5 \\ \hline \end{array}$

13. $\begin{array}{r} 9 \\ \times 10 \\ \hline \end{array}$

Name _____

Find the product.

14. $5 \times 1 =$ _____

15. _____ $= 10 \times 2$

16. _____ $= 4 \times 5$

17. $10 \times 10 =$ _____

18. $10 \times 0 =$ _____

19. $10 \times 5 =$ _____

20. _____ $= 1 \times 5$

21. _____ $= 5 \times 9$

22. $\begin{array}{r} 3 \\ \times 4 \\ \hline \end{array}$

23. $\begin{array}{r} 5 \\ \times 0 \\ \hline \end{array}$

24. $\begin{array}{r} 4 \\ \times 8 \\ \hline \end{array}$

25. $\begin{array}{r} 10 \\ \times 5 \\ \hline \end{array}$

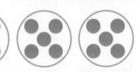 **Identify Relationships Algebra Use the pictures to find the unknown numbers.**

26.

$3 \times$ _____ $=$ _____

27.

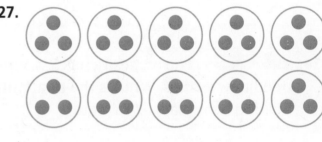

_____ $\times 3 =$ _____

MATHEMATICAL PRACTICE ④ Use a Diagram Complete the bar model to solve.

28. Marcel played 5 songs on the banjo. If each song lasted 8 minutes, how long did he play?

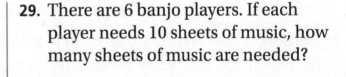

[   ] minutes

_____

29. There are 6 banjo players. If each player needs 10 sheets of music, how many sheets of music are needed?

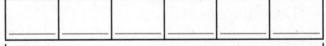

[   ] sheets

_____

30. **GO DEEPER** Chris has 5 stacks of DVDs on a shelf. Each stack has 10 DVDs. If Chris adds 2 more identical stacks of DVDs to the shelves, how many DVDs will Chris have?

_____

31. **GO DEEPER** Mark is making 10 kites. He uses 5 yards of ribbon for each kite. He has already made 2 of the kites. How many yards of ribbon will Mark need to make the rest of the kites?

_____

Problem Solving • Applications

Use the table for 32–34.

32. John and his dad own 7 banjos. They want to replace the strings on all of them. How many strings should they buy? Write a multiplication sentence to solve.

_____

33. GO DEEPER   Mr. Lemke has 5 guitars, 4 banjos, and 2 mandolins. What is the total number of strings on Mr. Lemke's instruments?

_____

Stringed Instruments	
Instrument	**Strings**
Guitar	6
Banjo	5
Mandolin	8
Violin	4

34. THINK SMARTER   The orchestra has 5 violins and 3 guitars that need new strings. What is the total number of strings that need to be replaced? Explain.

_____

_____

_____

35. WRITE ▸Math **What's the Error?** Mr. James has 3 banjos. Mr. Lewis has 5 times the number of banjos Mr. James has. Riley says Mr. Lewis has 12 banjos. Describe her error.

_____

_____

36. THINK SMARTER   Circle the number that makes the multiplication sentence true.

$$5 \times \boxed{\begin{matrix} 7 \\ 8 \\ 9 \end{matrix}} = 45$$

Multiply with 5 and 10

Common Core **COMMON CORE STANDARD—3.OA.A.3**
Represent and solve problems involving multiplication and division.

Find the product.

1. $5 \times 7 = \underline{35}$

2. $5 \times 1 = \underline{}$

3. $2 \times 10 = \underline{}$

4. $\underline{} = 8 \times 5$

5. $1 \times 10 = \underline{}$

6. $\underline{} = 4 \times 5$

7. $5 \times 10 = \underline{}$

8. $7 \times 5 = \underline{}$

9. $\begin{array}{r} 5 \\ \times\ 6 \\ \hline \end{array}$

10. $\begin{array}{r} 10 \\ \times\ 7 \\ \hline \end{array}$

11. $\begin{array}{r} 5 \\ \times\ 3 \\ \hline \end{array}$

12. $\begin{array}{r} 10 \\ \times\ 4 \\ \hline \end{array}$

13. $\begin{array}{r} 5 \\ \times\ 0 \\ \hline \end{array}$

14. $\begin{array}{r} 10 \\ \times\ 8 \\ \hline \end{array}$

15. $\begin{array}{r} 5 \\ \times\ 2 \\ \hline \end{array}$

16. $\begin{array}{r} 10 \\ \times\ 6 \\ \hline \end{array}$

Problem Solving

17. Ginger takes 10 nickels to buy some pencils at the school store. How many cents does Ginger have to spend?

18. The gym at Evergreen School has three basketball courts. There are 5 players on each of the courts. How many players are there?

_____

_____

19. **WRITE** ▸*Math* Michelle bought some pinwheels for a dollar and paid in dimes. How many dimes did she use? Explain.

_____

_____

Lesson Check (3.OA.A.3)

1. Mrs. Hinely grows roses. There are 6 roses on each of her 10 rose bushes. How many roses in all are on Mrs. Hinely's rose bushes?

_____

2. Find the product.

$$\begin{array}{r} 5 \\ \times\ 8 \\ \hline \end{array}$$

Spiral Review (3.OA.D.9, 3.NBT.A.1, 3.MD.B.3)

3. Mr. Miller's class voted on where to go for a field trip. Use the picture graph to find which choice had the most votes.

Field Trip Choices

Science Center	★★
Aquarium	★★★⯪
Zoo	★★★★
Museum	★★

Key: Each ★ = 2 votes.

_____

4. Zack made this table for his survey.

Favorite Juice

Flavor	Votes
Grape	16
Orange	10
Berry	9
Apple	12

How many votes were cast?

_____

5. Which of the following is an even number?

25, 28, 31, 37

_____

6. Estimate the sum.

$$\begin{array}{r} 479 \\ +\ \ 89 \\ \hline \end{array}$$

_____

FOR MORE PRACTICE
GO TO THE
Personal Math Trainer

Name _____

Multiply with 3 and 6

Essential Question What are some ways to multiply with 3 and 6?

Common Core Operations and Algebraic Thinking—3.OA.A.3 *Also 3.OA.A.1, 3.OA.C.7, 3.OA.D.9*

MATHEMATICAL PRACTICES
MP1, MP2, MP3, MP6

Unlock the Problem Real World

Sabrina is making triangles with toothpicks. She uses 3 toothpicks for each triangle. She makes 4 triangles. How many toothpicks does Sabrina use?

- Why does Sabrina need 3 toothpicks for each triangle?

_____

_____

Draw a picture. Hands On

STEP 1

Complete the 4 triangles.

STEP 2

Skip count by the number of sides. _____, _____, _____, _____

How many triangles are there in all? _____

How many toothpicks are in each triangle? _____

How many toothpicks are there in all?

$4 \times$ _____ = _____

4 triangles have _____ toothpicks.

So, Sabrina uses _____ toothpicks.

Math Talk

MATHEMATICAL PRACTICES ②

Reason Abstractly How can you use what you know about the number of toothpicks needed for 4 triangles to find the number of toothpicks needed for 8 triangles?

Try This! **Find the number of toothpicks needed for 6 triangles.**

Draw a quick picture to help you. How did you find the answer?

_____

_____

Jessica is using craft sticks to make 6 octagons.
How many craft sticks will she use?

▲ An octagon has 8 sides.

🔓 One Way Use 5s facts and addition.

To multiply a factor by 6, multiply the factor
by 5, and then add the factor.

$6 \times 7 = 5 \times 7 + 7 = 42$

$6 \times 6 = 5 \times 6 +$ _____ = _____

$6 \times 8 = 5 \times$ _____ + _____ = _____

$6 \times 9 =$ _____ $\times$ _____ + _____ = _____

So, Jessica will use _____ craft sticks.

5×8

$+ 8$

🔓 Other Ways

🅐 Use doubles.

When at least one factor is an even number,
you can use doubles.

First multiply with half of an even number.

After you multiply, double the product.

$6 \times 8 = \blacksquare$

$3 \times 8 =$ _____

_____ $+ 24 =$ _____

$6 \times 8 =$ _____

🅑 Use a multiplication table.

Hands On

Find the product 6×8 where
row 6 and column 8 meet.

$6 \times 8 =$ _____

- Shade the row for 3 in the table. Then,
  compare the rows for 3 and 6. What do
  you notice about their products?

_____

_____

×	0	1	2	3	4	5	6	7	8	9	10
0	0	0	0	0	0	0	0	0	0	0	0
1	0	1	2	3	4	5	6	7	8	9	10
2	0	2	4	6	8	10	12	14	16	18	20
3	0	3	6	9	12	15	18	21	24	27	30
4	0	4	8	12	16	20	24	28	32	36	40
5	0	5	10	15	20	25	30	35	40	45	50
6	0	6	12	18	24	30	36	42	48	54	60
7	0	7	14	21	28	35	42	49	56	63	70
8	0	8	16	24	32	40	48	56	64	72	80
9	0	9	18	27	36	45	54	63	72	81	90
10	0	10	20	30	40	50	60	70	80	90	100

Name _____

1. Use 5s facts and addition to find $6 \times 4 = $ ▪.

   $6 \times 4 = $ _____ $\times$ _____ $+$ _____ $=$ _____

   $6 \times 4 = $ _____

Math Talk MATHEMATICAL PRACTICES ⑥

Explain how you would use 5s facts and addition to find 6×3.

Find the product.

2. $6 \times 1 = $ _____   3. _____ $= 3 \times 7$ ✓ 4. _____ $= 6 \times 5$ ✓ 5. $3 \times 9 = $ _____

On Your Own

Find the product.

6. $2 \times 3 = $ _____   7. _____ $= 3 \times 6$ 8. _____ $= 3 \times 0$ 9. $1 \times 6 = $ _____

10.　　3
　　$\times 6$

11.　　8
　　$\times 3$

12.　　6
　　$\times 7$

13.　　3
　　$\times 3$

14.　　10
　　$\times\ 6$

MATHEMATICAL PRACTICE ② **Use Reasoning Algebra** Complete the table.

Multiply by 3.	
Factor	Product
15. 4	
16.	18

Multiply by 6.	
Factor	Product
17. 5	
18. 7	

Multiply by ▪.	
Factor	Product
19. 3	15
20. 2	

Problem Solving · Applications

Use the table for 21–22.

Quilt Pieces	
Shape	**Number in One Quilt Piece**
Square	6
Triangle	4
Circle	4

21. **GO DEEPER** The table tells about quilt pieces Jenna has made. How many squares and circles are there in 6 of Jenna's quilt pieces?

_____

22. **GO DEEPER** How many more squares than triangles are in 3 of Jenna's quilt pieces?

_____

23. **THINK SMARTER** Alli used some craft sticks to make shapes. If she used one craft stick for each side of the shape, would Alli use more craft sticks for 5 squares or 6 triangles? Explain.

_____

_____

_____

24. **MATHEMATICAL PRACTICE ③** **Apply** Draw a picture and use words to explain the Commutative Property of Multiplication with the factors 3 and 4.

_____

_____

25. **THINK SMARTER** Omar reads 6 pages in his book each night. How many pages does Omar read in 7 nights?

Use the array to explain how you know your answer is correct.

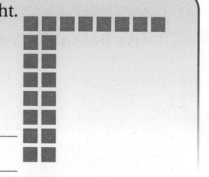

_____

_____

Multiply with 3 and 6

Common Core

COMMON CORE STANDARD—3.OA.A.3
Represent and solve problems involving
multiplication and division.

Find the product.

1. $6 \times 4 =$ __24__

2. $3 \times 7 =$ _____

3. _____ $= 2 \times 6$

4. _____ $= 3 \times 5$

Think: You can use doubles.
$3 \times 4 = 12$
$12 + 12 = 24$

5. $1 \times 3 =$ _____

6. _____ $= 6 \times 8$

7. $3 \times 9 =$ _____

8. _____ $= 6 \times 6$

9. $\begin{array}{r} 4 \\ \times\ 3 \\ \hline \end{array}$

10. $\begin{array}{r} 6 \\ \times\ 5 \\ \hline \end{array}$

11. $\begin{array}{r} 2 \\ \times\ 3 \\ \hline \end{array}$

12. $\begin{array}{r} 6 \\ \times\ 3 \\ \hline \end{array}$

13. $\begin{array}{r} 10 \\ \times\ 6 \\ \hline \end{array}$

14. $\begin{array}{r} 3 \\ \times\ 6 \\ \hline \end{array}$

15. $\begin{array}{r} 7 \\ \times\ 6 \\ \hline \end{array}$

16. $\begin{array}{r} 3 \\ \times\ 0 \\ \hline \end{array}$

Problem Solving

17. James got 3 hits in each of his baseball games. He has played 4 baseball games. How many hits has he had?

_____

18. Mrs. Burns is buying muffins. There are 6 muffins in each box. If she buys 5 boxes, how many muffins will she buy?

_____

19. **WRITE** ▸Math Explain how multiplying with 6 is like multiplying with 3.

_____

_____

Lesson Check (3.OA.A.3)

1. Paco buys a carton of eggs. The carton has 2 rows of eggs. There are 6 eggs in each row. How many eggs are in the carton?

_____

2. Find the product.

$$\begin{array}{r} 9 \\ \times\ 3 \\ \hline \end{array}$$

Spiral Review (3.OA.A.3, 3.NBT.A.2, 3.MD.B.3)

3. Find the difference.

$$\begin{array}{r} 568 \\ -\ 283 \\ \hline \end{array}$$

4. Dwight made double the number of baskets in the second half of the basketball game than in the first half. He made 5 baskets in the first half. How many baskets did he make in the second half?

_____

5. In Jane's picture graph, the symbol ☺ represents two students. One row in the picture graph has 8 symbols. How many students does that represent?

6. What multiplication sentence does this array show?

_____

FOR MORE PRACTICE
GO TO THE
Personal Math Trainer

Distributive Property

Essential Question How can you use the Distributive Property to find products?

Common Core **Operations and Algebraic Thinking—3.OA.B.5** *Also 3.OA.A.1, 3.OA.A.3, 3.OA.A.4, 3.OA.C.7*
MATHEMATICAL PRACTICES
MP2, MP3, MP7

Unlock the Problem

Mark bought 6 new fish for his aquarium. He paid $7 for each fish. How much money did he spend in all?

Find 6 × $7.

You can use the Distributive Property to solve the problem.

The **Distributive Property** states that multiplying a sum by a number is the same as multiplying each addend by the number and then adding the products.

- Describe the groups in this problem.

_____

- Circle the numbers you will use to solve the problem.

Remember

sum—the answer to an addition problem

addends—the numbers being added

Activity Materials ■ square tiles

Make an array with tiles to show 6 rows of 7.

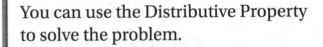

6 × 7 = ■

Break apart the array to make two smaller arrays for facts you know.

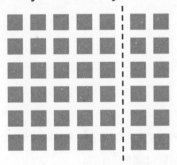

6 × 5   6 × 2

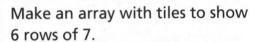

6 × 7 = ■
6 × 7 = 6 × (5 + 2)   **Think:** 7 = 5 + 2
6 × 7 = (6 × 5) + (6 × 2)   Multiply each addend by 6.

6 × 7 = _____ + _____   Add the products.

6 × 7 = _____

So, Mark spent $_____ for his new fish.

 Math Talk

MATHEMATICAL PRACTICES ②

Reason Quantitatively What other ways could you break apart the 6 × 7 array?

Try This!

Suppose Mark bought 9 fish for $6 each.

You can break apart a 9 × 6 array into two smaller arrays for facts you know. One way is to think of 9 as 5 + 4. Draw a line to show this way. Then find the product.

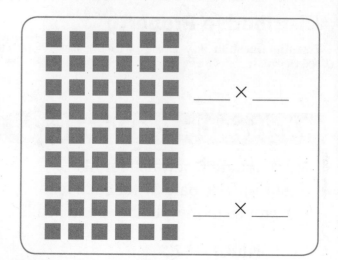

_____ × _____

_____ × _____

9 × 6 = (____ × ____) + (____ × ____)

9 × 6 = ____ + ____

So, Mark spent $____ for 9 fish.

Share and Show

MATH BOARD

Hands On

1. Draw a line to show how you could break apart this 6 × 8 array into two smaller arrays for facts you know.

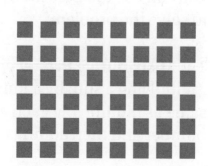

- What numbers do you multiply? ____ and ____

  ____ and ____

- What numbers do you add? ____ + ____

6 × 8 = 6 × (____ + ____)

6 × 8 = (____ × ____) + (____ × ____)

6 × 8 = ____ + ____

6 × 8 = ____

Write one way to break apart the array. Then find the product.

Math Talk

MATHEMATICAL PRACTICES ⑦

Look for Structure Why do you have to add to find the total product when you use the Distributive Property?

2.

_____

_____

3.

_____

_____

Name _____

4. *GO DEEPER* Shade tiles to make an array that shows a fact with 7, 8, or 9 as a factor. Write the fact. Explain how you found the product.

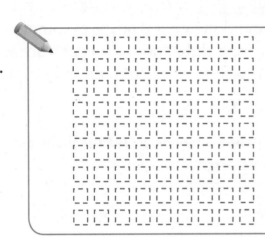

_____

_____

_____

_____

5. *THINK SMARTER* Robin says, "I can find 8×7 by multiplying 3×7 and doubling it." Does her statement make sense? Justify your answer.

_____

_____

6. *GO DEEPER* Kent buys 5 bags of potatoes that cost $7 each. He gives the clerk $40. How much change should Kent receive?

_____

7. *THINK SMARTER* For numbers 7a-7d, choose Yes or No to indicate whether the sum or product is equal to 7×5.

7a. $7 + (3 + 2) = \blacksquare$ ○ Yes   ○ No

7b. $7 \times (3 + 2) = \blacksquare$ ○ Yes   ○ No

7c. $(5 \times 4) + (5 \times 3) = \blacksquare$ ○ Yes   ○ No

7d. $(7 \times 2) + (7 \times 5) = \blacksquare$ ○ Yes   ○ No

Problem Solving • Applications

What's the Error?

8. **MATHEMATICAL PRACTICE 3** **Verify the Reasoning of Others**
Brandon needs 8 boxes of spinners for his
fishing club. The cost of each box is $9.
How much will Brandon pay?

$8 \times \$9 = \blacksquare$

Look at how Brandon solved the problem.
Find and describe his error.

$8 \times 9 = (4 \times 9) + (5 \times 9)$

$8 \times 9 = 36 + 45$

$8 \times 9 = 81$

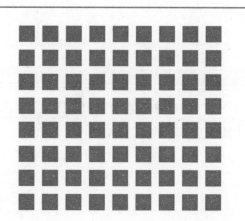

_____

_____

Use the array to help solve the problem
and correct his error.

$8 \times 9 = (4 + 4) \times 9$

$8 \times 9 = (\text{\_\_\_} \times \text{\_\_\_}) + (\text{\_\_\_} \times \text{\_\_\_})$

$8 \times 9 = \text{\_\_\_} + \text{\_\_\_}$

$8 \times 9 = \text{\_\_\_}$

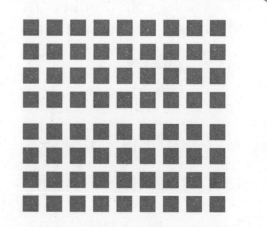

So, Brandon will pay $ _____ for the spinners.

Name _____

Distributive Property

 COMMON CORE STANDARD—3.OA.B.5
Understand properties of multiplication and the relationship between multiplication and division.

Write one way to break apart the array. Then find the product.

1.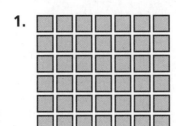

_____
$$(3 \times 7) + (3 \times 7)$$
_____
42
_____

2.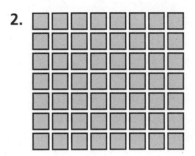

_____

_____

_____

Problem Solving Real World

3. There are 2 rows of 8 chairs set up in the library for a puppet show. How many chairs are set up? Use the Distributive Property to solve.

_____

4. A marching band has 4 rows of trumpeters with 10 trumpeters in each row. How many trumpeters are in the marching band? Use the Distributive Property to solve.

_____

5. **WRITE** ▸*Math* What are some ways you could break apart 7×9 using the Distributive Property?

_____

_____

Lesson Check (3.OA.B.5)

1. Complete the number sentence to show the Distributive Property.

$7 \times 6 =$

_____

_____

_____

2. What is one way to break apart the array?

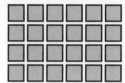

_____

_____

_____

Spiral Review (3.NBT.A.1, 3.NBT.A.2, 3.MD.B.3)

3. The school auditorium has 448 chairs set out for the third-grade performance. What is 448 rounded to the nearest ten?

_____

4. Find the difference.

$$\begin{array}{r} 400 \\ -\ 296 \\ \hline \end{array}$$

5. There are 622 fruit snacks in one crate and 186 in another crate. How many fruit snacks are there?

$$\begin{array}{r} 622 \\ +\ 186 \\ \hline \end{array}$$

_____

6. Which sport do exactly 6 students play?

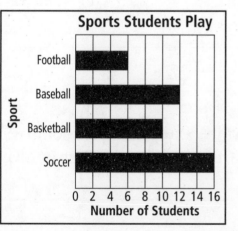

_____

FOR MORE PRACTICE GO TO THE Personal Math Trainer

Name _____

Multiply with 7

Essential Question What strategies can you use to multiply with 7?

Common Core **Operations and Algebraic Thinking—3.OA.C.7** *Also 3.OA.A.1, 3.OA.A.3, 3.OA.A.4, 3.OA.B.5*

MATHEMATICAL PRACTICES
MP1, MP7, MP8

Unlock the Problem

Jason's family has a new puppy. Jason takes a turn walking the puppy once a day. How many times will Jason walk the puppy in 4 weeks?

Find 4×7.

- How often does Jason walk the puppy?

  _____

- How many days are in 1 week?

  _____

One Way Use the Commutative Property of Multiplication.

If you know 7×4, you can use that fact to find 4×7.
You can change the order of the factors and the product is the same.

$7 \times 4 =$ _____, so $4 \times 7 =$ _____.

So, Jason will walk the puppy _____ times in 4 weeks.

Other Ways

A Use the Distributive Property.

STEP 1 Complete the array to show 4 rows of 7.

STEP 2 Draw a line to break the array into two smaller arrays for facts you know.

STEP 3 Multiply the facts for the smaller arrays. Add the products.

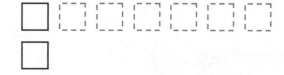

$4 \times$ _____ = _____ $4 \times$ _____ = _____

_____ + _____ = _____

So, $4 \times 7 =$ _____.

MATHEMATICAL PRACTICES ⑧

Generalize Why would you use the Distributive Property as a strategy to multiply?

B Use a fact you know.

Multiply. $4 \times 7 =$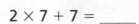

- Start with a fact you know. $2 \times 7 =$ ____

- Add a group of 7 for 3×7. $2 \times 7 + 7 =$ ____

- Then add 7 more for 4×7. $3 \times 7 + 7 =$ ____

So, $4 \times 7 =$ ____.

Share and Show MATH BOARD

1. **Explain** how you could break apart an array to find 6×7. Draw an array to show your work.

_____

_____

Math Talk   MATHEMATICAL PRACTICES ①

Apply How can you use doubles to find 8×7?

Find the product.

2. $9 \times 7 =$ ____   3. ____ $= 5 \times 7$ ✓ 4. ____ $= 7 \times 3$ ✓ 5. $1 \times 7 =$ ____

On Your Own

Find the product.

6. ____ $= 7 \times 7$ 7. $6 \times 7 =$ ____   8. ____ $= 7 \times 10$ 9. ____ $= 7 \times 2$

10. 7
    $\times 3$

11. 6
    $\times 7$

12. 9
    $\times 7$

13. 8
    $\times 7$

14. 1
    $\times 7$

15. 4
    $\times 7$

16. **GO DEEPER** Anders makes 7 fruit cups. He puts 2 green grapes, 2 red grapes, and 2 black grapes in each fruit cup. How many grapes does Anders use for the fruit cups?

_____

Problem Solving • Applications

Use the table for 17–19.

17. Lori has a dog named Rusty. How many baths will Rusty have in 7 months?

_____

18. **THINK SMARTER** How many more cups of water than food will Rusty get in 1 week?

_____

19. **GO DEEPER** Tim's dog, Midnight, eats 28 cups of food in a week. Midnight eats the same amount each day. In one day, how many more cups of food will Midnight eat than Rusty? Explain.

_____

_____

_____

Rusty's Care	
Food	3 cups a day
Water	4 cups a day
Bath	2 times a month

WRITE *Math* • **Show Your Work**

20. José walks his dog 10 miles every week. How many miles do they walk in 7 weeks?

_____

21. **MATHEMATICAL PRACTICE ⑦ Look for Structure** Dave takes Zoey, his dog, for a 3-mile walk twice a day. How many miles do they walk in one week?

_____

22. **THINK SMARTER** Alia arranges some playing cards in 7 equal rows with 7 cards in each row. How many cards does Alia arrange?

_____

Connect to Reading

Summarize

To help you stay healthy, you should eat a balanced diet and exercise every day.

The table shows the recommended daily servings for third graders. You should eat the right amounts of the food groups.

Suppose you want to share with your friends what you learned about healthy eating. How could you summarize what you learned?

When you *summarize,* you restate the most important information in a shorter way to help you understand what you have read.

Recommended Daily Servings

Food Group	Servings
Whole Grains (bread, cereal)	6 ounces
Vegetables (carrot, corn)	2 cups
Fruits (apples, oranges)	1 cup
Dairy Products (milk, cheese)	3 cups
Meat, Beans, Fish, Eggs, Nuts	5 ounces
8 ounces = 1 cup	

- To stay healthy, you should eat a balanced

    _____ and _____ every day.

- A third grader should eat 3 cups of _____, such as milk and cheese, each day.

- A third grader should eat _____ of vegetables and fruits each day.

    How many cups of vegetables and fruits should a third

    grader eat in 1 week? _____

    Remember: 1 week = 7 days

- A third grader should eat _____ of whole grains, such as bread and cereal, each day.

    How many ounces of whole grains should a third grader

    eat in 1 week? _____

Multiply with 7

COMMON CORE STANDARD—3.OA.C.7
Multiply and divide within 100.

Find the product.

1. $6 \times 7 =$ **42**   2. _____ $= 7 \times 9$ 3. _____ $= 1 \times 7$ 4. $3 \times 7 =$ _____

5. $7 \times 7 =$ _____   6. _____ $= 2 \times 7$ 7. $7 \times 8 =$ _____   8. _____ $= 4 \times 7$

9. $\begin{array}{r} 7 \\ \times\ 5 \\ \hline \end{array}$ 10. $\begin{array}{r} 7 \\ \times\ 1 \\ \hline \end{array}$ 11. $\begin{array}{r} 6 \\ \times\ 7 \\ \hline \end{array}$ 12. $\begin{array}{r} 7 \\ \times\ 4 \\ \hline \end{array}$ 13. $\begin{array}{r} 2 \\ \times\ 7 \\ \hline \end{array}$

14. $\begin{array}{r} 10 \\ \times\ 7 \\ \hline \end{array}$ 15. $\begin{array}{r} 3 \\ \times\ 7 \\ \hline \end{array}$ 16. $\begin{array}{r} 7 \\ \times\ 9 \\ \hline \end{array}$ 17. $\begin{array}{r} 8 \\ \times\ 7 \\ \hline \end{array}$ 18. $\begin{array}{r} 7 \\ \times\ 0 \\ \hline \end{array}$

Problem Solving

19. Julie buys a pair of earrings for $7. Now she would like to buy the same earrings for 2 of her friends. How much will she spend for all 3 pairs of earrings?

20. Owen and his family will go camping in 8 weeks. There are 7 days in 1 week. How many days are in 8 weeks?

_____   _____

21. **WRITE** ▸*Math* Explain how you would use the Commutative Property of Multiplication to answer 7×3.

_____

_____

Lesson Check (3.OA.C.7)

1. Find the product.

$$\begin{array}{r} 7 \\ \times\ 8 \\ \hline \end{array}$$

2. What product does the array show?

_____

Spiral Review (3.OA.A.3, 3.OA.D.9, 3.NBT.A.1, 3.MD.B.3)

3. Which numbers below are even?

6, 12, 15, 24, 30

_____

4. How many more people chose retriever than poodle?

Favorite Breed of Dog	
Dog	**Number**
Shepherd	58
Retriever	65
Poodle	26

_____

5. What is 94 rounded to the nearest ten?

6. Jack has 5 craft sticks. He needs 4 times that number for a project. How many craft sticks does Jack need altogether?

_____

FOR MORE PRACTICE
GO TO THE
Personal Math Trainer

✓ Mid-Chapter Checkpoint

Personal Math Trainer
Online Assessment
and Intervention

Vocabulary

Choose the best term from the box to complete the sentence.

Vocabulary
Commutative Property of Multiplication
Distributive Property
multiple

1. A _____ of 4 is any product that has 4 as one of its factors. (p. 197)

2. This is an example of the _____ Property.

$$3 \times 8 = (3 \times 6) + (3 \times 2)$$

This property states that multiplying a sum by a number is the same as multiplying each addend by the number and then adding the products. (p. 209)

Concepts and Skills

**Write one way to break apart the array.
Then find the product.** (3.OA.B.5)

3.

_____

_____

4.

_____

_____

Find the product. (3.OA.A.3, 3.OA.C.7)

5. $3 \times 1 =$ ____   6. $5 \times 6 =$ ____   7. ____ $= 7 \times 7$ 8. $2 \times 10 =$ ____

9. $\begin{array}{r} 2 \\ \times 1 \\ \hline \end{array}$ 10. $\begin{array}{r} 6 \\ \times 6 \\ \hline \end{array}$ 11. $\begin{array}{r} 8 \\ \times 7 \\ \hline \end{array}$ 12. $\begin{array}{r} 6 \\ \times 0 \\ \hline \end{array}$ 13. $\begin{array}{r} 3 \\ \times 8 \\ \hline \end{array}$

14. Lori saw 6 lightning bugs. They each had 6 legs. How many legs did the lightning bugs have in all?

(3.OA.A.3)

_____

15. GO DEEPER   Zach walked his dog twice a day, for 7 days. Moira walked her dog three times a day for 5 days. Whose dog was walked more times? How many more?

(3.OA.A.3)

_____

16. GO DEEPER   Annette buys 4 boxes of pencils. There are 8 pencils in each box. Jordan buys 3 boxes of pencils with 10 pencils in each box. Who buys more pencils? How many more? (3.OA.A.3)

_____

17. Shelly can paint 4 pictures in a day. How many pictures can she paint in 7 days? (3.OA.C.7)

_____

Name _____

Associative Property of Multiplication

Essential Question How can you use the Associative Property of Multiplication to find products?

 Operations and Algebraic Thinking—3.OA.B.5 *Also 3.OA.A.1, 3.OA.A.3, 3.OA.A.4, 3.OA.C.7*
MATHEMATICAL PRACTICES
MP2, MP4, MP8

CONNECT You have learned the Associative Property of Addition. When the grouping of the addends is changed, the sum stays the same.

$$(2 + 3) + 4 = 2 + (3 + 4)$$

The **Associative Property of Multiplication** states that when the grouping of the factors is changed, the product is the same. It is also called the Grouping Property of Multiplication.

$$2 \times (3 \times 4) = (2 \times 3) \times 4$$

> **Math Idea**
> Always multiply the numbers inside the parentheses first.

Unlock the Problem Real World

Each car on the roller coaster has 2 rows of seats. Each row has 2 seats. There are 3 cars in each train. How many seats are on each train?

- Underline what you need to find.
- Describe the grouping of the seats.

_____

Use an array.
You can use an array to show $3 \times (2 \times 2)$.

$3 \times (2 \times 2) = \blacksquare$

$3 \times$ _____ = _____

So, there are 3 cars with 4 seats in each car.

There are _____ seats on each roller coaster train.

You can change the grouping with parentheses and the product is the same.

$(3 \times 2) \times 2 = \blacksquare$

_____ $\times 2 =$ _____

Math Talk MATHEMATICAL PRACTICES ⑧

Generalize Why does changing the placement of the parentheses not change the answer when multiplying 3 numbers together?

Example Use the Commutative and Associative Properties.

You can also change the order of the factors.
The product is the same.

$(4 \times 3) \times 2 = $ ▪

$4 \times (3 \times 2) = $ ▪   Associative Property

$4 \times \underline{\hspace{1cm}} = \underline{\hspace{1cm}}$

$4 \times (3 \times 2) = $ ▪

$4 \times (2 \times 3) = $ ▪   Commutative Property

$(4 \times 2) \times 3 = $ ▪   Associative Property

$\underline{\hspace{1cm}} \times 3 = \underline{\hspace{1cm}}$

Share and Show

1. Find the product of 5, 2, and 3. Write another way to group the factors. Is the product the same? Why?

_____

_____

Write another way to group the factors. Then find the product.

2. $(2 \times 1) \times 7$

_____

_____

3. $3 \times (3 \times 4)$

_____

_____

✅ 4. $5 \times (2 \times 5)$

_____

_____

✅ 5. $3 \times (2 \times 6)$

_____

_____

6. $2 \times (2 \times 5)$

_____

_____

7. $(1 \times 3) \times 6$

_____

_____

MATHEMATICAL PRACTICES ②

Use Reasoning Why would you use both the Commutative and Associative Properties when solving a multiplication problem?

Name _____

On Your Own

Write another way to group the factors. Then find the product.

8. $(2 \times 3) \times 3$

_____

_____

9. $(8 \times 3) \times 2$

_____

_____

10. $2 \times (5 \times 5)$

_____

_____

11. $(3 \times 2) \times 4$

_____

_____

12. $(6 \times 1) \times 4$

_____

_____

13. $2 \times (2 \times 6)$

_____

_____

Practice: Copy and Solve Use parentheses and multiplication properties. Then, find the product.

14. $6 \times 5 \times 2$

15. $2 \times 3 \times 5$

16. $3 \times 1 \times 6$

17. $2 \times 5 \times 6$

18. $2 \times 0 \times 8$

19. $1 \times 9 \times 4$

THINK SMARTER **Algebra** Find the unknown factor.

20. $7 \times (2 \times \underline{\quad}) = 56$

21. $30 = 6 \times (5 \times \underline{\quad})$

22. $\underline{\quad} \times (2 \times 2) = 32$

23. $42 = 7 \times (2 \times \underline{\quad})$

24. $8 \times (5 \times \underline{\quad}) = 40$

25. $0 = \underline{\quad} \times (25 \times 1)$

26. **GO DEEPER** What number sentence does this array represent? Write another way to group the factors.

_____

_____

27. **GO DEEPER** Jamal has 65 quilt patches. He makes 2 quilts with 5 rows of 6 patches in each quilt. How many quilt patches will be left over?

_____

_____

Problem Solving · Applications

Use the graph for 28–29.

28. MATHEMATICAL PRACTICE ② **Represent a Problem**
Each car on the Steel Force train has 3 rows with 2 seats in each row. How many seats are on the train? Draw a quick picture.

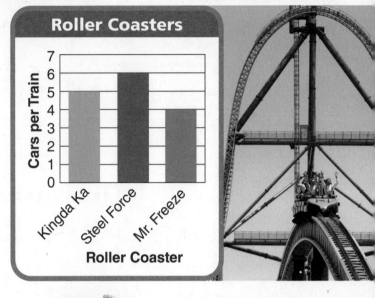

_____

29. THINK SMARTER A Kingda Ka train has 4 seats per car, but the last car has only 2 seats. How many seats are on one Kingda Ka train?

_____

30. GO DEEPER **Sense or Nonsense?** Each week, Kelly works 2 days for 4 hours each day and earns $5 an hour. Len works 5 days for 2 hours each day and earns $4 an hour. Kelly says they both earn the same amount. Does this statement make sense? Explain.

_____

_____

WRITE ▸ Math
Show Your Work

31. THINK SMARTER Clayton packs 3 boxes. He puts 3 lunch bags in each box. There are 4 sandwiches in each lunch bag. How many sandwiches does Clayton pack? Show your work.

_____

Associative Property of Multiplication

Common Core

COMMON CORE STANDARD—3.OA.B.5
Understand properties of multiplication and the relationship between multiplication and division.

**Write another way to group the factors.
Then find the product.**

1. $(3 \times 2) \times 5$

   $\underline{\quad 3 \times (2 \times 5) \quad}$

   $\underline{\quad\quad 30 \quad\quad}$

2. $(4 \times 3) \times 2$

   _____

   _____

3. $2 \times (2 \times 8)$

   _____

   _____

4. $9 \times (2 \times 1)$

   _____

   _____

5. $2 \times (3 \times 6)$

   _____

   _____

6. $(2 \times 4) \times 5$

   _____

   _____

**Use parentheses and multiplication properties.
Then, find the product.**

7. $9 \times 1 \times 5 =$ _____

8. $3 \times 3 \times 2 =$ _____

9. $2 \times 4 \times 3 =$ _____

10. $7 \times 2 \times 3 =$ _____

11. $4 \times 1 \times 3 =$ _____

12. $10 \times 2 \times 4 =$ _____

Problem Solving · Real World

13. Beth and Maria are going to the county fair. Admission costs $4 per person for each day. They plan to go for 3 days. How much will the girls pay for all 3 days?

    _____

14. Randy's garden has 3 rows of carrots with 3 plants in each row. Next year, he plans to plant 4 times the number of rows. How many plants will he have next year?

    _____

15. **WRITE** ▸ *Math* Why would you use the Associative Property of Multiplication to solve $(10 \times 4) \times 2$? How would you regroup the factors?

    _____

Lesson Check (3.OA.B.5)

1. There are 2 benches in each car of a train ride. Two people ride on each bench. If a train has 5 cars, how many people can be on a train?

   _____

2. Crystal has 2 CDs in each box. She has 3 boxes on each of her 6 shelves. How many CDs does Crystal have?

   _____

Spiral Review (3.OA.A.3, 3.NBT.A.1, 3.NBT.A.2, 3.MD.B.3)

3. Find the sum.

$$
\begin{array}{r}
472 \\
+\ 186 \\
\hline
\end{array}
$$

4. Trevor made a picture graph to show how many minutes each student biked last week. This is his key.

   Each ⊛ = 10 minutes.

   What does ⊛ ⊛ ☾ stand for?

   _____

5. Madison has 142 stickers in her collection. What is 142 rounded to the nearest ten?

   _____

6. There are 5 pages of photos. Each page has 6 photos. How many photos are there?

   _____

FOR MORE PRACTICE
GO TO THE
Personal Math Trainer

Name _____

Patterns on the Multiplication Table

Essential Question How can you use properties to explain patterns on the multiplication table?

 Operations and Algebraic Thinking—3.OA.D.9 *Also 3.OA.B.5*

MATHEMATICAL PRACTICES
MP1, MP3, MP7

 **Unlock the Problem** *Real World*

You can use a multiplication table to explore number patterns.

🔒 Activity 1

Materials ■ MathBoard

- Write the products for the green squares. What do you notice about the products?

_____

_____

_____

Write the multiplication sentences for the products on your MathBoard. What do you notice about the factors?

_____

- Will this be true in the yellow squares? **Explain** using a property you know.

_____

Write the products for the yellow squares.

- Complete the columns for 1, 5, and 6. Look across each row and compare the products. What do you notice?

_____

What property does this show?

_____

×	0	1	2	3	4	5	6	7	8	9	10
0											
1											
2											
3											
4											
5											
6											
7											
8											
9											
10											

 Math Talk MATHEMATICAL PRACTICES ❼

Look for a Pattern How can you use patterns on a multiplication chart to find other products?

Activity 2

Materials ■ yellow and blue crayons

- Shade the rows for 0, 2, 4, 6, 8, and 10 yellow.

- What pattern do you notice about each shaded row? _____

  _____

- Compare the rows for 2 and 4. What do you notice about the products?

  _____

- Shade the columns for 1, 3, 5, 7, and 9 blue.

- What do you notice about the products for each shaded column?

  _____

- Compare the products for the green squares. What do you notice? What do you notice about the factors?

  _____

- What other patterns do you see?

  _____

×	0	1	2	3	4	5	6	7	8	9	10
0	0	0	0	0	0	0	0	0	0	0	0
1	0	1	2	3	4	5	6	7	8	9	10
2	0	2	4	6	8	10	12	14	16	18	20
3	0	3	6	9	12	15	18	21	24	27	30
4	0	4	8	12	16	20	24	28	32	36	40
5	0	5	10	15	20	25	30	35	40	45	50
6	0	6	12	18	24	30	36	42	48	54	60
7	0	7	14	21	28	35	42	49	56	63	70
8	0	8	16	24	32	40	48	56	64	72	80
9	0	9	18	27	36	45	54	63	72	81	90
10	0	10	20	30	40	50	60	70	80	90	100

Share and Show

1. Use the table to write the products for the row for 2.

   _____, _____, _____, _____, _____,

   _____, _____, _____, _____, _____, _____

   Describe a pattern you see.

   _____

Math Talk

MATHEMATICAL PRACTICES ①

Analyze What do you notice about the product of any number and 2?

Is the product even or odd? Write *even* or *odd*.

2. 5 × 8 _____   **3.** 6 × 3 _____   **4.** 3 × 5 _____   ✔ **5.** 4 × 4 _____

Name _____

Use the multiplication table. Describe a pattern you see.

6. in the column for 10

_____

_____

☑ **7.** in the column for 8

_____

_____

On Your Own

Is the product even or odd? Write *even* or *odd*.

8. 4×8 _____

9. 5×5 _____

10. 7×4 _____

11. 2×9 _____

12. GO DEEPER Use the multiplication table. Rewrite the correct pattern.

6, 12, 18, 22, 30, 36 _____

Problem Solving • Applications Real World

Complete the table. Then describe a pattern you see in the products.

13.

×	2	4	6	8	10
5					

_____

_____

14.

×	1	3	5	7	9
5					

_____

_____

15. THINK SMARTER **Explain** how patterns of the ones digits in the products relate to the factors in Exercises 13 and 14.

_____

_____

_____

Personal Math Trainer

16. THINK SMARTER ➕ Helene selected an odd number to multiply by the factors in this table. Write *even* or *odd* to describe each product.

×	1	2	3	4	5
odd number					

Sense or Nonsense?

17. **MATHEMATICAL PRACTICE ③** **Make Arguments** Whose statement makes sense? Whose statement is nonsense? Explain your reasoning.

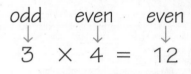
The product of an odd number and an even number is even.

The product of two even numbers is even.

Gunter's Work

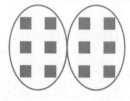

odd   even   even
$3 \times 4 = 12$

I can circle 2 equal groups of 6 with no tiles left over. So, the product is even.

Giselle's Work

even   even   even
$2 \times 6 = 12$

I can circle 6 pairs with no tiles left over. So, the product is even.

18. **GO DEEPER** Write a statement about the product of two odd numbers. Give an example to show why your statement is true.

Patterns on the Multiplication Table

Common Core

COMMON CORE STANDARD—3.OA.D.9
Solve problems involving the four operations, and identify and explain patterns in arithmetic.

Is the product even or odd? Write *even* or *odd*.

1. $2 \times 7 =$ __even__   Think: Products with 2 as a factor are even.

2. $4 \times 6 =$ _____

3. $8 \times 3 =$ _____

Use the multiplication table. Describe a pattern you see.

4. in the column for 5

_____

_____

5. in the row for 10

_____

_____

6. in the rows for 3 and 6

_____

_____

×	0	1	2	3	4	5	6	7	8	9	10
0	0	0	0	0	0	0	0	0	0	0	0
1	0	1	2	3	4	5	6	7	8	9	10
2	0	2	4	6	8	10	12	14	16	18	20
3	0	3	6	9	12	15	18	21	24	27	30
4	0	4	8	12	16	20	24	28	32	36	40
5	0	5	10	15	20	25	30	35	40	45	50
6	0	6	12	18	24	30	36	42	48	54	60
7	0	7	14	21	28	35	42	49	56	63	70
8	0	8	16	24	32	40	48	56	64	72	80
9	0	9	18	27	36	45	54	63	72	81	90
10	0	10	20	30	40	50	60	70	80	90	100

Problem Solving (Real World)

7. Carl shades a row in the multiplication table. The products in the row are all even. The ones digits in the products repeat 0, 4, 8, 2, 6. What row does Carl shade?

_____

8. Jenna says that no row or column contains products with only odd numbers. Do you agree? Explain.

_____

_____

_____

9. |WRITE ▶Math Draw a picture that shows an example of a product of two even numbers. Write the matching multiplication sentence.

_____

Lesson Check

1. Is the product of 4×9 even or odd?

2. Describe a pattern you see.

10, 15, 20, 25, 30

_____

_____

Spiral Review (3.OA.A.3, 3.OA.B.5, 3.NBT.A.2, 3.MD.B.3)

3. Lexi has 2 cans of tennis balls. There are 3 tennis balls in each can. She buys 2 more cans. How many tennis balls does she now have?

4. Use the picture graph.

Color of Eyes

Blue	● ● ●
Green	● ● ● ●
Brown	● ● ● ● ●

Key: Each ● = 4 students.

How many students have green eyes?

_____

_____

5. Sasha bought 3 boxes of pencils. If each box has 6 pencils, how many pencils did Sasha buy?

6. Find the sum.

$$\begin{array}{r} 219 \\ + \ 763 \\ \hline \end{array}$$

_____

FOR MORE PRACTICE
GO TO THE
Personal Math Trainer

Name _____

Multiply with 8

Essential Question What strategies can you use to multiply with 8?

Common Core
Operations and Algebraic Thinking—3.OA.C.7 *Also 3.OA.A.1, 3.OA.A.3, 3.OA.A.4, 3.OA.B.5, 3.OA.D.9*
MATHEMATICAL PRACTICES
MP1, MP3, MP6

Unlock the Problem

A scorpion has 8 legs. How many legs do 5 scorpions have?

Find 5×8.

One Way Use doubles.

$5 \times 8 = \blacksquare$

$\swarrow \searrow$

$4 + 4$

Think: The factor 8 is an even number. $4 + 4 = 8$

$5 \times 4 = $ _____

20 doubled is _____.

$5 \times 8 = $ _____

So, 5 scorpions have _____ legs.

Another Way Use a number line.

Use the number line to show 5 jumps of 8.

• How many legs does one scorpion have?

_____

• What are you asked to find?

_____

_____

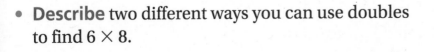

0 2 4 6 8 10 12 14 16 18 20 22 24 26 28 30 32 34 36 38 40

So, 5 jumps of 8 is _____.   _____ $\times$ _____ = _____

! **ERROR Alert**

Be sure to count the spaces between the tick marks, not the tick marks.

• **Describe** two different ways you can use doubles to find 6×8.

_____

_____

Chapter 4 235

🔑 Example Use the Associative Property of Multiplication.

Scorpions have two eyes on the top of the head, and usually two to five pairs along the front corners of the head. If each scorpion has 6 eyes, how many eyes would 8 scorpions have?

$8 \times 6 = \blacksquare$

$8 \times 6 = (2 \times 4) \times 6$ Think: $8 = 2 \times 4$

$8 \times 6 = 2 \times (4 \times 6)$ Use the Associative Property.

$8 \times 6 = 2 \times \underline{\hspace{1cm}}$ Multiply. 4×6

$8 \times 6 = \underline{\hspace{1cm}} + \underline{\hspace{1cm}}$ Double the product.

$8 \times 6 = \underline{\hspace{1cm}}$

MATHEMATICAL PRACTICES ❸

Apply When you multiply with 8, will the product always be even?

Share and Show 🖊 MATH BOARD

1. Explain one way you can find 4×8.

_____

Find the product.

2. $3 \times 8 = $ _____   **3.** _____ $= 8 \times 2$ ⨀ **4.** _____ $= 7 \times 8$ ⨀ **5.** $9 \times 8 = $ _____

On Your Own

Find the product.

6. _____ $= 6 \times 8$ **7.** $10 \times 8 = $ _____   **8.** _____ $= 8 \times 3$ **9.** $1 \times 8 = $ _____

10. $4 \times 8 = $ _____   **11.** $5 \times 8 = $ _____   **12.** $0 \times 8 = $ _____   **13.** $8 \times 8 = $ _____

14.   6   **15.**   8   **16.**   5   **17.**   3   **18.**   10   **19.**   7
    $\times 8$ $\times 2$ $\times 8$ $\times 8$ $\times 8$ $\times 8$

20.  Jamal buys 4 sets of animal postcards and 5 sets of nature postcards. Each set has 6 cards. How many postcards does Jamal buy?

_____

Name _____

Use the table for 21–24.

21. About how much rain falls in the Chihuahuan Desert in 6 years? **Explain** how you can use doubles to find the answer.

_____

_____

Average Yearly Rainfall in North American Deserts	
Desert	Inches
Chihuahuan	8
Great Basin	9
Mojave	4
Sonoran	9

22. _GO DEEPER_   In 2 years, about how many more inches of rain will fall in the Sonoran Desert than in the Chihuahuan Desert? **Explain**.

_____

_____

23. _MATHEMATICAL PRACTICE 6_ **Describe a Method** Look back at Exercise 22. Write and show how to solve a similar problem by comparing two different deserts.

_____

_____

24. _THINK SMARTER_   How can you find about how many inches of rain will fall in the Mojave Desert in 20 years?

_____

_____

25. _THINK SMARTER_   For numbers 25a–25d, select True or False for each multiplication sentence.

25a. $3 \times (2 \times 4) = 24$ ○ True   ○ False

25b. $4 \times 8 = 32$ ○ True   ○ False

25c. $7 \times 8 = 72$ ○ True   ○ False

25d. $2 \times (5 \times 8) = 80$ ○ True   ○ False

There are 90 species of scorpions that live in the United States. Only 3 species of scorpions live in Arizona. They are the Arizona bark scorpion, the Desert hairy scorpion, and the Stripe-tailed scorpion.

Facts About Scorpions

Scorpions:

- are between 1 and 4 inches long
- mostly eat insects
- glow under ultraviolet light

They have:

- 8 legs for walking
- 2 long, claw-like pincers used to hold their food
- a curled tail held over their body with a stinger on the tip

▲ Scorpions glow under ultraviolet light.

26. How many species of scorpions do *not* live in Arizona?

_____

27. Students saw 8 scorpions. What multiplication sentences can help you find how many pincers and legs the 8 scorpions had?

_____

28. **GO DEEPER** Three scorpions were in a display with ultraviolet light. Eight groups of 4 students saw the display. How many students saw the glowing scorpions?

_____

© Houghton Mifflin Harcourt Publishing Company • Image Credits: (cr) ©Raul Gonzalez Perez/Photo Researchers, Inc.

Multiply with 8

Common
Core

COMMON CORE STANDARD—3.OA.C.7
Multiply and divide within 100.

Find the product.

1. $8 \times 10 =$ __80__

2. $8 \times 8 =$ ____

3. $8 \times 5 =$ ____

4. $3 \times 8 =$ ____

5. ____ $= 4 \times 8$

6. $8 \times 7 =$ ____

7. $6 \times 8 =$ ____

8. ____ $= 9 \times 8$

9. $\begin{array}{r} 8 \\ \times\ 8 \\ \hline \end{array}$

10. $\begin{array}{r} 9 \\ \times\ 8 \\ \hline \end{array}$

11. $\begin{array}{r} 8 \\ \times\ 3 \\ \hline \end{array}$

12. $\begin{array}{r} 8 \\ \times\ 1 \\ \hline \end{array}$

13. $\begin{array}{r} 4 \\ \times\ 8 \\ \hline \end{array}$

Problem Solving Real World

14. There are 6 teams in the basketball league. Each team has 8 players. How many players are there?

_____

15. Lynn has 4 stacks of quarters. There are 8 quarters in each stack. How many quarters does Lynn have?

_____

16. Tomas is packing 7 baskets for a fair. He is placing 8 apples in each basket. How many apples are there in the baskets?

_____

17. There are 10 pencils in each box. If Jenna buys 8 boxes, how many pencils will she buy?

_____

18. **WRITE** ▸*Math* What two facts can you double to find 8×4? Explain.

_____

_____

Lesson Check (3.OA.C.7)

1. Find the product.

$$5 \times 8 =$$

_____

2. There are 7 tarantulas in the spider exhibit at the zoo. Each tarantula has 8 legs. How many legs do the 7 tarantulas have?

_____

Spiral Review (3.OA.A.3, 3.NBT.A.1, 3.NBT.A.2, 3.MD.B.3)

3. Find the difference.

$$
\begin{array}{r}
652 \\
-99 \\
\hline
\end{array}
$$

4. The school library received an order of 232 new books. What is 232 rounded to the nearest ten?

_____

5. Sam's picture graph shows that 8 students chose pizza as their favorite lunch. This is the key for the graph.

Each ☺ = 2 students.

How many ☺ should be next to pizza on Sam's graph?

_____

6. Tashia buys 5 packages of oranges. Each package has 4 oranges. How many oranges does Tashia buy?

_____

FOR MORE PRACTICE GO TO THE Personal Math Trainer

Name _____

Multiply with 9

Essential Question What strategies can you use to multiply with 9?

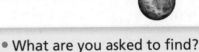

Operations and Algebraic Thinking—
3.OA.C.7 *Also 3.OA.A.1, 3.OA.A.3,
3.OA.A.4, 3.OA.B.5, 3.OA.D.9*

MATHEMATICAL PRACTICES
MP2, MP5, MP6

Unlock the Problem

Olivia's class is studying the solar system. Seven students are making models of the solar system. Each model has 9 spheres (eight for the planets and one for Pluto, a dwarf planet). How many spheres do the 7 students need for all the models?

Find 7 × 9.

• **What are you asked to find?**

_____

_____

• **How many students are making**

models? _____

One Way Use the Distributive Property.

A **With multiplication and addition**

$$7 \times 9 = \blacksquare$$

Think: 9 = 3 + 6   7 × 9 = 7 × (3 + 6)

Multiply each addend by 7.   7 × 9 = (7 × 3) + (7 × 6)

Add the products.   7 × 9 = _____ + _____

7 × 9 = _____

B **With multiplication and subtraction**

$$7 \times 9 = \blacksquare$$

Think: 9 = 10 − 1   7 × 9 = 7 × (10 − 1)

Multiply each number by 7.   7 × 9 = (7 × 10) − (7 × 1)

Subtract the products.   7 × 9 = _____ − _____

7 × 9 = _____

So, 7 students need _____ spheres for all the models.

🔓 Another Way Use patterns of 9.

The table shows the 9s facts.

Multiply by 9.	
Factors	**Product**
1 × 9	9
2 × 9	18
3 × 9	27
4 × 9	36
5 × 9	45
6 × 9	54
7 × 9	
8 × 9	
9 × 9	

- What do you notice about the tens digit in the product?

  The tens digit is _____ less than the factor that is multiplied with 9.

- What do you notice about the sum of the digits in the product?

  The sum of the digits in the product is always _____.

  So, to multiply 7 × 9, think the tens digit is _____

  and the ones digit is _____. The product is _____.

Try This! Complete the table above.

Use the patterns to find 8 × 9 and 9 × 9.

Share and Show MATH BOARD

Math Talk MATHEMATICAL PRACTICES ⑤

Use Patterns Explain how you can easily find the product of 3 × 9.

1. What is the tens digit in the product

   3 × 9? _____

   Think: What number is 1 less than 3?

Find the product.

2. 9 × 8 = _____   3. _____ = 2 × 9   ✅ 4. _____ = 6 × 9   ✅ 5. 9 × 1 = _____

On Your Own

Find the product.

6. 4 × 9 = _____   7. 5 × 9 = _____   8. 10 × 9 = _____   9. 1 × 9 = _____

10. 9   11. 9   12. 6   13. 7   14. 4
    × 5   × 3   × 9   × 9   × 9

© Houghton Mifflin Harcourt Publishing Company

Name _____

15. 2×9 ◯ 3×6 **16.** 5×9 ◯ 6×7 **17.** 1×9 ◯ 3×3

18. 9×4 ◯ 7×5 **19.** 9×0 ◯ 2×3 **20.** 5×8 ◯ 3×9

Problem Solving • Applications

Use the table for 21–24.

21. The number of moons for one of the planets can be found by multiplying 7×9. Which planet is it?

_____

22. GO DEEPER   This planet has 9 times the number of moons that Mars and Earth have together. Which planet is it? **Explain** your answer.

_____

_____

_____

Moons	
Planet	Number of Moons
Earth	1
Mars	2
Jupiter	63
Saturn	47
Uranus	27
Neptune	13

23. THINK SMARTER   Uranus has 27 moons. What multiplication fact with 9 can be used to find the number of moons Uranus has? Describe how you can find the fact.

_____

_____

_____

24. MATHEMATICAL PRACTICE ② **Use Reasoning** Nine students made models of Mars and its moons. The answer is 18. What's the question?

_____

Unlock the Problem

25. The school library has 97 books about space. John and 3 of his friends each check out 9 books. How many space books are still in the school library?

a. What do you need to find? _____

_____

b. Describe one way you can find the answer. _____

_____

c. Show the steps you used to solve the problem.

d. Complete the sentences.

The library has _____ space books.

Multiply _____ × _____ to find how many books John and his 3 friends check out in all.

After you find the number of books

they check out, _____

to find the number of books still in the library.

So, there are _____ space books still in the library.

26. **THINK SMARTER** Circle the symbol that makes the multiplication sentence true.

$$9 \times 7 \quad \boxed{\begin{array}{c} > \\ < \\ = \end{array}} \quad 3 \times (3 \times 7)$$

Name _____

Multiply with 9

Common Core   **COMMON CORE STANDARD—3.OA.C.7**
Multiply and divide within 100.

Find the product.

1. $10 \times 9 =$ __90__

2. $2 \times 9 =$ _____

3. $9 \times 4 =$ _____

4. $0 \times 9 =$ _____

5. $1 \times 9 =$ _____

6. $8 \times 9 =$ _____

7. $9 \times 5 =$ _____

8. $6 \times 9 =$ _____

9. $\begin{array}{r} 10 \\ \times\ 9 \\ \hline \end{array}$

10. $\begin{array}{r} 3 \\ \times\ 9 \\ \hline \end{array}$

11. $\begin{array}{r} 9 \\ \times\ 8 \\ \hline \end{array}$

12. $\begin{array}{r} 6 \\ \times\ 9 \\ \hline \end{array}$

13. $\begin{array}{r} 9 \\ \times\ 1 \\ \hline \end{array}$

 Problem Solving Real World

14. There are 9 positions on the softball team. Three people are trying out for each position. How many people are trying out?

_____

15. Carlos bought a book for $9. Now he would like to buy 4 other books for the same price. How much will he have to pay for the other 4 books?

_____

16. **WRITE** ▸*Math* Explain how you know whether to add or subtract when you use the Distributive Property to multiply.

_____

_____

Lesson Check (3.OA.C.7)

1. Find the product.

$$7 \times 9 =$$

2. Clare buys 5 tickets for the high school musical. Each ticket costs $9. How much do the tickets cost?

_____

_____

Spiral Review (3.OA.A.3, 3.OA.C.7, 3.MD.B.3)

3. The table shows the hair color of girls in Kim's class. How many girls have brown hair?

Kim's Class	
Hair Color	**Number of Girls**
Brown	卅 l
Black	lll
Blonde	llll
Red	l

4. Miles picked up 9 shirts from the dry cleaners. It costs $4 to clean each shirt. How much did Miles spend to have all the shirts cleaned?

_____

_____

5. In a picture graph, each picture of a baseball is equal to 5 games won by a team. The row for the Falcons has 7 baseballs. How many games have the Falcons won?

6. An array has 8 rows with 4 circles in each row. How many circles are in the array?

_____

_____

FOR MORE PRACTICE
GO TO THE
Personal Math Trainer

Name _____

Problem Solving • Multiplication

Essential Question How can you use the strategy *make a table* to solve multiplication problems?

Operations and Algebraic Thinking—3.OA.D.8, 3.OA.D.9
Also 3.OA.A.3, 3.OA.C.7

MATHEMATICAL PRACTICES
MP2, MP4, MP7

Unlock the Problem

Scott has a stamp album. Some pages have 1 stamp on them, and other pages have 2 stamps on them. If Scott has 18 stamps, show how many different ways he could put them in the album. Use the graphic organizer below to solve the problem.

Read the Problem	Solve the Problem
What do I need to find? _____ _____ _____	Make a table to show the number of pages with 1 stamp and with 2 stamps. Each row must equal _____, the total number of stamps.

What information do I need to use?

Scott has _____ stamps. Some of the

pages have _____ stamp on them, and

the other pages have _____ stamps.

Pages with 2 Stamps	Pages with 1 Stamp	Total Stamps
8	2	18
7	4	18
6	6	18
5		18
	10	18
3	12	
2		

How will I use the information?

I will make a _____ showing all the different ways of arranging the stamps in the album.

So, there are _____ different ways.

1. What number patterns do you see in the table?

_____

_____

🔓 Try Another Problem

What if Scott bought 3 more stamps and now has 21 stamps? Some album pages have 1 stamp and some pages have 2 stamps. Show how many different ways he could put the odd number of stamps in the album.

Read the Problem	Solve the Problem
What do I need to find?	_____
	_____
What information do I need to use?	_____
	_____
	_____
	_____
	_____
	_____
How will I use the information?	_____
	_____
	_____
	So, there are _____ different ways.

2. What patterns do you see in this table? _____

_____

3. How are these patterns different from the patterns in

the table on page 247? _____

_____

_____

Name _____

1. Aaron's mother is making lemonade. For each pitcher, she uses 1 cup of lemon juice, 1 cup of sugar, and 6 cups of water. What is the total number of cups of ingredients she will use to make 5 pitchers of lemonade?

First, make a table to show the number of cups of lemon juice, sugar, and water that are in 1 pitcher of lemonade.

Next, multiply to find the number of cups of water needed for each pitcher of lemonade.

Last, use the table to solve the problem.

Think: For every pitcher, the number of cups of water increases by 6.

Number of Pitchers	1	2	3		5
Cups of Lemon Juice	1		3		
Cups of Sugar	1	2			
Cups of Water	6	12		24	
Total Number of Cups of Ingredients	8				

So, in 5 pitchers of lemonade, there are _____ cups of

lemon juice, _____ cups of sugar, and _____ cups of water.

This makes a total of _____ cups of ingredients.

2. What if it takes 4 lemons to make 1 cup of lemon juice? How many lemons would it take to make 5 pitchers? Explain how you can use the table to help you find the answer.

_____

_____

3. What pattern do you see in the total number of cups of ingredients?

_____

_____

On Your Own

4. Julie saw 3 eagles each day she went bird-watching. How many eagles did Julie see in 6 days?

_____

5. (MATHEMATICAL PRACTICE ②) **Use Reasoning** Greg has a dollar bill, quarters, and dimes. How many ways can he make $1.75?

Name the ways. _____

_____

_____

6. [THINK SMARTER] Cammi needs 36 postcards. She buys 4 packages of 10 postcards. How many postcards will Cammi have left over? Explain.

_____

_____

_____

7. [GO DEEPER] Phillip has 8 books on each of 3 bookshelves. His aunt gives him 3 new books. How many books does Phillip have now?

_____

Personal Math Trainer

8. [THINK SMARTER +] Stuart has some 2-ounce, 3-ounce, and 4-ounce weights. How many different ways can Stuart combine the weights to make a total of 12 ounces? List the ways.

_____

_____

_____

Problem Solving • Multiplication

Solve.

1. Henry has a new album for his baseball cards. He uses pages that hold 6 cards and pages that hold 3 cards. If Henry has 36 cards, how many different ways can he put them in his album?

Pages with 6 Cards	1	2	3	4	5
Pages with 3 Cards	10	8	6	4	2
Total Cards	36	36	36	36	36

Henry can put the cards in his album ___5___ ways.

---

2. Ms. Hernandez has 17 tomato plants that she wants to plant in rows. She will put 2 plants in some rows and 1 plant in the others. How many different ways can she plant the tomato plants? Make a table to solve.

Rows with 2 Plants	
Rows with 1 Plant	
Total Plants	

Ms. Hernandez can plant the tomato plants _____ ways.

---

3. **WRITE** ▶*Math* Write a problem you can use the *make a table* strategy to solve. Then solve the problem.

_____

_____

Lesson Check (3.OA.D.8)

1. The table shows different ways that Cameron can display his 12 model cars on shelves. How many shelves will display 2 cars if 8 of the shelves each display 1 car?

Shelves with 1 Car	2	4	6	8	10
Shelves with 2 Cars	5	4	3	■	■
Total cars	12	12	12	12	12

_____

Spiral Review (3.OA.A.3, 3.NBT.A.1, 3.NBT.A.2, 3.MD.B.3)

2. Find the sum.

$$\begin{array}{r} 317 \\ + \ 151 \\ \hline \end{array}$$

3. The school cafeteria has an order for 238 hot lunches. What is 238 rounded to the nearest ten?

_____

4. Tyler made a picture graph to show students' favorite colors. This is the key for his graph.

Each ⬤ = 3 votes.

If 12 students voted for green, how many ⬤ should there be in the green row of the graph?

5. There are 5 bikes in each bike rack at the school. There are 6 bike racks. How many bikes are in the bike racks?

© Houghton Mifflin Harcourt Publishing Company

FOR MORE PRACTICE
GO TO THE
Personal Math Trainer

✓ Chapter 4 Review/Test

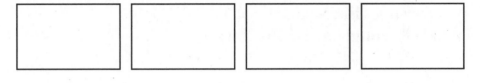

Personal Math Trainer
Online Assessment and Intervention

1. Mrs. Ruiz sorted spools of thread into 4 boxes. Each box holds 5 spools. How many spools of thread does Mrs. Ruiz have?

Draw circles to model the problem. Then solve.

[ ] [ ] [ ] [ ]

_____

_____

2. For numbers 2a–2d, select True or False for each multiplication sentence.

2a. $2 \times 8 = 16$ ○ True   ○ False

2b. $5 \times 8 = 40$ ○ True   ○ False

2c. $6 \times 8 = 56$ ○ True   ○ False

2d. $8 \times 8 = 64$ ○ True   ○ False

3. Bella is planning to write in a journal. Some pages will have one journal entry on them, and other pages will have two journal entries on them. If Bella wants to make 10 entries, how many different ways can she write them in her journal?

[   ]

4. There are 7 days in 1 week. How many days are there in 4 weeks?

_____ days

5. Circle groups to show $3 \times (2 \times 3)$.

6. Dale keeps all of his pairs of shoes in his closet. Select the number of shoes that Dale could have in his closet. Mark all that apply.

(A) 3

(B) 4

(C) 6

(D) 7

(E) 8

7. **GO DEEPER** Lisa completed the table to describe the product of a mystery one-digit factor and each number.

×	1	2	3	4	5
?	even	even	even	even	even

Part A

Give all of the possible numbers that could be Lisa's mystery one-digit factor.

_____

Part B

Explain how you know that you have selected all of the correct possibilities.

_____

_____

_____

Name _____

8. Kate drew 7 octagons. An octagon has 8 sides.
How many sides did Kate draw?

_____ sides

9. José buys 6 bags of flour. Each bag weighs 5 pounds.
How many pounds of flour did José buy?

_____ pounds

10. Break apart the array to show $8 \times 6 = (4 \times 6) + (4 \times 6)$.

11. Circle the symbol that makes the multiplication sentence
true.

$$9 \times 6 \quad \boxed{\begin{array}{c} > \\ < \\ = \end{array}} \quad 3 \times (3 \times 9)$$

12. Roberto wants to display his 18 sports cards in an album.
Some pages hold 2 cards and others hold 3 cards . How
many different ways can Roberto display his figures?

_____ different ways

13. A carpenter builds stools that have 3 legs each. How many legs does the carpenter use to build 5 stools? Use the array to explain how you know your answer is correct.

_____

_____

14. Etta buys some ribbon and cuts it into 7 pieces that are the same length. Each piece is 9 inches long. How long was the ribbon that Etta bought?

_____ inches

15. Antoine and 3 friends divide some pennies evenly among themselves. Each friend separates his pennies into 3 equal stacks with 5 pennies in each stack.

Write a multiplication sentence that shows the total number of pennies.

_____

16. Luke is making 4 first-aid kits. He wants to put 3 large and 4 small bandages in each kit. How many bandages does he need for the kits? Show your work.

_____ bandages

Name _____

17. For numbers 17a–17d, select True or False for each equation.

17a. $3 \times 7 = 21$ ○ True   ○ False

17b. $5 \times 7 = 28$ ○ True   ○ False

17c. $8 \times 7 = 49$ ○ True   ○ False

17d. $9 \times 7 = 63$ ○ True   ○ False

18. Circle the number that makes the multiplication sentence true.

$$10 \times \boxed{\begin{array}{c} 4 \\ 5 \\ 8 \end{array}} = 40$$

19. For numbers 19a–19d, select Yes or No to indicate whether the sum or product is equal to 8×6.

19a. $8 + (4 \times 2) = \blacksquare$ ○ Yes   ○ No

19b. $(8 \times 4) + (8 \times 2) = \blacksquare$ ○ Yes   ○ No

19c. $(6 \times 4) + (6 \times 2) = \blacksquare$ ○ Yes   ○ No

19d. $6 \times (4 + 4) = \blacksquare$ ○ Yes   ○ No

20. Chloe bought 4 movie tickets. Each ticket cost $6. What was the total cost of the movie tickets?

$ _____

21. Write a multiplication sentence using the following numbers and symbols.

| 6 | 60 | 5 | 2 | ( ) | = |

_____

22. [THINK SMARTER +] Louis started a table showing a multiplication pattern.

Part A

Complete the table. Describe a pattern you see in the products.

×	1	2	3	4	5	6	7	8	9	10
3	3	6	9							

_____

_____

Part B

If you multiplied 3 × 37, would the product be an even number or an odd number? Use the table to explain your reasoning.

_____

_____

_____

_____

_____

23. Use the number line to show the product of 4 × 8.

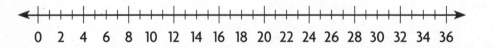

0 2 4 6 8 10 12 14 16 18 20 22 24 26 28 30 32 34 36

4 × 8 = _____

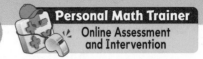

✓ Show What You Know

Check your understanding of important skills.

Name _____

▶ **Add Tens** Write how many tens. Then add. (1.NBT.C.4)

1. 30 + 30 = ■

_____ tens + _____ tens =

_____ tens

30 + 30 = _____

2. 40 + 50 = ■

_____ tens + _____ tens =

_____ tens

40 + 50 = _____

▶ **Regroup Tens as Hundreds** Write the missing numbers. (2.NBT.A.1a)

3. 35 tens = _____ hundreds _____ tens

4. 52 tens = _____ hundreds _____ tens

5. 97 tens = _____ hundreds _____ tens

▶ **Multiplication Facts Through 9** Find the product. (3.OA.C.7)

6. 3 × 9 = _____   **7.** 4 × 5 = _____   **8.** 7 × 6 = _____   **9.** 8 × 2 = _____

The butterfly exhibit at the museum will display 60 different butterfly species arranged in an array. Each row has 6 butterflies. How many rows are in the butterfly exhibit?

The butterfly exhibit will open soon.

Vocabulary Builder

▶ **Visualize It** ●●●●●●●●●●●●●●●●●●●●●●●●●●●●●

Complete the tree map by using the words with a ✓.

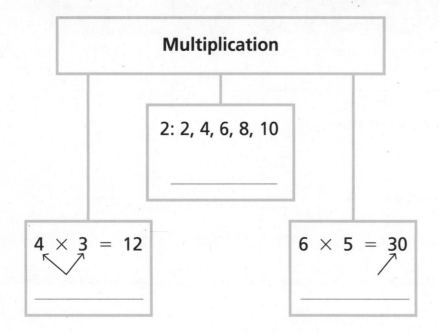

Multiplication

2: 2, 4, 6, 8, 10

_____

4 × 3 = 12

_____

6 × 5 = 30

_____

▶ **Understand Vocabulary** ●●●●●●●●●●●●●●●●●●●●

**Read the definition. Write the preview word
or review word that matches it.**

1. An ordered set of numbers or objects
   in which the order helps you predict
   what will come next.   _____

2. A set of objects arranged in rows
   and columns.   _____

3. A number sentence that uses the equal
   sign to show that two amounts are equal.   _____

4. The property that states that multiplying
   a sum by a number is the same as
   multiplying each addend by the number
   and then adding the products.   _____

5. The value of each digit in a number, based
   on the location of the digit.   _____

GO DIGITAL
• **Interactive Student Edition**
• **Multimedia eGlossary**

Chapter 5 Vocabulary

array

matriz

4

Commutative Property of Multiplication

Propiedad conmutativa de la multiplicación

9

Distributive Property

Propiedad distributiva

13

equation

ecuación

22

factor

factor

25

Pattern

patrón

57

place value

valor posicional

62

product

producto

65

The property that states that you can multiply two factors in any order and get the same product

Example: 4 × 3 = 3 × 4

A set of objects arranged in rows and columns

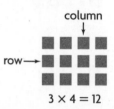

3 × 4 = 12

A number sentence that uses the equal sign to show that two amounts are equal

Example: 9 × 2 = 18 is an equation

The property that states that multiplying a sum by a number is the same as multiplying each addend by the number and then adding the products

Example: 5 × 8 = 5 × (4 + 4)
5 × 8 = (5 × 4) + (5 × 4)
5 × 8 = 20 + 20
5 × 8 = 40

An ordered set of numbers or objects in which the order helps you predict what will come next

Examples: 2, 4, 6, 8, 10, 2, 4, 6, 8, 10

A number that is multiplied by another number to find a product

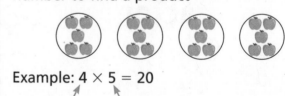

Example: 4 × 5 = 20

factor   factor

The answer in a multiplication problem

Example: 4 × 5 = 20

product

The value of each digit in a number, based on the location of the digit

MILLIONS			THOUSANDS			ONES		
Hundreds	Tens	Ones	Hundreds	Tens	Ones	Hundreds	Tens	Ones
		1,	3	9	2,	0	0	0
		1 × 1,000,000	3 × 100,000	9 × 10,000	2 × 1,000	0 × 100	0 × 10	0 × 1
		1,000,000	300,000	90,000	2,000	0	0	0

Pick It

For 3 players

Materials

- 4 sets of word cards

How to Play

1. Each player is dealt 5 cards. The remaining cards are a draw pile.

2. To take a turn, ask any player if he or she has a word that matches one of your word cards.

3. If the player has the word, he or she gives the word card to you.

   - If you are correct, keep the card and put the matching pair in front of you. Take another turn.

   - If you are wrong, return the card. Your turn is over.

4. If the player does not have the word, he or she answers, "Pick it." Then you take a card from the draw pile.

5. If the card you draw matches one of your word cards, follow the directions for Step 3 above. If it does not, your turn is over.

6. The game is over when one player has no cards left. The player with the most pairs wins.

Word Box
array
Commutative Property of Multiplication
Distributive Property
equation
factors
pattern
place value
product

The Write Way

Reflect

Choose one idea. Write about it.

- Work with a partner to explain and illustrate two ways to multiply with multiples of 10. Use a separate piece of paper for your drawing.

- Write a paragraph that uses at least three of these words.

  equation   factors   pattern   place value   product

- Think about what you learned in class today. Complete one of these sentences.

  I learned that I _____.

  I was surprised that I _____.

  I noticed that I _____.

  I discovered that I _____.

  I was pleased that I _____.

_____

_____

_____

_____

_____

_____

_____

Describe Patterns

Essential Question What are some ways you can describe a pattern in a table?

 Common Core **Operations and Algebraic Thinking—**
3.OA.D.9 *Also 3.OA.A.3, 3.OA.C.7*
MATHEMATICAL PRACTICES
MP1, MP4, MP7

Unlock the Problem

The outdoor club is planning a camping trip. Each camper will need a flashlight. One flashlight uses 4 batteries. How many batteries are needed for 8 flashlights?

You can describe a pattern in a table.

Flashlights	1	2	3	4	5	6	7	8
Batteries	4	8	12	16	20	24	28	

Think: Count by 1s.

Think: Count by 4s.

🔑 One Way Describe a pattern across the rows.

STEP 1 Look for a pattern to complete the table. As you look across the rows, you can see that the number of batteries increases by 4 for each flashlight.

So, for every flashlight add _____ batteries.

STEP 2 Use the pattern to find the number of batteries in 8 flashlights.

Add _____ to 28 batteries. $28 + 4 =$ _____

So, _____ batteries are needed for 8 flashlights.

🔑 Another Way Describe a pattern in the columns.

STEP 1 Look for a pattern by comparing the columns in the table. You can multiply the number of flashlights by 4 to find the number of batteries that are needed.

STEP 2 Use the pattern to find how many batteries are needed for 8 flashlights.

$8 \times 4 =$ _____

> **! ERROR Alert**
> Check that your pattern will work for all the numbers in the table.

 Math Talk

MATHEMATICAL PRACTICES 7

Look for a Pattern
Do you notice any other patterns in the Flashlights/Batteries table?

Try This! Describe a pattern. Then complete the table.

The campers need 5 packs of batteries. If there are 8 batteries in each pack, how many batteries will be in 5 packs?

Packs of Batteries	Number of Batteries
1	8
2	16
3	
4	32
5	

Use addition.

Describe a pattern.

Add _____ batteries for each pack.

Use multiplication.

Describe a pattern.

Multiply the number of packs of batteries

by _____ .

So, there will be _____ batteries in 5 packs.

Share and Show

1. How can you describe a pattern to find the cost of 4 packs of batteries?

_____

_____

Packs of Batteries	1	2	3	4
Cost	$3	$6	$9	

Describe a pattern in the table. Then complete the table.

2.

Tents	Lanterns
2	4
3	6
4	8
5	10
6	
7	

3.

Adults	1	2	3	4	5
Campers	6	12	18		

_____

Math Talk

MATHEMATICAL PRACTICES ①

Describe how you use your description for a pattern to complete a table.

Name _____

Describe a pattern in the table. Then complete the table.

4.

Hours	1	2	3	4	5
Miles Hiked	2	4	6		

_____

5.

Cabins	3	4	5	6	7
Campers	27	36	45		

_____

6.

Cabins	Beds
1	5
2	10
3	
4	20
5	
6	

7.

Adults	Students
2	12
3	18
4	
5	30
6	
7	

8. **THINK SMARTER** Students made a craft project at camp. They used 2 small pine cone patterns and 1 large pine cone pattern. Complete the table to find how many patterns were used for the different numbers of projects.

Projects	1	2	3						
Small Pattern	2								
Large Pattern	1								

9. **GO DEEPER** Isaac uses 4 red beads and 3 blue beads to make a belt. How many beads will Isaac use to make 4 belts?

_____

10. **GO DEEPER** Corey uses 5 yellow tiles and 4 green tiles to make a design. How many tiles will he need to repeat the design 5 times?

_____

Problem Solving • Applications

MATHEMATICAL PRACTICE ④ Use Graphs Use the picture graph for 11–13.

Cost of Fishing Supplies

Corks	🐟🐟
Poles	🐟🐟🐟🐟🐟
Worms	🐟🐟🐟🐟

Key: Each 🐟 = $2.

11. Jena bought 3 fishing poles. How much money did she spend?

_____

12. **GO DEEPER** Noah bought 1 fishing pole, 2 corks, and 1 carton of worms. What was the total cost?

_____

13. **WRITE ▸ Math** Ryan bought 8 corks. Explain how you can use the Commutative Property to find the cost.

_____

_____

14. **GO DEEPER** The cost to rent a raft is $7 per person. A raft can hold up to 6 people. There is a $3 launch fee per raft. What is the total cost for a group of 6? Explain.

_____

15. A group of students and adults are going on a field trip in vans. In each van, there will be 8 students and 2 adults. How many people will be in 4 vans?

_____

Personal Math Trainer

16. **THINK SMARTER +** Complete the table. Amir said a rule for the pattern shown in this table is "Multiply by 4." Is he correct? Explain how you know your answer is reasonable.

Cans	2	3	4		6
Peaches	8	12		20	

_____

_____

Describe Patterns

Common Core COMMON CORE STANDARD—3.OA.D.9
Solve problems involving the four operations, and identify and explain patterns in arithmetic.

Describe a pattern for the table. Then complete the table.

1.

Pans	1	2	3	4	5
Muffins	6	12	18	24	30

Add 6 muffins for each pan;

Multiply the number of pans by 6.

_____

2.

Wagons	2	3	4	5	6
Wheels	8	12	16		

_____

_____

_____

3.

Vases	2	3	4	5	6
Flowers	14		28		42

_____

_____

4.

Spiders	1	2	3	4	5
Legs	8		24		40

_____

_____

Problem Solving *Real World*

5. Caleb buys 5 cartons of yogurt. Each carton has 8 yogurt cups. How many yogurt cups does Caleb buy?

_____

6. Libby bought 4 packages of pencils. Each package has 6 pencils. How many pencils did Libby buy?

_____

7. **WRITE** ▸ *Math* How does finding a pattern help you complete a table?

_____

_____

Lesson Check (3.OA.D.9)

1. Describe a pattern in the table.

Tables	1	2	3	4	5
Chairs	5	10	15	20	25

_____

2. What number completes this table?

Butterflies	3	4	5	6	7
Wings	12	16	20	■	28

_____

Spiral Review (3.OA.A.3, 3.OA.C.7)

3. Jennilee buys 7 packs of crayons. There are 6 crayons in each pack. How many crayons does Jennilee buy?

_____

4. Maverick has 5 books of circus tickets. Each book has 5 tickets. How many tickets does Maverick have?

_____

5. Bailey walked his dog 2 times each day for 9 days. How many times did Bailey walk his dog?

_____

6. Drew's Tree Company delivers pear trees in groups of 4. Yesterday, the company delivered 8 groups of pear trees. How many pear trees were delivered?

_____

FOR MORE PRACTICE
GO TO THE
Personal Math Trainer

Name _____

Find Unknown Numbers

Essential Question How can you use an array or a multiplication table to find an unknown factor or product?

 Common Core **Operations and Algebraic Thinking—3.OA.A.4** Also 3.OA.A.1, 3.OA.A.3, 3.OA.C.7
MATHEMATICAL PRACTICES
MP1, MP4, MP7

Unlock the Problem

Tanisha plans to invite 24 people to a picnic. The invitations come in packs of 8. How many packs of invitations does Tanisha need to buy?

An **equation** is a number sentence that uses the equal sign to show that two amounts are equal.

A symbol or letter can stand for an unknown number. You can write the equation, $n \times 8 = 24$, to find how many packs of invitations Tanisha needs. Find the number, n, that makes the equation true.

- How many people is Tanisha inviting? _____
- How many invitations are in 1 pack? _____

Use an array.

- Show an array of 24 tiles with 8 tiles in each row by completing the drawing.

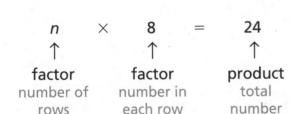

n	$\times$	8	$=$	24
↑		↑		↑
factor		factor		product
number of rows		number in each row		total number

Math Talk **MATHEMATICAL PRACTICES ⑥**

Explain how the array represents the problem. How do the factors relate to the array?

- Count how many rows of 8 tiles there are.   **Think:** What number times 8 equals 24?

There are _____ rows of 8 tiles. The unknown factor is _____. $n =$ _____

_____ $\times 8 = 24$ Check.

_____ $= 24$ ✓ The equation is true.

So, Tanisha needs _____ packs of invitations.

🔑 **Use a multiplication table.**

$$3 \times 8 = \blacksquare$$

Think: The symbol, ▨, stands for the unknown product.

Find the product 3×8 where row 3 and column 8 meet.

The unknown product is _____.

$$\blacksquare = \underline{\hspace{1cm}}$$

$$3 \times 8 = \underline{\hspace{1cm}} \quad \text{Check.}$$

$$24 = \underline{\hspace{1cm}} \checkmark \text{ The equation is true.}$$

×	0	1	2	3	4	5	6	7	8	9	10
0	0	0	0	0	0	0	0	0	0	0	0
1	0	1	2	3	4	5	6	7	8	9	10
2	0	2	4	6	8	10	12	14	16	18	20
3	0	3	6	9	12	15	18	21	24	27	30
4	0	4	8	12	16	20	24	28	32	36	40
5	0	5	10	15	20	25	30	35	40	45	50
6	0	6	12	18	24	30	36	42	48	54	60
7	0	7	14	21	28	35	42	49	56	63	70
8	0	8	16	24	32	40	48	56	64	72	80
9	0	9	18	27	36	45	54	63	72	81	90
10	0	10	20	30	40	50	60	70	80	90	100

Share and Show

1. What is the unknown factor shown by this array?

$$5 \times \blacksquare = 35$$

$$\blacksquare = \underline{\hspace{1cm}}$$

Find the unknown number.

2. $d \times 3 = 27$

$d = \underline{\hspace{1cm}}$

3. $6 \times 5 = \blacktriangle$

$\blacktriangle = \underline{\hspace{1cm}}$

✅ 4. $c = 5 \times 4$

$c = \underline{\hspace{1cm}}$

✅ 5. $\blacksquare \times 2 = 14$

$\blacksquare = \underline{\hspace{1cm}}$

6. $b = 4 \times 9$

$b = \underline{\hspace{1cm}}$

7. $8 \times e = 64$

$e = \underline{\hspace{1cm}}$

8. $7 \times \bigstar = 42$

$\bigstar = \underline{\hspace{1cm}}$

9. $8 \times 9 = z$

$z = \underline{\hspace{1cm}}$

Math Talk

MATHEMATICAL PRACTICES ②

Use Reasoning How do you know if you are looking for the number of rows or the number in each row when you make an array to find an unknown factor?

On Your Own

Find the unknown number.

10. $\blacksquare = 9 \times 2$

$\blacksquare =$ _____

11. $28 = 4 \times m$

$m =$ _____

12. $y \times 3 = 9$

$y =$ _____

13. $7 \times 9 = g$

$g =$ _____

14. $a = 6 \times 4$

$a =$ _____

15. $7 = 7 \times n$

$n =$ _____

16. $w \times 3 = 15$

$w =$ _____

17. $\bigstar = 8 \times 6$

$\bigstar =$ _____

MATHEMATICAL PRACTICE ② Reason Quantitatively Algebra Find the unknown number.

18. $3 \times 6 = k \times 9$

$k =$ _____

19. $4 \times y = 2 \times 6$

$y =$ _____

20. $5 \times g = 36 - 6$

$g =$ _____

21. $6 \times 4 = \blacksquare \times 3$

$\blacksquare =$ _____

22. $9 \times d = 70 + 2$

$d =$ _____

23. $8 \times h = 60 - 4$

$h =$ _____

24. **GO DEEPER** Invitations cost $3 for a pack of 8. Lori gives the cashier $20 to buy invitations and gets $11 in change. How many packs of invitations does Lori buy? Explain.

_____

_____

25. **GO DEEPER** Coz and Amelia each make a tile design with 36 tiles. Coz puts his in rows of 4. Amelia puts hers in rows of 6. How many more tiles are in each of Coz's rows than Amelia's?

_____

Problem Solving • Applications

Use the table for 26–29.

Picnic Supplies		
Item	Number in 1 Pack	Cost
Bowls	6	$10
Cups	8	$3
Tablecloth	1	$2
Napkins	36	$2
Forks	50	$3

26. Tanisha needs 40 cups for the picnic. How many packs of cups should she buy?

_____

27. GO DEEPER   Ms. Hill buys 3 tablecloths and 2 packs of napkins. How much money does she spend?

_____

28. THINK SMARTER   What if Tanisha needs 40 bowls for the picnic? Explain how to write an equation with a letter for an unknown factor to find the number of packs she should buy. Then find the unknown factor.

_____

_____

_____

29. MATHEMATICAL PRACTICE ① **Analyze** What if Randy needs an equal number of bowls and cups for his picnic? How many packs of each will he need to buy?

_____

_____

30. THINK SMARTER   For numbers 30a–30d, choose Yes or No to show whether the unknown factor is 8.

30a. $8 \times \blacksquare = 64$ ○ Yes   ○ No

30b. $\blacksquare \times 3 = 27$ ○ Yes   ○ No

30c. $6 \times \blacksquare = 42$ ○ Yes   ○ No

30d. $\blacksquare \times 7 = 56$ ○ Yes   ○ No

Find Unknown Numbers

Common Core **COMMON CORE STANDARD—3.OA.A.4**
Represent and solve problems involving multiplication and division.

Find the unknown number.

1. $n \times 3 = 12$

Think: How many groups of 3 equal 12?

$n = \underline{\quad 4 \quad}$

2. $s \times 8 = 64$

$s = \underline{\quad\quad}$

3. $21 = 7 \times n$

$n = \underline{\quad\quad}$

4. $y \times 2 = 18$

$y = \underline{\quad\quad}$

5. $5 \times p = 10$

$p = \underline{\quad\quad}$

6. $56 = 8 \times t$

$t = \underline{\quad\quad}$

7. $m \times 4 = 28$

$m = \underline{\quad\quad}$

8. $\star \times 1 = 9$

$\star = \underline{\quad\quad}$

9. $b \times 6 = 54$

$b = \underline{\quad\quad}$

10. $5 \times \blacktriangle = 40$

$\blacktriangle = \underline{\quad\quad}$

11. $30 = d \times 3$

$d = \underline{\quad\quad}$

12. $7 \times k = 42$

$k = \underline{\quad\quad}$

Problem Solving

13. Carmen spent $42 for 6 hats. How much did each hat cost?

_____

14. Mark has a baking tray with 24 muffins. The muffins are arranged in 4 equal rows. How many muffins are in each row?

_____

15. **WRITE** ▸*Math* Explain why it does not matter what letter or symbol is used to find an unknown number.

_____

_____

Lesson Check (3.OA.A.4)

1. What is the unknown number?

$$b \times 7 = 56$$

2. What is the unknown number shown by this array?

$$3 \times \blacksquare = 24$$

_____

Spiral Review (3.OA.A.3, 3.OA.B.5)

3. The number sentence $4 \times 6 = 6 \times 4$ is an example of what property?

_____

_____

_____

4. Find the product.

$$5 \times (4 \times 2)$$

_____

_____

5. The number sentence $4 \times 7 = (4 \times 3) + (4 \times 4)$ is an example of what property?

6. In a group of 10 boys, each boy had 2 hats. How many hats did they have?

_____

_____

FOR MORE PRACTICE
GO TO THE
Personal Math Trainer

Name _____

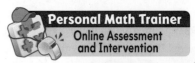

Vocabulary

Vocabulary
array
equation

Choose the best term from the box.

1. An _____ is a number sentence that uses the equal sign to show that two amounts are equal. (p. 267)

Concepts and Skills

Describe a pattern in the table. Then complete the table. (3.OA.D.9)

2.

Weeks	1	2	3	4	5
Days	7	14	21		

_____

3.

Tickets	2	3	4	5	6
Cost	$8	$12	$16		

_____

4.

Project Teams	Members
3	9
4	12
5	
6	18
7	

_____

5.

Tables	Chairs
1	8
2	16
3	
4	32
5	

_____

Find the unknown number. (3.OA.A.4)

6. $m \times 5 = 30$

$m = $ _____

7. $\blacksquare \times 6 = 48$

$\blacksquare = $ _____

8. $n = 2 \times 10$

$n = $ _____

9. $4 \times 8 = p$

$p = $ _____

10. $25 = y \times 5$

$y = $ _____

11. $\blacklozenge \times 10 = 10$

$\blacklozenge = $ _____

12. Describe a pattern in the table. (3.OA.D.9)

Packages	1	2	3	4	5
Stickers	6	12	18	24	30

_____

13. What number makes the equation true? (3.OA.A.4)

$$a \times 8 = 72$$

_____

14. Mia bought 2 copies of the same book. She spent $18. What was the cost of one book? (3.OA.A.4)

_____

15. Kyle saves $10 every week for 6 weeks. How much money will Kyle have in Week 6? (3.OA.D.9)

Weeks	1	2	3	4	5	6
Amount	$10	$20	$30	■	■	■

_____

16. **GO DEEPER** Tennis balls cost $7 for a can of 3. Steve gives the cashier $40 to buy balls and receives $12 in change. How many tennis balls did Steve buy? (3.OA.A.4)

_____

Name _____

Problem Solving •
Use the Distributive Property

Essential Question How can you use the strategy *draw a diagram* to multiply with multiples of 10?

 Number and Operations in Base Ten—3.NBT.A.3 *Also 3.OA.A.3, 3.OA.B.5, 3.OA.C.7*
MATHEMATICAL PRACTICES
MP1, MP2, MP3, MP4

Unlock the Problem

The school assembly room has 5 rows of chairs with 20 chairs in each row. If the third-grade classes fill 3 rows of chairs, how many third graders are at the assembly?

Read the Problem	Solve the Problem
What do I need to find? I need to find how many _____ are at the assembly.	Draw a diagram. Finish the shading to show 3 rows of 20 chairs. 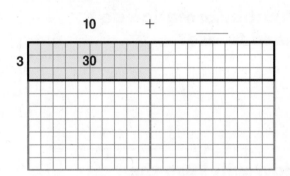 I can use the sum of the products of the smaller rectangles to find how many third graders are at the assembly. $3 \times 10 =$ _____ $3 \times 10 =$ _____ _____ $+$ _____ $=$ _____ $3 \times 20 =$ _____ So, _____ third graders are at the assembly.
What information do I need to use? There are _____ chairs in each row. The third graders fill _____ rows of chairs.	
How will I use the information? The Distributive Property tells me I can _____ the factor 20 to multiply. $3 \times 20 = 3 \times (10 +$ _____$)$	

1. Explain how breaking apart the factor 20 makes finding the

product easier. _____

⬛ Try Another Problem

Megan is watching a marching band practice. The band marches by with 4 rows of people playing instruments. She counts 30 people in each row. How many people march in the band?

Read the Problem	Solve the Problem
What do I need to find?	**Record the steps you used to solve the problem.** 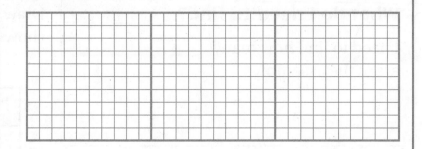
What information do I need to use?	
How will I use the information?	

2. How can you check to see if your answer is reasonable?

_____

_____

3. Explain how you can use the Distributive Property to help you find a product.

_____

_____

Name _____

Unlock the Problem

√ Circle the numbers you will use.

√ Use the Distributive Property and break apart a greater factor to use facts you know.

√ Draw a diagram to help you solve the problem.

1. People filled all the seats in the front section of the theater. The front section has 6 rows with 40 seats in each row. How many people are in the front section of the theater?

First, draw and label a diagram to break apart the problem into easier parts to solve.

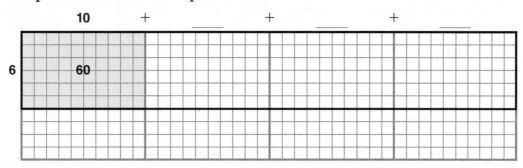

Next, find the products of the smaller rectangles.

6 × 10 = _____   _____ × _____ = _____

_____ × _____ = _____   _____ × _____ = _____

Then, find the sum of the products.

_____ + _____ + _____ + _____ = _____

So, there are _____ people in the front section of the theater.

2. What if seats are added to the front section of the theater so that there are 6 rows with 50 seats in each row? How many seats are in the front section?

_____

On Your Own

3. THINK SMARTER Tova sewed 60 pieces of blue ribbon together to make a costume. Each piece of ribbon was 2 meters long. She also sewed 40 pieces of red ribbon together that were each 3 meters long. Did Tova use more blue ribbon or red ribbon? Explain.

_____

4. MATHEMATICAL PRACTICE ③ **Verify the Reasoning of Others**
Carina draws this diagram to show that $8 \times 30 = 210$.
Explain her error.

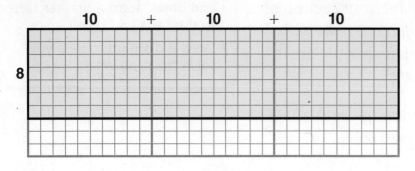

_____

_____

_____

_____

5. WRITE ▸Math Tamika wants to display 10 trophies on a
table in a rectangular array. How many different ways can
Tamika arrange the trophies? Explain your answer.

_____

_____

6. GO DEEPER The drama club has 350 tickets to sell. They sell
124 tickets on Monday and 98 tickets on Tuesday. How
many tickets does the drama club have left to sell?

_____

7. THINK SMARTER Select the equations that show the
Distributive Property. Mark all that apply.

Ⓐ $3 \times 20 = (3 \times 10) + (3 \times 10)$

Ⓑ $(7 + 3) + 8 = 7 + (3 + 8)$

Ⓒ $(5 \times 10) + (5 \times 10) = 5 \times 20$

Ⓓ $(9 \times 2) + (9 \times 4) = 9 \times 6$

Problem Solving • Use the Distributive Property

COMMON CORE STANDARD—3.NBT.A.3
Use place value understanding and properties of operations to perform multi-digit arithmetic.

Read each problem and solve.

1. Each time a student turns in a perfect spelling test, Ms. Ricks puts an achievement square on the bulletin board. There are 6 rows of squares on the bulletin board. Each row has 30 squares. How many perfect spelling tests have been turned in?

   Think: $6 \times 30 = 6 \times (10 + 10 + 10)$

   $= 60 + 60 + 60 = 180$

   ___**180 spelling tests**___

2. Norma practices violin for 50 minutes every day. How many minutes does Norma practice violin in 7 days?

   _____

3. A kitchen designer is creating a new backsplash for the wall behind a kitchen sink. The backsplash will have 5 rows of tiles. Each row will have 20 tiles. How many tiles are needed for the entire backsplash?

   _____

4. A bowling alley keeps shoes in rows of cubbyholes. There are 9 rows of cubbyholes, with 20 cubbyholes in each row. If there is a pair of shoes in every cubbyhole, how many pairs of shoes are there?

   _____

5. **WRITE** ▸*Math* Write a description of how a diagram can help you solve 2×40.

   _____

   _____

Lesson Check (3.NBT.A.3)

1. Each snack pack holds 20 crackers. How many crackers in all are there in 4 snack packs?

2. A machine makes 70 springs each hour. How many springs will the machine make in 8 hours?

Spiral Review (3.OA.A.1, 3.NBT.A.1, 3.MD.B.4)

3. Lila read 142 pages on Friday and 168 pages on Saturday. Estimate how many pages Lila read on Friday and Saturday combined.

4. Jessica wrote 6 + 6 + 6 + 6 on the board. What is another way to show 6 + 6 + 6 + 6?

Use the line plot for 5–6.

5. Eliot made a line plot to record the number of birds he saw at his bird feeder. How many more sparrows than blue jays did he see?

6. How many robins and cardinals combined did Eliot see?

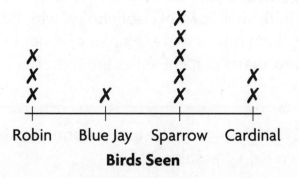

Birds Seen

FOR MORE PRACTICE GO TO THE Personal Math Trainer

Multiplication Strategies with Multiples of 10

Essential Question What strategies can you use to multiply with multiples of 10?

Common Core Number and Operations in Base Ten—**3.NBT.A.3** *Also 3.OA.A.3, 3.OA.B.5, 3.OA.C.7*
MATHEMATICAL PRACTICES
MP1, MP5, MP8

Unlock the Problem

You can use models and place value to multiply with multiples of 10.

- What is a product of 10 and the counting numbers 1, 2, 3, and so on?

  _____

Activity Model multiples of 10.

Materials ■ base-ten blocks

Model the first nine multiples of 10.

 1 × 10
1 × 1 ten
1 ten
10

2 × 10
2 × 1 ten
2 tens
20

 3 × 10
3 × 1 ten
3 tens
30

What are the first nine multiples of 10?

10, 20, 30, _____ , _____ , _____ , _____ , _____ , _____

Best Care Veterinary Clinic offered free pet care classes for 5 days. Erin attended the pet care class for 30 minutes each day. How many minutes did Erin attend the class?

One Way Use a number line.

5 × 30 = ■   **Think:** 30 = 3 tens

STEP 1 Complete the number line. Write the labels for the multiples of 10.

STEP 2 Draw jumps on the number line to show 5 groups of 3 tens.

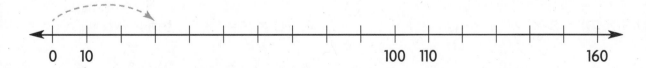

0   10   100 110   160

5 × 30 = _____

So, Erin attended the pet care class for _____ minutes.

Another Way Use place value.

MODEL

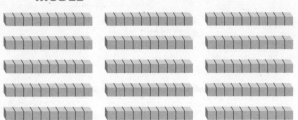

So, $5 \times 30 =$ _____ .

THINK

$5 \times 30 = 5 \times$ _____ tens

$= $ _____ tens $=$ _____

Try This!

$4 \times 50 =$ _____ $\times$ _____ tens

$= $ _____ tens $=$ _____

Math Talk

Make Sense of Problems Why does 5×30 have one zero in the product and 4×50 has two zeros in the product?

Share and Show

Use a number line to find the product.

1. $3 \times 40 =$ _____   **Think:** There are 3 jumps of 40.

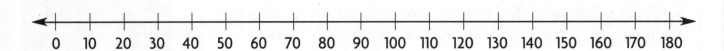

2. $8 \times 20 =$ _____

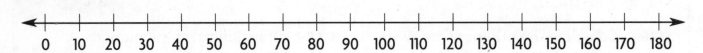

Use place value to find the product.

3. $3 \times 70 = 3 \times$ _____ tens

$= $ _____ tens $=$ _____

4. $50 \times 2 =$ _____ tens $\times$ 2

$= $ _____ tens $=$ _____ .

Math Talk

Use Repeated Reasoning Why will the product of a multiplication problem be the same when the factors are reversed?

Name _____

Use a number line to find the product.

5. $7 \times 20 =$ _____

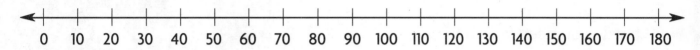

6. $3 \times 50 =$ _____

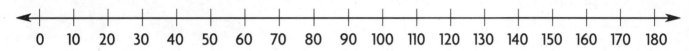

Use place value to find the product.

7. $6 \times 60 = 6 \times$ _____ tens

  $=$ _____ tens $=$ _____

8. $50 \times 7 =$ _____ tens $\times 7$

  $=$ _____ tens $=$ _____

Problem Solving • Applications

Use the table for 9–11.

9. GO DEEPER A bottle of shampoo costs $8 and a package of cat toys costs $7. If the clinic sells its entire supply of shampoo and cat toys, how much money will it receive?

_____

10. What's the Question? Each bag of treats has 30 treats. The answer is 240.

_____

11. THINK SMARTER There are 4 bottles of vitamins in each box of vitamins. Each bottle of vitamins has 20 vitamins. If the clinic wants to have a supply of 400 vitamins, how many more boxes should it order?

_____

Best Care Clinic Pet Supplies	
Item	**Amount**
Cat toys	10 packs
Treats	8 bags
Shampoo	20 bottles
Vitamins	3 boxes

? Unlock the Problem (Real World)

12. **MATHEMATICAL PRACTICE ①** **Make Sense of Problems** Hiromi needs to set up chairs for 155 people to attend the school career day program. So far she has set up 6 rows with 20 chairs in each row. How many more chairs does Hiromi need to set up?

a. What do you need to find?

_____

b. What operations will you use to find how many more chairs Hiromi needs to set up?

_____

c. Write the steps you will use to solve the problem.

d. Complete the sentences.

Hiromi needs to set up _____ chairs for people to attend the program.

She has set up _____ rows with _____ chairs in each row.

So, Hiromi needs to set up _____ more chairs.

13. **Go DEEPER** Last week, Dr. Newman examined the paws of 30 dogs at her clinic. She examined the paws of 20 cats. What is the total number of paws Dr. Newman examined last week?

_____

14. **THINK SMARTER** Nick made this multiplication model. Complete the equation that represents the model.

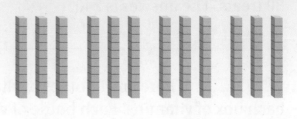

_____ × _____ = _____

Name _____

Multiplication Strategies with Multiples of 10

Common Core **COMMON CORE STANDARD—3.NBT.A.3**
Use place value understanding and properties of operations to perform multi-digit arithmetic.

Use a number line to find the product.

1. $2 \times 40 =$ ___80___

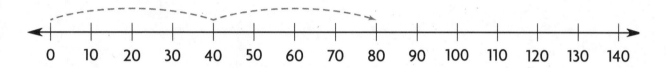

2. $4 \times 30 =$ _____

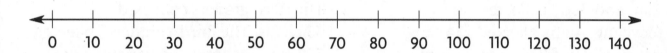

Use place value to find the product.

3. $5 \times 70 = 5 \times$ _____ tens

$=$ _____ tens $=$ _____

4. $60 \times 4 =$ _____ tens $\times 4$

$=$ _____ tens $=$ _____

Problem Solving · Real World

5. One exhibit at the aquarium has 5 fish tanks. Each fish tank holds 50 gallons of water. How much water do the 5 tanks hold?

_____

6. In another aquarium display, there are 40 fish in each of 7 large tanks. How many fish are in the display?

_____

7. **WRITE** ▸*Math* Which strategy do you prefer to use to multiply with multiples of 10: base ten blocks, a number line, or place value? Explain why.

_____

_____

Lesson Check (3.NBT.A.3)

1. Each bag of pattern blocks contains 50 blocks. To make a class pattern, the teacher combines 4 bags of blocks. How many pattern blocks are there?

2. A deli received 8 blocks of cheese. Each block of cheese weighs 60 ounces. What is the total weight of the cheeses?

Spiral Review (3.NBT.A.1, 3.NBT.A.2, 3.MD.B.3)

3. Alan and Betty collected cans for recycling. Alan collected 154 cans. Betty collected 215 cans. How many cans did they collect?

4. The third graders collected 754 cans. The fourth graders collected 592 cans. Estimate how many more cans the third graders collected.

Use the bar graph for 5–6.

5. How many more books did Ed read than Bob?

6. How many books did the four students read in June?

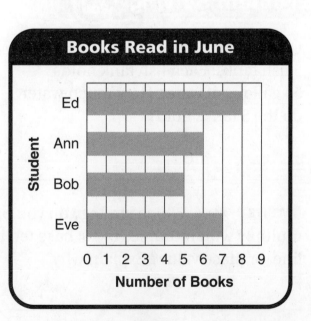

Books Read in June

Student — Ed, Ann, Bob, Eve

Number of Books — 0 1 2 3 4 5 6 7 8 9

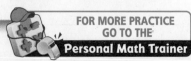

FOR MORE PRACTICE
GO TO THE
Personal Math Trainer

Multiply 1-Digit Numbers by Multiples of 10

Essential Question How can you model and record multiplying 1-digit whole numbers by multiples of 10?

Common Core **Number and Operations in Base Ten—3.NBT.A.3**
Also 3.OA.A.3, 3.OA.C.7
MATHEMATICAL PRACTICES
MP1, MP2, MP4, MP7

Unlock the Problem Real World

The community center offers 4 dance classes. If 30 students sign up for each class, how many students sign up for dance class?

- How many equal groups are there? _____
- How many are in each group? _____

Activity Use base-ten blocks to model 4 × 30.

Materials ■ base-ten blocks

STEP 1 Model 4 groups of 30.

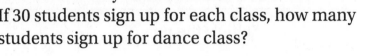

STEP 2 Combine the tens. Regroup 12 tens as 1 hundred 2 tens.

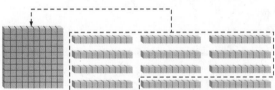

4 × 30 = _____

So, _____ students sign up for dance class.

Math Idea
If one factor is a multiple of 10, then the product will also be a multiple of 10.

Try This! Find 7 × 40.

Use a quick picture to record your model. Draw a stick for each ten. Draw a square for each hundred.

STEP 1 Model _____ groups of

_____.

STEP 2 Combine the tens. Regroup 28 tens as

_____ hundreds _____ tens.

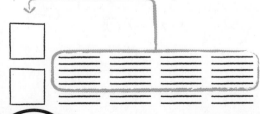

So, 7 × 40 = _____.

Math Talk

MATHEMATICAL PRACTICES ⑦

Look for Structure Why will the product of 7 × 40 be the same as 4 × 70?

© Houghton Mifflin Harcourt Publishing Company

🔑 Example Use place value and regrouping.

Find 9×50.

	MODEL	THINK	RECORD
STEP 1	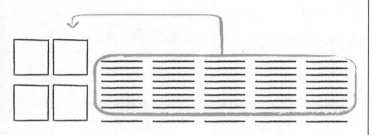	Multiply the ones. 9×0 ones = ____ ones	$\begin{array}{r} 5\,0 \\ \times\ 9 \\ \hline 0 \end{array}$
STEP 2		Multiply the tens. 9×5 tens = 45 tens. Regroup the ____ tens as ____ hundreds ____ tens.	$\begin{array}{r} 5\,0 \\ \times\ 9 \\ \hline 4\,5\,0 \end{array}$

So, $9 \times 50 =$ _____.

Share and Show 📝 MATH BOARD

1. Use the quick picture to find 5×40.

$5 \times 40 =$ _____

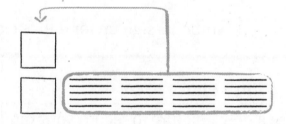

Find the product. Use base-ten blocks or draw a quick picture on your MathBoard.

✔ **2.** $7 \times 30 =$ _____   **3.** _____ $= 2 \times 90$ **4.** $8 \times 40 =$ _____   **5.** _____ $= 4 \times 60$

Find the product.

✔ **6.** $\begin{array}{r} 80 \\ \times\ 9 \\ \hline \end{array}$ **7.** $\begin{array}{r} 70 \\ \times\ 7 \\ \hline \end{array}$ **8.** $\begin{array}{r} 90 \\ \times\ 4 \\ \hline \end{array}$ **9.** $\begin{array}{r} 60 \\ \times\ 8 \\ \hline \end{array}$

Math Talk

MATHEMATICAL PRACTICES ①

Analyze Explain why a 1-digit number multiplied by a multiple of 10 is easily computed mentally.

Name _____

**Find the product. Use base-ten blocks or draw a
quick picture on your MathBoard.**

10. $2 \times 70 =$ _____   **11.** $8 \times 50 =$ _____   **12.** _____ $= 3 \times 90$ **13.** $2 \times 80 =$ _____

Find the product.

14.
$$\begin{array}{r} 80 \\ \times\ 3 \\ \hline \end{array}$$

15.
$$\begin{array}{r} 60 \\ \times\ 9 \\ \hline \end{array}$$

16.
$$\begin{array}{r} 90 \\ \times\ 8 \\ \hline \end{array}$$

17.
$$\begin{array}{r} 80 \\ \times\ 8 \\ \hline \end{array}$$

Practice: Copy and Solve **Find the product.**

18. 6×70 **19.** 9×90 **20.** 70×8 **21.** 90×7

MATHEMATICAL PRACTICE ② **Reason Quantitatively** **Algebra** **Find the unknown factor.**

22. $a \times 80 = 480$ **23.** $b \times 30 = 30$ **24.** $7 \times \blacksquare = 420$ **25.** $50 \times \blacktriangle = 0$

$a =$ _____ $b =$ _____ $\blacksquare =$ _____ $\blacktriangle =$ _____

Problem Solving • Applications

26. (THINK SMARTER) Ava's class bought 6 packages of balloons for a school
celebration. Each package had 30 balloons. If 17 balloons were left
over, how many balloons were used for the party?

_____

27. **Sense or Nonsense?** Lori says that 8 is not a factor of 80 because
8 does not end in zero. Does Lori's statement make sense? Explain.

_____

28. **MATHEMATICAL PRACTICE ④** **Model Mathematics** The book club members read
200 books in all. Each member read 5 books. Write an equation to
find the number of members in the book club. Use a letter to stand
for the unknown factor.

_____

Unlock the Problem Real World

29. **GO DEEPER** Frank has a 2-digit number on his baseball uniform. The number is a multiple of 10 and has 3 for one of its factors. What three numbers could Frank have on his uniform?

a. What do you need to find?

_____

b. What information do you need to use?

_____

c. How can you solve the problem?

d. Complete the sentences.

Frank has a _____ on his uniform.

The number is a multiple of _____.

One factor of the number is _____.

Frank could have _____, _____, or

_____ on his uniform.

Personal Math Trainer

30. **THINK SMARTER +** Baker Farm grows and sells carrots to local grocery stores. The stores bundle the carrots to sell. Which grocery store bought the greatest number of carrots from Baker Farm? How many carrots did the store buy?

Grocery Store	Number of Carrots in 1 Bundle	Number of Bundles
Buy–More Foods	6	90
Lower Price Foods	8	60
Yummy Foods	7	80
Healthy Foods	9	70

_____

Multiply 1-Digit Numbers by Multiples of 10

COMMON CORE STANDARD—3.NBT.A.3
Use place value understanding and properties of
operations to perform multi-digit arithmetic.

**Find the product. Use base-ten blocks or draw a
quick picture.**

1. $4 \times 50 =$ ___200___

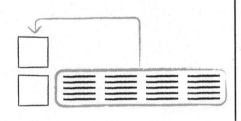

2. $60 \times 3 =$ _____

3. _____ $= 60 \times 5$

Find the product.

4.   80
    $\times\ 3$

5.   50
    $\times\ 2$

6.   60
    $\times\ 7$

7.   70
    $\times\ 4$

8. $6 \times 90 =$ ____

9. $9 \times 70 =$ ____

10. $8 \times 90 =$ ____

11. ____ $= 6 \times 80$

Problem Solving · Real World

12. Each model car in a set costs $4. There
are 30 different model cars in the set.
How much would it cost to buy all the
model cars in the set?

_____

13. Amanda exercises for 50 minutes
each day. How many minutes will she
exercise in 7 days?

_____

14. **WRITE** ▸*Math* Explain how to find 4×80. Show your work.

_____

_____

Lesson Check (3.NBT.A.3)

1. Each shelf in one section of the library holds 30 books. There are 9 shelves in that section. How many books will these shelves hold?

2. One can of juice mix makes 30 ounces of juice. How many ounces of juice can be made from 6 cans of juice mix?

Spiral Review (3.OA.A.3, 3.OA.B.5, 3.OA.D.8)

3. Sue bought 7 cans of tennis balls. There are 3 balls in each can. How many balls did Sue buy?

4. Use the Commutative Property of Multiplication to write a related multiplication sentence.

$$3 \times 4 = 12$$

5. Lyn drew this bar model to solve a problem. What operation should she use to find the unknown number?

90 flowers	54 flowers

▨ flowers

6. Joe drew this bar model to find the unknown number of balls. Find the unknown number.

106 balls	▨ balls

250 balls

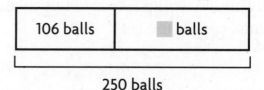

FOR MORE PRACTICE
GO TO THE
Personal Math Trainer

✓ Chapter 5 Review/Test

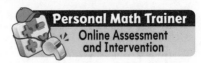

1. The camping club wants to rent rafts. Each raft can hold 8 people. Which equation could be used to find how many rafts are needed for 32 people?

Ⓐ $8 \times 32 = $ ▪

Ⓑ $32 \times $ ▪ $ = 8$

Ⓒ ▪ $\times 8 = 32$

Ⓓ $32 \times 8 = $ ▪

2. Select the equations that show the Distributive Property. Mark all that apply.

Ⓐ $8 \times 20 = 8 \times (10 + 10)$

Ⓑ $5 \times 60 = 5 \times (20 + 40)$

Ⓒ $30 \times 6 = 6 \times 30$

Ⓓ $9 \times (4 + 3) = 9 \times 7$

3. Choose the number from the box that makes the sentence true.

A library has 48 shelves of fiction books. There are 6 shelves in each cabinet.

There are
7
8
9
cabinets of fiction books in the library.

4. For numbers 4a–4d, choose True or False for each equation.

4a. $5 \times (4 + 4) = 8 \times 5$ ○ True   ○ False

4b. $8 \times (3 + 3) = 8 \times 5$ ○ True   ○ False

4c. $(3 \times 5) + (5 \times 5) = 8 \times 5$ ○ True   ○ False

4d. $(3 \times 2) + (8 \times 3) = 8 \times 5$ ○ True   ○ False

5. Alya planted 30 trays of flowers. Each tray held 8 flowers. Javon planted 230 flowers. Did Alya plant more flowers than Javon, the same number of flowers as Javon, or fewer flowers than Javon?

Ⓐ   She planted more flowers than Javon.

Ⓑ   She planted the exact same number of flowers as Javon.

Ⓒ   She planted fewer flowers than Javon.

6. For numbers 6a–6d, choose Yes or No to show whether the unknown number is 6.

6a. $4 \times \blacksquare = 32$ ○ Yes   ○ No

6b. $\blacksquare \times 6 = 36$ ○ Yes   ○ No

6c. $8 \times \blacksquare = 49$ ○ Yes   ○ No

6d. $\blacksquare \times 30 = 180$ ○ Yes   ○ No

7. Each train can carry 20 cars. Use the number line to find how many cars 6 trains can carry.

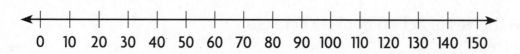

0   10   20   30   40   50   60   70   80   90   100   110   120   130   140   150

_____ cars

Name _____

8. Samantha made this multiplication model. Complete the equation that represents the model.

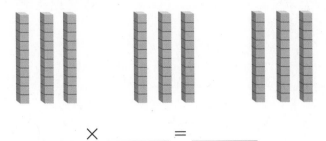

_____ × _____ = _____

9. A printer prints newsletters for many groups every month. Which group uses the greatest number of pieces of paper?

Group	Number of pieces of paper in newsletter	Number of copies of newsletter printed
Garden Ladies	5	70
Book Lovers Club	6	80
Model Train Fans	7	60
Travel Club	8	50

_____

10. **GO DEEPER** A store has 30 boxes of melons. Each box holds 4 bags. Each bag holds 2 melons. What is the total number of melons in the store?

_____ melons

11. Heather's puppy weighs 23 pounds. He has been gaining 3 pounds every month as he grows. If this pattern continues, how much will the puppy weigh 5 months from now?

_____

12. Tim describes a pattern. He says the pattern shown in the table is "Add 3." Is Tim correct? Explain how you know.

Packages	1	2	3	4	5
Markers	4	8	12	16	20

_____

_____

_____

13. This shows a part of a multiplication table. Find the missing numbers. Explain how you found the numbers.

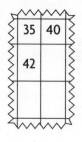

_____

_____

_____

_____

_____

14. Describe a pattern for this table.

Tanks	3	4	5	6	7
Fish	240	320	400	480	560

Pattern: _____

How would the table change if the pattern was "Multiply the number of tanks by 8"? Explain.

_____

_____

15. Devon has 80 books to pack in boxes. She packs 20 books in each box. How many boxes does she need?

Write an equation using the letter *n* to stand for the unknown factor. Explain how to find the unknown factor.

_____

_____

_____

16.  The bookstore has 6 shelves of books about animals. There are 30 books on each shelf. How many books about animals does the bookstore have?

Shade squares to make a diagram to show how you can use the Distributive Property to find the number of books about animals in the bookstore.

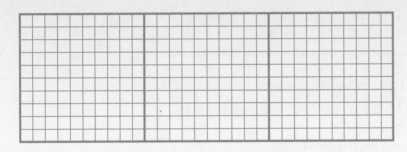

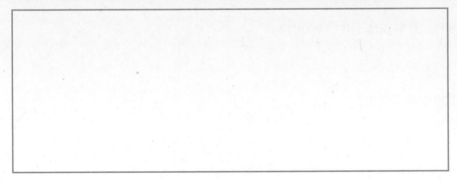

_____ animal books

17. Cody saves all his nickels. Today he is getting them out of his piggy bank and wrapping them to take to the bank. He finds he has 360 nickels. It takes 40 nickels to fill each paper wrapper and make a roll. How many wrappers does he need?

Part A

Write an equation using *n* for the unknown number. Find the number of wrappers needed.

_____ × _____ = _____

Part B

Explain how you solved this problem and how you know your answer is correct.

_____

_____

_____

_____

18. Ruben is collecting cans for the recycling contest at school. He makes two plans to try to collect the most cans.

Plan A: Collect 20 cans each week for 9 weeks.

Plan B: Collect 30 cans each week for 7 weeks.

Part A

Which plan should Ruben choose? _____

Part B

Explain how you made your choice.

_____

_____

_____

_____

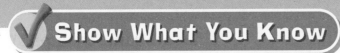

Show What You Know

Personal Math Trainer
Online Assessment
and Intervention

Check your understanding of important skills.

Name _____

▶ **Count Back to Subtract** **Use the number line. Write the difference.** (1.OA.C.5)

1. $8 - 5 =$ _____

0 1 2 3 4 5 6 7 8 9 10

2. $9 - 4 =$ _____

0 1 2 3 4 5 6 7 8 9 10

▶ **Count Equal Groups** **Complete.** (2.OA.C.4)

3.

_____ groups

_____ in each group

4.

_____ groups

_____ in each group

▶ **Multiplication Facts Through 9** **Find the product.** (3.OA.C.7)

5. $8 \times 5 =$ _____   **6.** _____ $= 7 \times 7$ **7.** $3 \times 9 =$ _____

The table shows 3 different ways to score points in basketball. Corina scored 12 points in a basketball game. Find the greatest number of field goals she could have scored. Then find the greatest number of 3-pointers she could have scored.

Scoring Points in Basketball	
free throw	1 point
field goal	2 points
3-pointer	3 points

Vocabulary Builder

▶ **Visualize It**

Complete the bubble map by using the words with a ✓ .

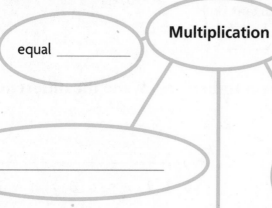

What is it like?

equal _____

Multiplication

What are some examples?

4 groups with 3 in each group

$$6 \quad \times \quad 3 \quad = \quad 18$$
$$6 \quad \times \quad 4 \quad = \quad 24$$
$$\uparrow \qquad \qquad \uparrow \qquad \qquad \uparrow$$
factor $\times$ _____ = _____

$5 + 5 + 5 = 3 \times 5 = 15$

▶ **Understand Vocabulary** •

Draw a line to match each word or term with its definition.

Preview Words	Definitions
1. dividend	A set of related multiplication and division equations
2. related facts	The number that divides the dividend
3. divisor	The number that is to be divided in a division problem

Review Words

array
✓ equal groups
equation
✓ factor
Identity Property of Multiplication
✓ product
✓ repeated addition

Preview Words

divide
dividend
divisor
inverse operations
quotient
related facts

GO DIGITAL
• **Interactive Student Edition**
• **Multimedia eGlossary**

Chapter 6 Vocabulary

divide

dividir

14

dividend

dividendo

15

divisor

divisor

16

equal groups

grupos iguales

20

factor

factor

25

inverse operations

operaciones inversas

37

quotient

cociente

67

related facts

operaciones
relacionadas

70

The number that is to be divided in a division problem

Examples: $32 \div 4 = 8$ $4\overline{)32}$ with quotient 8

dividend   dividend

To separate into equal groups; the opposite operation of multiplication

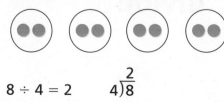

$8 \div 4 = 2$ $4\overline{)8}$ with quotient 2

Groups that have the same number of objects

The number that divides the dividend

Examples: $32 \div 4 = 8$ $4\overline{)32}$ with quotient 8

divisor   divisor

Opposite operations, or operations that undo one another, such as addition and subtraction or multiplication and division

Examples: $16 + 8 = 24;\ 24 - 8 = 16$
$4 \times 3 = 12;\ 12 \div 4 = 3$

A number that is multiplied by another number to find a product

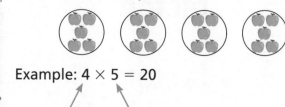

Example: $4 \times 5 = 20$

factor   factor

A set of related addition and subtraction, or multiplication and division, number sentences

Examples: $4 \times 7 = 28$ $28 \div 4 = 7$
$7 \times 4 = 28$ $28 \div 7 = 4$

The number, not including the remainder, that results from division

Example: $35 \div 7 = 5$

quotient

Bingo

Word Box
divide
dividend
divisor
equal groups
inverse operations
factors
quotient
related facts

For 3–6 players

Materials

- 1 set of word cards
- 1 Bingo board for each player
- counters, paperclips, or coins for game markers

How to Play

1. The caller chooses a card and reads the definition. Then the caller puts the card in a second pile.
2. Players put a marker on the word that matches the definition each time they find it on their Bingo boards.
3. Repeat Steps 1 and 2 until a player marks 5 boxes in a line going down, across, or on a slant and calls "Bingo."
4. Check the answers. Have the player who said "Bingo" read the words aloud while the caller checks the definitions on the cards in the second pile.

The Write Way

Reflect

Choose one idea. Write about it.

- Explain equal groups and how they relate to division.
- Write a division word problem using the numbers 24 and 6.
- Suppose that you write a math advice column, and a reader needs help understanding the division rules for 1. Write a response that explains the rules.

Problem Solving • Model Division

Essential Question How can you use the strategy *act it out* to solve problems with equal groups?

 Common Core Operations and Algebraic Thinking—3.OA.A.3 *Also 3.OA.A.2*
MATHEMATICAL PRACTICES
MP1, MP6, MP8

Unlock the Problem

Stacy has 16 flowers. She puts an equal number of flowers in each of 4 vases. How many flowers does Stacy put in each vase?

Use the graphic organizer below to solve the problem.

Read the Problem

What do I need to find?

I need to find the number

of _____ Stacy puts in

each _____.

What information do I need to use?

Stacy has _____ flowers.
She puts an equal number
of flowers in each of

_____ vases.

How will I use the information?

I will act out the problem

by making equal _____ with
counters.

Solve the Problem

Describe how to act out the problem to solve.

First, count out _____ counters.

Next, make _____ equal groups. Place
1 counter at a time in each group until
all 16 counters are used.

Last, draw the equal groups by completing
the picture below.

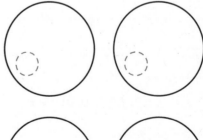

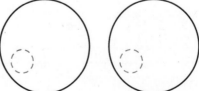 So, Stacy puts _____ flowers in each vase.

🔓 Try Another Problem

Jamal is at the pet store. He buys 21 dog treats. If he plans to give each dog 3 treats, how many dogs does he feed?

Read the Problem	Solve the Problem
What do I need to find?	**Describe how to act out the problem to solve.**
What information do I need to use?	
How will I use the information?	

• How can you check your answer is reasonable? _____

_____

_____

© Houghton Mifflin Harcourt Publishing Company

MATHEMATICAL PRACTICES ⑧

Generalize How does a strategy like *acting it out* help you solve a problem?

Name _____

Unlock the Problem

√ Use the Problem Solving MathBoard
√ Underline important facts.
√ Choose a strategy you know.

1. Mariana is having a party. She has 16 cups. She puts them in 2 equal stacks. How many cups are in each stack?

First, decide how to act out the problem.
You can use counters to represent the _____.

You can draw _____ to represent the stacks.

Then, draw to find the number of _____ in each stack.

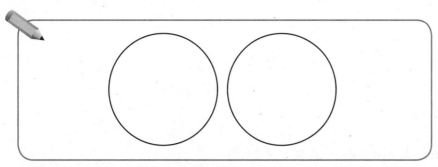

There are _____ groups. There are _____ counters in each group.

So, there are _____ cups in each stack.

2. **MATHEMATICAL PRACTICE 1 Make Sense of Problems** What if Mariana has 24 cups and puts 4 cups in each stack? If she already made 4 stacks, how many more stacks can she make with the remaining cups?

_____

On Your Own

3. *THINK SMARTER* At Luke's school party, the children make teams of 5 to play a game. If there are 20 boys and 15 girls, how many teams are there?

_____

4. *GO DEEPER* Anne put 20 party hats and 20 balloons on 4 tables. She put an equal number of hats and an equal number of balloons on each table. How many hats and how many balloons did she put on each table?

_____

Use the table for 5–6.

5. Sadie's plates came in packages of 5 plates. How many packages of plates did she buy?

_____

6. **MATHEMATICAL PRACTICE** ⑥ **Explain a Method** Sadie bought 4 packages of napkins and 3 packages of cups. Which type of package had more items in it? How many more items are in each package? Explain.

_____

_____

_____

_____

_____

Sadie's Party Supplies	
Item	Number
Plates	30
Napkins	28
Cups	24

7. **GO DEEPER** Ira and his brother share a model car collection. Ira has 25 cars, and his brother has 15 cars. They store the model cars on a bookshelf and place the same number of cars on each shelf. There are 5 shelves. How many model cars are on each shelf?

_____

WRITE ▸ *Math* · **Show Your Work**

Personal Math Trainer

8. **THINK SMARTER +** Miguel gave 2 party favors to each of the children at his party. He gave away 18 party favors. How many children were at Miguel's party?

Circle equal groups to model the problem.

_____ children

Problem Solving • Model Division

Common Core   **COMMON CORE STANDARD—3.OA.A.3**
*Represent and solve problems involving
multiplication and division.*

Solve each problem.

1. Six customers at a toy store bought 18 jump
   ropes. Each customer bought the same
   number of jump ropes. How many jump ropes
   did each customer buy?

   _____
   3 jump ropes

2. Hiro has 36 pictures of his summer trip. He
   wants to put them in an album. Each page of
   the album holds 4 pictures. How many pages
   will Hiro need for his pictures?

   _____

3. Katia has 42 crayons in a box. She buys a
   storage bin that has 6 sections. She puts the
   same number of crayons in each section. How
   many crayons does Katia put in each section of
   the storage bin?

   _____

4. Ms. Taylor's students give cards to each of
   the 3 class parent helpers. There are
   24 cards. How many cards will each helper
   get if the students give an equal number of
   cards to each helper?

   _____

5. **WRITE** ▸*Math* Write a word problem about equal groups
   and act it out to solve.

   _____

   _____

Lesson Check (3.OA.A.3)

1. Maria buys 15 apples at the store and places them into bags. She puts 5 apples into each bag. How many bags does Maria use for all the apples?

2. Tom's neighbor is fixing a section of his walkway. He has 32 bricks that he is placing in 8 equal rows. How many bricks will Tom's neighbor place in each row?

Spiral Review (3.OA.A.1, 3.OA.A.4, 3.OA.B.5, 3.MD.B.4)

3. Find the unknown factor.

$$7 \times \blacksquare = 56$$

4. How many students practiced the piano more than 3 hours?

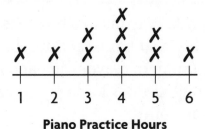

Piano Practice Hours

5. Count equal groups to find how many counters there are.

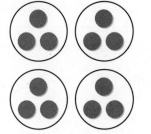

6. What is another way to group the factors?

$$(3 \times 2) \times 5$$

FOR MORE PRACTICE
GO TO THE
Personal Math Trainer

Size of Equal Groups

Essential Question How can you model a division problem to find how many in each group?

Common Core
**Operations and Algebraic Thinking—
3.OA.A.2** *Also 3.OA.A.3*
MATHEMATICAL PRACTICES
MP1, MP3, MP4

Unlock the Problem (Real World)

Hector has 12 rocks from a nearby state park. He puts an equal number of his rocks in each of 3 boxes. How many rocks are in each box?

When you multiply, you put equal groups together. When you **divide**, you separate into equal groups.

You can divide to find the number in each group.

- What do you need to find?

  _____

- Circle the numbers you need to use.

Activity Use counters to model the problem.

Materials ■ counters ■ MathBoard

STEP 1

Use 12 counters.

_____

STEP 2

Draw 3 circles on your MathBoard. Place 1 counter at a time in each circle until all 12 counters are used. Draw the rest of the counters to show your work.

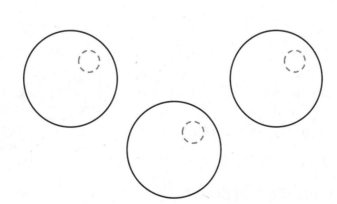

There are _____ counters in each group.

So, there are _____ rocks in each box.

Try This!

Madison has 15 rocks. She puts an equal number of rocks in each of 5 boxes. How many rocks are in each box?

STEP 1

Draw 5 squares to show 5 boxes.

_____

STEP 2

Draw 1 counter in each square to show the rocks. Continue drawing 1 counter at a time in each box until all 15 counters are drawn.

There are _____ counters in each group.

So, there are _____ rocks in each box.

MATHEMATICAL PRACTICES ①

Describe another way to arrange 15 counters to make equal groups.

1. How many counters did you draw? _____

2. How many equal groups did you make? _____

3. How many counters are in each group? _____

Name _____

1. Jon has 8 counters. He makes 4 equal groups.
   Draw a picture to show the number of counters
   in each group.

Math Talk

MATHEMATICAL PRACTICES ④

Use Models Explain how you made the groups equal.

**Use counters or draw a quick picture on your
MathBoard. Make equal groups. Complete the table.**

	Counters	Number of Equal Groups	Number in Each Group
✓2.	10	2	
✓3.	24	6	

On Your Own

**Use counters or draw a quick picture on your
MathBoard. Make equal groups. Complete the table.**

	Counters	Number of Equal Groups	Number in Each Group
4.	14	7	
5.	21	3	

6. **GO DEEPER** Cameron and Jody collected 20 stamps. Cameron says
   they can put an equal number of stamps on each of 5 pages of
   their album. Jody says they can put an equal number on each of
   4 pages. Whose statement makes sense? Explain.

_____

_____

Problem Solving • Applications Real World

Use the table for 7–8.

Photos	
Name	**Number of Photos**
Madison	28
Joe	25
Ella	15

7. Madison puts all of her photos in a photo album. She puts an equal number of photos on each of 4 pages in her album. How many photos are on each page?

_____

8. **THINK SMARTER** Joe and Ella combine their photos. Then they put an equal number on each page of an 8-page photo album. How many photos are on each page?

_____

9. **MATHEMATICAL PRACTICE ③** **Make Arguments** Rebekah found 28 seashells. Can she share all the seashells equally among the 6 people in her family? Explain.

_____

_____

_____

10. **THINK SMARTER** Zana has 9 rocks from a trip. She puts an equal number of rocks in each of 3 bags. How many rocks are in each bag?

Circle the amount to complete the sentence.

There are
| 3 |
| 6 |
| 12 |
| 27 |
 rocks in each bag.

Size of Equal Groups

COMMON CORE STANDARD—3.OA.A.2
Represent and solve problems involving multiplication and division.

Use counters or draw a quick picture. Make equal groups. Complete the table.

	Counters	Number of Equal Groups	Number in Each Group
1.	15	3	5
2.	21	7	
3.	28	7	
4.	32	4	
5.	9	3	
6.	35	5	
7.	24	3	

Problem Solving (Real World)

8. Alicia has 12 eggs that she will use to make 4 different cookie recipes. If each recipe calls for the same number of eggs, how many eggs will she use in each recipe?

9. Brett picked 27 flowers from the garden. He plans to give an equal number of flowers to each of 3 people. How many flowers will each person get?

_____

_____

10. **WRITE** ▸*Math* Describe how to divide 18 strawberries equally between 2 of your friends.

_____

_____

Lesson Check (3.OA.A.2)

1. Ryan has 21 pencils. He wants to put the same number of pencils in each of 3 pencil holders. How many pencils will he put in each pencil holder?

2. Corrine is setting out 24 plates on 6 tables for a dinner. She sets the same number of plates on each table. How many plates does Corrine set on each table?

Spiral Review (3.OA.A.1, 3.OA.A.4, 3.OA.B.5, 3.OA.D.9)

3. Each table has 4 legs. How many legs do 4 tables have?

4. Tina has 3 stacks of 5 CDs on each of 3 shelves. How many CDs does she have?

5. What is the unknown factor?

$$7 \times \blacksquare = 35$$

6. Describe a pattern in the table.

Number of packs	1	2	3	4	5
Number of yo-yos	3	6	9	12	?

FOR MORE PRACTICE GO TO THE Personal Math Trainer

Number of Equal Groups

Essential Question How can you model a division problem to find how many equal groups?

 Common Core **Operations and Algebraic Thinking—3.OA.A.2** *Also 3.OA.A.3*
MATHEMATICAL PRACTICES
MP1, MP3, MP6

CONNECT You have learned how to divide to find the number in each group. Now you will learn how to divide to find the number of equal groups.

Unlock the Problem Real World

Juan has 12 shells and some boxes. He wants to put each group of 3 shells in a box. How many boxes does he need for his shells?

- Underline what you need to find.
- How many shells does Juan want to put in each box?

_____

🔒 **Make equal groups.**

- Look at the 12 counters.
- Circle a group of 3 counters.
- Continue circling groups of 3 until all 12 counters are in groups.

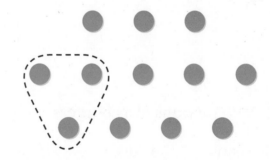

There are _____ groups of counters.

So, Juan needs _____ boxes for his shells.

 Math Talk

MATHEMATICAL PRACTICES ❻

Compare How would the drawing change if Juan wanted to put his shells in groups of 4?

Try This!

Sarah has 15 shells. She wants to put each group of 5 shells in a box.
How many boxes does she need for her shells?

STEP 1

Draw 15 counters.

_____

STEP 2

Make a group of 5 counters by
drawing a circle around them.
Continue circling groups of 5
until all 15 counters are in groups.

There are _____ groups of 5 counters.

So, Sarah needs _____ boxes for her shells.

- **THINK SMARTER** What if Sarah puts her 15 shells in
groups of 3?

How many boxes does she need? _____
Draw a quick picture to show your work.

Name _____

1. Tamika has 12 counters. She puts them in groups of 2. Draw a picture to show the number of groups.

Math Talk

MATHEMATICAL PRACTICES ③

Apply How do you find the number of equal groups when you divide?

Draw counters on your MathBoard. Then circle equal groups. Complete the table.

	Counters	Number of Equal Groups	Number in Each Group
✓2.	20		4
✓3.	24		3

On Your Own

Draw counters on your MathBoard. Then circle equal groups. Complete the table.

	Counters	Number of Equal Groups	Number in Each Group
4.	18		2
5.	16		8

6. **THINK SMARTER** A store has 18 red beach balls and 17 green beach balls in boxes of 5 beach balls each. How many boxes of beach balls are at the store?

_____

Unlock the Problem (Real World)

7. **MATHEMATICAL PRACTICE ①** **Make Sense of Problems** A store has 24 beach towels in stacks of 6 towels each. How many stacks of beach towels are at the store?

a. What do you need to find? _____

_____

b. How will you use what you know about making equal groups

to solve the problem? _____

_____

c. Draw equal groups to find how many stacks of beach towels there are at the store.

d. Complete the sentences.

The store has _____ beach towels.

There are _____ towels in each stack.

So, there are _____ stacks of beach towels at the store.

8. **GO DEEPER** Write a problem about dividing beach toys into equal groups. Then solve the problem.

_____

_____

_____

_____

9. **THINK SMARTER** Dan's train is 27 inches long. If each train car is 3 inches long, how many train cars are there?

Choose a number from the box to complete the sentence.

| 6 |
| 7 |
| 8 |
| 9 |

There are _____ train cars.

Number of Equal Groups

Common Core
COMMON CORE STANDARD—3.OA.A.2
Represent and solve problems involving multiplication and division.

Draw counters on your MathBoard. Then circle equal groups. Complete the table.

	Counters	Number of Equal Groups	Number in Each Group
1.	24	3	8
2.	35		7
3.	30		5
4.	16		4
5.	12		6
6.	36		9
7.	18		3

Problem Solving Real World

8. In his bookstore, Toby places 21 books on shelves, with 7 books on each shelf. How many shelves does Toby need?

9. Mr. Holden has 32 quarters in stacks of 4 on his desk. How many stacks of quarters are on his desk?

_____   _____

10. **WRITE** ▸*Math* Write and solve a math problem in which you need to find how many equal groups.

_____

_____

Lesson Check (3.OA.A.2)

1. Ramon works at a clothing store. He puts 24 pairs of jeans into stacks of 8. How many stacks does Ramon make?

_____

2. There are 36 people waiting in line for a hay ride. Only 6 people can ride on each wagon. If each wagon is full, how many wagons are needed for all 36 people?

_____

Spiral Review (3.OA.A.3, 3.OA.D.8, 3.OA.D.9, 3.NBT.A.3)

3. What multiplication sentence does the array show?

_____

_____

4. Austin buys 4 boxes of nails for his project. There are 30 nails in each box. How many nails does Austin buy in all?

_____

_____

5. What property does the number sentence show?

$$8 + 0 = 8$$

_____

_____

6. Each month for 6 months, Kelsey completes 5 paintings. How many more paintings does she need to complete before she has completed 38 paintings?

_____

_____

FOR MORE PRACTICE GO TO THE Personal Math Trainer

Name _____

Model with Bar Models

Essential Question How can you use bar models to solve division problems?

 Operations and Algebraic Thinking—3.OA.A.2 *Also 3.OA.A.3*
MATHEMATICAL PRACTICES
MP2, MP4, MP6

Unlock the Problem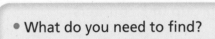

A dog trainer has 20 dog treats for 5 dogs in his class. If each dog gets the same number of treats, how many treats will each dog get?

* What do you need to find?
_____

Activity 1 Use counters to find how many in each group.

Materials ■ counters ■ MathBoard

* Use 20 counters.
* Draw 5 circles on your MathBoard.
* Place 1 counter at a time in each circle until all 20 counters are used.
* Draw the rest of the counters to show your work.

There are _____ counters in each of the 5 groups.

A bar model can show how the parts of a problem are related.

* Complete the bar model to show 20 dog treats divided into 5 equal groups.

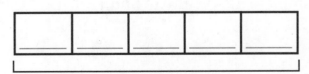
20 dog treats

So, each dog will get _____ treats.

🔓 Activity 2 Draw to find how many equal groups.

A dog trainer has 20 dog treats. If the dog trainer gives 5 treats to each dog in the class, how many dogs are in the class?

- Look at the 20 counters.

- Circle a group of 5 counters.

- Continue circling groups of 5 until all 20 counters are in groups.

There are _____ groups of 5 counters.

- Complete the bar model to show 20 treats divided into groups of 5 treats.

So, there are _____ dogs in the class.

_____ dogs

5		5

20 dog treats

Here are two ways to record division.

Write: 20 ÷ 5 = 4

↑ **dividend**   ↑ **divisor**   ↑ **quotient**

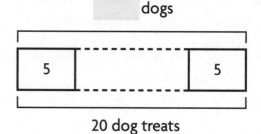

divisor → 5)20   ← quotient

↑ dividend

Read: Twenty divided by five equals four.

1. Complete the picture to find 12 ÷ 4. _____

Math Talk

MATHEMATICAL PRACTICES 6

Use Math Vocabulary Describe how you solved the problem in Activity 2. Use the terms *dividend, divisor,* and *quotient* in your explanation.

Math Talk

MATHEMATICAL PRACTICES 2

Reason Quantitatively How do you know how many groups to make?

320

Name _____

Write a division equation for the picture.

 2.   **3.**

_____   _____

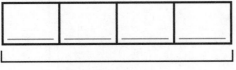 **On Your Own**

Write a division equation for the picture.

4. 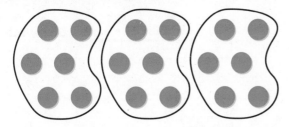   **5.**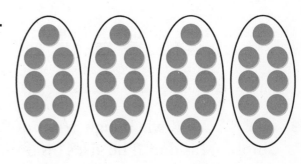

_____   _____

Practice: Copy and Solve Make equal groups to find
the quotient. Draw a quick picture to show your work.

6. $20 \div 2$ **7.** $27 \div 9$

8. $20 \div 5$ **9.** $18 \div 3$

**Complete the bar model to solve. Then write a
division equation for the bar model.**

10. There are 24 books in 4 equal
stacks. How many books are
in each stack?

24 books

_____

11. There are 8 matching socks.
How many pairs of socks can
you make?

[   ] pairs

2	----	----	2

8 socks

_____

Problem Solving • Applications

Use the table for 12–13.

Dog Treats	
Type	**Number in Box**
Chew Sticks	14
Chewies	25
Dog Bites	30
Puppy Chips	45

12. **MATHEMATICAL PRACTICE ④ Write an Equation** Pat bought one box of Chew Sticks to share equally between his 2 dogs. Mia bought one box of Chewies to share equally among her 5 dogs. How many more treats will each of Pat's dogs get than each of Mia's dogs? Explain.

_____

_____

_____

_____

WRITE ▸ *Math* • **Show Your Work**

13. **THINK SMARTER** Kevin bought a box of Puppy Chips for his dog. If he gives his dog 5 treats each day, for how many days will one box of treats last?

_____

14. **GO DEEPER** Write and solve a problem for $42 \div 7$ in which the quotient is the number of groups.

_____

_____

_____

15. **THINK SMARTER** Ed buys 5 bags of treats. He buys 15 treats in all. How many treats are in each bag?

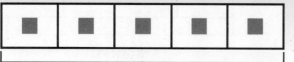

15 treats

_____ treats

Model with Bar Models

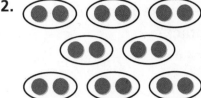 **COMMON CORE STANDARD—3.OA.A.2**
Represent and solve problems involving multiplication and division.

Write a division equation for the picture.

1.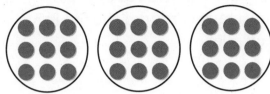

   27 ÷ 3 = 9 or 27 ÷ 9 = 3

2. _____

Complete the bar model to solve. Then write a division equation for the bar model.

3. There are 15 postcards in 3 equal stacks. How many postcards are in each stack?

   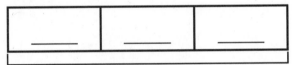

   15 postcards

   _____

4. There are 21 key rings. How many groups of 3 key rings can you make?

   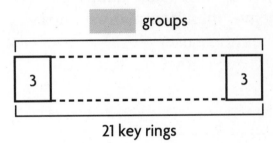

   21 key rings

   _____

![Problem Solving Real World]

5. Jalyn collected 24 stones. She put them in 4 equal piles. How many stones are in each pile?

   _____

6. Tanner has 30 stickers. He puts 6 stickers on each page. On how many pages does he put stickers?

   _____

7. **WRITE** ▸*Math* Describe how to find the number of $4 train tickets you can buy with $32.

   _____

   _____

Lesson Check (3.OA.A.2)

1. Jack and his little sister are stacking 24 blocks. They put the blocks in 3 equal stacks. How many blocks are in each stack?

_____

2. Melissa made 45 greeting cards. She put them in 5 equal piles. How many cards did she put in each pile?

_____

Spiral Review (3.OA.B.5, 3.OA.C.7, 3.MD.B.4)

3. Angie puts 1 stamp on each envelope. She puts stamps on 7 envelopes. How many stamps does Angie use?

_____

4. A carnival ride has 8 cars. Each car holds 4 people. How many people are on the ride if all the cars are full?

_____

Use the line plot for 5–6.

5. How many families have exactly 1 computer at home?

_____

6. How many families have more than 1 computer at home?

_____

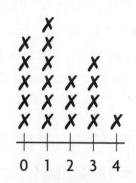

Number of Computers at Home

FOR MORE PRACTICE GO TO THE Personal Math Trainer

Relate Subtraction and Division

Essential Question How is division related to subtraction?

Common Core **Operations and Algebraic Thinking—**
3.OA.A.3 *Also 3.OA.A.2, 3.OA.C.7*
MATHEMATICAL PRACTICES
MP1, MP4, MP7

Unlock the Problem

Serena and Mandy brought a total of 12 newspapers to school for the recycling program. Each girl brought in one newspaper each day. For how many days did the girls bring in newspapers?

- How many newspapers were brought in altogether?

  _____

- How many newspapers did the two girls bring in altogether each day?

  _____

One Way Use repeated subtraction.

- Start with 12.

- Subtract 2 until you reach 0.

- Count the number of times you subtract 2.

$$\begin{array}{cc} 12 \\ -\ 2 \\ \hline 10 \end{array} \nearrow \begin{array}{cc} 10 \\ -\ 2 \\ \hline 8 \end{array} \nearrow \begin{array}{cc} 8 \\ -\ 2 \\ \hline \end{array} \nearrow \begin{array}{cc} 6 \\ -\ 2 \\ \hline \end{array} \nearrow \begin{array}{cc} 4 \\ -\ 2 \\ \hline \end{array} \nearrow \begin{array}{cc} 2 \\ -\ 2 \\ \hline \end{array}$$

Number of times you subtract 2: 1   2   3   4   5   6

! ERROR Alert
Be sure to keep subtracting 2 until you are unable to subtract 2 anymore.

Since you subtract 2 six times,

there are _____ groups of 2 in 12.

So, Serena and Mandy brought in

newspapers for _____ days.

Write: $12 \div 2 = 6$ or $2\overline{)12}^{\;6}$

Read: Twelve divided by two equals six.

🔑 Another Way Count back on a number line.

- Start at 12.
- Count back by 2s as many times as you can. Draw the rest of the jumps on the number line.
- Count the number of times you jumped back 2.

You jumped back by 2 six times.

There are _____ jumps of 2 in 12.

$12 \div 2 =$ _____

Math Talk

Use Diagrams How does using a number line make solving a division problem easier?

- What do your jumps of 2 represent? _____

_____

Share and Show MATH BOARD

1. Draw the rest of the jumps on the number line to complete the division equation. $12 \div 4 =$ _____

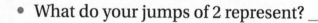

0 1 2 3 4 5 6 7 8 9 10 11 12

Math Talk

Identify Relationships How is counting back on a number line like using repeated subtraction to solve a division problem?

Write a division equation.

✓2.
```
  10
 − 5
 ────
   5
```
```
   5
 − 5
 ────
   0
```

✓3.

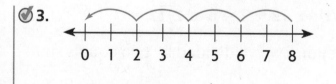

0 1 2 3 4 5 6 7 8

_____

_____

Name _____

On Your Own

Write a division equation.

4.
$$
\begin{array}{cccc}
28 & 21 & 14 & 7 \\
-7 & -7 & -7 & -7 \\
\hline
21 & 14 & 7 & 0
\end{array}
$$

_____

5.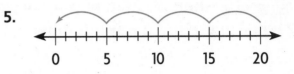

_____

Use repeated subtraction or a number line to solve.

6. $18 \div 6 =$ _____

7. $9\overline{)27}$

8. **THINK SMARTER** Write a word problem that can be solved by using one of the division equations above.

_____

_____

9. Jeff has a booklet of 30 stickers. He uses one page of stickers. If there are 6 stickers on each page, how many pages are left?

_____

10. Tara has 32 beads. She takes out 4 red beads, then sorts the rest into 4 equal groups. How many beads are in each group?

_____

11. **GO DEEPER** Tim has 30 grapes. He keeps 9 grapes for himself. Then he gives 7 grapes each to some of his friends. To how many friends does Tim give grapes?

_____

12. **GO DEEPER** There are 16 dolphins in a pod. Each pod has the same number of males and females. The female dolphins are swimming in pairs. How many pairs of female dolphins are there?

_____

Problem Solving • Applications Real World

Use the graph for 13–15.

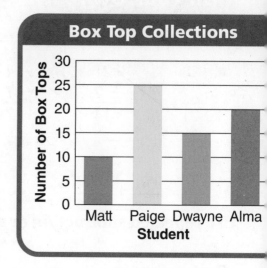

Box Top Collections

13. **MATHEMATICAL PRACTICE ① Analyze** Matt puts his box tops in 2 equal piles. How many box tops are in each pile?

_____

14. **THINK SMARTER** Paige brought an equal number of box tops to school each day for 5 days. Alma also brought an equal number of box tops each day for 5 days. How many box tops did the two students bring in altogether each day? Explain.

_____

_____

_____

15. **GO DEEPER** Dwayne collects another 15 box tops and puts all his box tops into bins. He puts an equal number in each bin. The answer is 5. What's the question?

_____

_____

Personal Math Trainer

16. **THINK SMARTER +** Maya collected 4 box tops each day. She collected 20 box tops in all. For how many days did Maya collect box tops?

Draw jumps on the number line to model the problem.

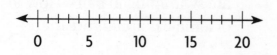

0   5   10   15   20   _____ days

Relate Subtraction and Division

COMMON CORE STANDARD—3.OA.A.3
Represent and solve problems involving multiplication and division.

Write a division equation.

1.
$$\begin{array}{r} 16 \\ -\ 4 \\ \hline 12 \end{array} \nearrow \begin{array}{r} 12 \\ -\ 4 \\ \hline 8 \end{array} \nearrow \begin{array}{r} 8 \\ -\ 4 \\ \hline 4 \end{array} \nearrow \begin{array}{r} 4 \\ -\ 4 \\ \hline 0 \end{array}$$

$$16 \div 4 = 4$$

2.
$$\begin{array}{r} 20 \\ -\ 5 \\ \hline 15 \end{array} \nearrow \begin{array}{r} 15 \\ -\ 5 \\ \hline 10 \end{array} \nearrow \begin{array}{r} 10 \\ -\ 5 \\ \hline 5 \end{array} \nearrow \begin{array}{r} 5 \\ -\ 5 \\ \hline 0 \end{array}$$

_____

Use repeated subtraction or a number line to solve.

3. $28 \div 7 =$ _____

4. $18 \div 6 =$ _____

5. $8\overline{)40}$

6. $9\overline{)36}$

Problem Solving (Real World)

7. Mrs. Costa has 18 pencils. She gives 9 pencils to each of her children for school. How many children does Mrs. Costa have?

_____

8. Boël decides to plant rose bushes in her garden. She has 24 bushes. She places 6 bushes in each row. How many rows of rose bushes does she plant in her garden?

_____

9. **WRITE** ▸*Math* Explain why you can use subtraction to solve a division problem.

_____

_____

Lesson Check (3.OA.A.3)

1. What division equation is shown?

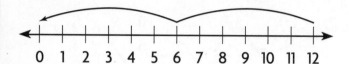

2. Isabella has 35 cups of dog food. She feeds her dogs 5 cups of food each day. For how many days will the dog food last?

_____

_____

_____

Spiral Review (3.OA.A.3, 3.OA.D.8, 3.MD.B.3)

3. Ellen buys 4 bags of oranges. There are 6 oranges in each bag. How many oranges does Ellen buy?

4. Each month for 7 months, Samuel mows 3 lawns. How many more lawns does he need to mow before he has mowed 29 lawns?

_____

_____

Use the graph for 5–6.

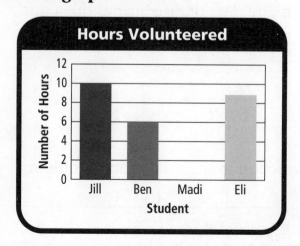

5. How many hours did Eli volunteer?

_____

6. Madi volunteered 2 hours less than Jill. At what number should the bar for Madi end?

_____

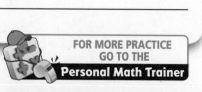

FOR MORE PRACTICE
GO TO THE
Personal Math Trainer

✓ Mid-Chapter Checkpoint

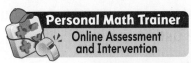

Personal Math Trainer
Online Assessment and Intervention

Vocabulary

Choose the best term from the box to complete the sentence.

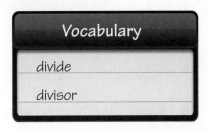

Vocabulary

divide

divisor

1. You _____ when you separate into equal groups. (p. 307)

Concepts and Skills

Use counters or draw a quick picture on your MathBoard. Make or circle equal groups. Complete the table. (3.OA.A.2)

	Counters	Number of Equal Groups	Number in Each Group
2.	6	2	
3.	30		5
4.	28	7	

Write a division equation for the picture. (3.OA.A.2)

5.

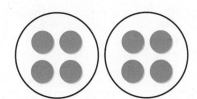

_____

6.

_____

Write a division equation. (3.OA.A.3)

7.
$$\begin{array}{r} 36 \\ -\ 9 \\ \hline 27 \end{array} \quad \begin{array}{r} 27 \\ -\ 9 \\ \hline 18 \end{array} \quad \begin{array}{r} 18 \\ -\ 9 \\ \hline 9 \end{array} \quad \begin{array}{r} 9 \\ -\ 9 \\ \hline 0 \end{array}$$

_____

8.
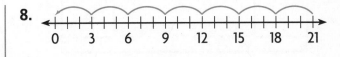

0   3   6   9   12   15   18   21

_____

9. Victor plants 14 seeds in some flowerpots. If he puts 2 seeds in each pot, how many flowerpots does he use? (3.OA.A.2)

_____

10. GO DEEPER Desiree had 35 stickers. She gave each of 3 friends the same number of stickers. She now has 20 stickers left. She then gives the same number of stickers to each of another 5 friends. How many stickers did she give each of her 3 friends? Each of her 5 friends? (3.OA.A.2)

_____

11. Jayden modeled a division equation with some counters. What division equation could Jayden have modeled? (3.OA.A.2)

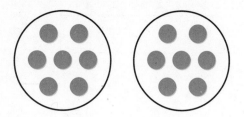

_____

12. Lillian bought 24 cans of cat food. There were 4 cans in each pack. How many packs of cat food did Lillian buy? (3.OA.A.2)

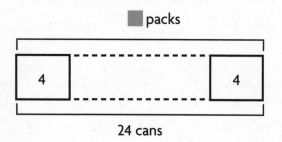

_____

Name _____

Model with Arrays

Essential Question How can you use arrays to solve division problems?

Common Core Operations and Algebraic Thinking—**3.OA.A.3** *Also 3.OA.A.2*
MATHEMATICAL PRACTICES
MP4, MP7, MP8

Investigate

Hands On

Materials ■ square tiles

You can use arrays to model division and find equal groups.

A. Count out 30 tiles. Make an array to find how many rows of 5 are in 30.

B. Make a row of 5 tiles.

C. Continue to make as many rows of 5 tiles as you can.

How many rows of 5 did you make? _____

Draw Conclusions

1. Explain how you used the tiles to find the number of rows of 5 in 30.

_____

_____

2. What multiplication equation could you write for the array? Explain.

_____

_____

3. Tell how to use an array to find how many rows of 6 are in 30.

_____

_____

Make Connections

You can write a division equation to show how
many rows of 5 are in 30. Show the array you made
in Investigate by completing the drawing below.

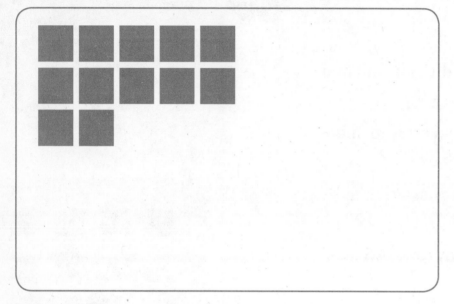

$30 \div 5 =$

There are _____ rows of 5 tiles in 30.

So, $30 \div 5 =$ _____.

Try This!

Count out 24 tiles. Make an array with the same number of tiles in
4 rows. Place 1 tile in each of the 4 rows. Then continue placing 1 tile in
each row until you use all the tiles. Draw your array below.

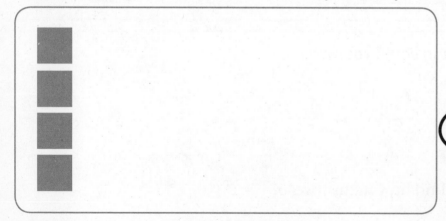

Math Talk

MATHEMATICAL PRACTICES ④

Use Models How does
making an array help
you divide?

- How many tiles are in each row? _____

- What division equation can you write for your array? _____

Name _____

Use square tiles to make an array. Solve.

1. How many rows of 3 are in 18?

   _____

2. How many rows of 6 are in 12?

   _____

3. How many rows of 7 are in 21?

   _____

4. How many rows of 8 are in 32?

   _____

Make an array. Then write a division equation.

5. 25 tiles in 5 rows

   _____

6. 14 tiles in 2 rows

   _____

7. 28 tiles in 4 rows

   _____

8. 27 tiles in 9 rows

   _____

Problem Solving • Applications

9. **THINK SMARTER** Tell how to use an array to find how many rows of 8 are in 40.

   _____

   _____

10. **MATHEMATICAL PRACTICE ④ Model Mathematics** Show two ways you could make an array with tiles for $18 \div 6$. Shade squares on the grid to record the arrays.

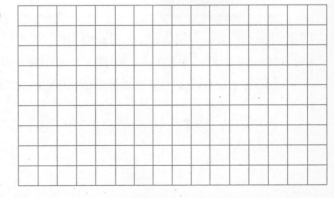

Unlock the Problem

11. **MATHEMATICAL PRACTICE ⑦** **Look for Structure** Thomas has 28 tomato seedlings to plant in his garden. He wants to plant 4 seedlings in each row. How many rows of tomato seedlings will Thomas plant?

a. What do you need to find? _____

_____

b. What operation could you use to solve the problem? _____

_____

c. Draw an array to find the number of rows of tomato seedlings.

d. What is another way you could have solved the problem?

_____

_____

e. Complete the sentences.

Thomas has _____ tomato seedlings.

He wants to plant _____ seedlings in each row.

So, Thomas will plant _____ rows of tomato seedlings.

12. **GO DEEPER** There were 20 plants sold at a store on Saturday, and 30 plants sold at the store on Sunday. Customers bought 5 plants each. How many customers in all bought the plants?

_____

13. **THINK SMARTER** Paige walked her dog 15 times in 5 days. She walked him the same number of times each day. How many times did Paige walk her dog each day?

Shade squares to make an array to model the problem.

_____ times

Model with Arrays

COMMON CORE STANDARD—3.OA.A.3
*Represent and solve problems involving
multiplication and division.*

Use square tiles to make an array. Solve.

1. How many rows of 4 are in 12?

_____3 rows_____

2. How many rows of 3 are in 21?

_____

Make an array. Then write a division equation.

3. 20 tiles in 5 rows

_____

4. 28 tiles in 7 rows

_____

 **Problem Solving** Real World

5. A dressmaker has 24 buttons. He needs 3 buttons to make one dress. How many dresses can he make with 24 buttons?

_____

6. Liana buys 36 party favors for her 9 guests. She gives an equal number of favors to each guest. How many party favors does each guest get?

_____

7. **WRITE** ▸*Math* Draw an array to show how to arrange 20 chairs into 5 equal rows. Explain what each part of the array represents.

_____

_____

Lesson Check (3.OA.A.3)

1. Mr. Canton places 24 desks in 6 equal rows. How many desks are in each row?

_____

_____

2. Which division equation is shown by the array?

_____

_____

Spiral Review (3.OA.A.1, 3.OA.A.4, 3.OA.B.5, 3.OA.C.7)

3. Amy has 2 rows of 4 sports trophies on each of her 3 shelves. How many sports trophies does Amy have?

_____

4. What is the unknown factor?

$$9 \times p = 45$$

_____

5. Sam has 7 stacks with 4 quarters each. How many quarters does Sam have?

_____

6. Skip count. How many counters are there in all?

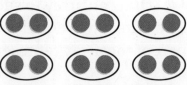

_____

FOR MORE PRACTICE
GO TO THE
Personal Math Trainer

Name _____

Relate Multiplication and Division

Essential Question How can you use multiplication to divide?

 Common Core Operations and Algebraic Thinking—**3.OA.B.6** *Also 3.OA.A.2, 3.OA.A.3, 3.OA.A.4, 3.OA.C.7*
MATHEMATICAL PRACTICES
MP3, MP4, MP5, MP6

 Unlock the Problem Real World

Pam went to the fair. She went on the same ride 6 times and used the same number of tickets each time. She used 18 tickets. How many tickets did she use each time she went on the ride?

- **What do you need to find?**

  _____

  _____

- **Circle the numbers you need to use.**

One Way Use bar models.

You can use bar models to understand how multiplication and division are related.

Complete the bar model to show 18 tickets divided into 6 equal groups.

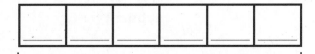

18 tickets

Write: 18 ÷ 6 = _____

So, Pam used _____ tickets each time she went on the ride.

What if the problem said Pam went on the ride 6 times and used 3 tickets each time? How many tickets did Pam use in all?

Complete the bar model to show 6 groups of 3 tickets.

3	3	3	3	3	3

_____ tickets

Write: 6 × 3 = _____

Multiplication and division are opposite operations, or **inverse operations**.

You can think about multiplication to solve a division problem.

To solve 18 ÷ 6 = ■, think 6 × ■ = 18.

Since 6 × 3 = 18, then 18 ÷ 6 = 3.

Math Talk MATHEMATICAL PRACTICES ⑤

Use a Concrete Model What information is given in each of the bar models?

❶ **Another Way** Use an array.

You can use an array to see how multiplication and division are related.

Show an array with 18 counters in 3 equal rows by completing the drawing.

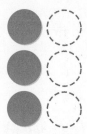

There are _____ counters in each row.

Write: 18 ÷ 3 = _____

The same array can be used to find the total number if you know there are 3 rows with 6 counters in each row.

Write: 3 × 6 = _____

Share and Show **MATH BOARD**

1. Use the array to complete the equation.

Think: There are 3 counters in each row.

6 ÷ 2 = _____

Complete.

2.

3 rows of ____ = 15

3 × ____ = 15

15 ÷ 3 = ____

3.

2 rows of _____ = 12

2 × _____ = 12

12 ÷ 2 = _____

☑ 4.

3 rows of _____ = 21

3 × _____ = 21

21 ÷ 3 = _____

Complete the equations.

5. 5 × ____ = 40   40 ÷ 5 = ____

☑ 6. 6 × ____ = 18   18 ÷ 6 = ____

Name _____

Complete.

7.

5 rows of _____ = 30

5 × _____ = 30

30 ÷ 5 = _____

8.

4 rows of _____ = 20

4 × _____ = 20

20 ÷ 4 = _____

9.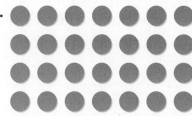

4 rows of _____ = 28

4 × _____ = 28

28 ÷ 4 = _____

Complete the equations.

10. 7 × _____ = 21   21 ÷ 7 = _____

11. 8 × _____ = 16   16 ÷ 8 = _____

MATHEMATICAL PRACTICE ⑥ Attend to Precision Algebra Complete.

12. 3 × 3 = 27 ÷ _____

13. 16 ÷ 2 = _____ × 2

14. 9 = _____ ÷ 4

15. Justin and Ivan went to the fair when all rides were $2 each. They each went on the same number of rides. Each boy spent $10. How many rides did each boy go on?

_____

16. GO DEEPER Roshan has 18 crackers. He shares the crackers equally with his brother. Then Roshan eats 3 crackers. How many crackers does Roshan have left?

_____

17. GO DEEPER Paul is in charge of the egg toss at the World Egg Day fair. There are 48 people participating in teams of 8 people. Each team needs 1 egg. Paul is buying eggs in cartons that each have 6 eggs. How many cartons does Paul need?

_____

Problem Solving • Applications

Use the table for 18–19.

18. Mr. Jerome paid $24 for some students to get into the fair. How many students did Mr. Jerome pay for?

_____

Ventura County Fair	
Price of Admission	
Adults	$6
Students	$3
Children 5 and under free	

19. **THINK SMARTER** Garrett is 8 years old. He and his family are going to the county fair. What is the price of admission for Garrett, his 2 parents, and baby sister?

_____

20. **MATHEMATICAL PRACTICE ④ Use a Diagram** There are 20 seats on the Wildcat ride. The number of seats in each car is the same. If there are 5 cars on the ride, how many seats are in each car? Complete the bar model to show the problem. Then answer the question.

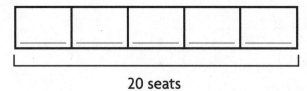

20 seats

_____

_____

21. **GO DEEPER** How many days are there in 2 weeks? Write and solve a related word problem to represent the inverse operation.

_____

_____

22. **THINK SMARTER** There are 35 prizes in 5 equal rows. How many prizes are in each row?

Complete each equation to represent the problem.

5 × _____ = 35   35 ÷ 5 = _____

_____ prizes

Relate Multiplication and Division

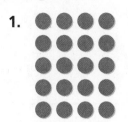

COMMON CORE STANDARD—3.OA.B.6
Understand properties of multiplication and the relationship between multiplication and division.

Complete.

1. 5 rows of __4__ = 20

   5 × __4__ = 20

   20 ÷ 5 = __4__

2. 4 rows of _____ = 24

   4 × _____ = 24

   24 ÷ 4 = _____

3. 3 rows of _____ = 24

   3 × _____ = 24

   24 ÷ 3 = _____

Complete the equations.

4. 4 × _____ = 28   28 ÷ 4 = _____

5. 6 × _____ = 36   36 ÷ 6 = _____

6. 4 × _____ = 36   36 ÷ 4 = _____

7. 8 × _____ = 40   40 ÷ 8 = _____

Problem Solving

8. Mr. Martin buys 36 muffins for a class breakfast. He places them on plates for his students. If he places 9 muffins on each plate, how many plates does Mr. Martin use?

9. Ralph read 18 books during his summer vacation. He read the same number of books each month for 3 months. How many books did he read each month?

_____

_____

10. **WRITE** ▸*Math* Use examples to show that multiplication and division are inverse operations.

_____

_____

Lesson Check (3.OA.B.6)

1. What number will complete the equations?

$$6 \times \blacksquare = 24$$

$$24 \div 6 = \blacksquare$$

_____

2. Alice has 14 seashells. She divides them equally between her 2 sisters. How many seashells does each sister get?

_____

Spiral Review (3.OA.A.1, 3.OA.B.5, 3.MD.B.3)

3. Sam and Jesse can wash 5 cars each hour. They work for 7 hours each day over 2 days. How many cars did Sam and Jesse wash?

_____

4. Keisha skip counted to find how many counters in all. How many equal groups are there?

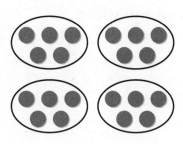

_____ groups of 5

5. The key for a picture graph showing the number of books students read is: Each 📖 = 2 books. How many books did Nancy read if she has 📖📖📖 by her name?

_____

6. Jan surveyed her friends to find their favorite season. She recorded 𝍸𝍷 |||| for summer. How many people chose summer as their favorite season?

_____

FOR MORE PRACTICE
GO TO THE
Personal Math Trainer

Write Related Facts

Essential Question How can you write a set of related multiplication and division facts?

Common Core **Operations and Algebraic Thinking—**
3.OA.C.7 *Also 3.OA.A.2, 3.OA.A.3*
MATHEMATICAL PRACTICES
MP3, MP6, MP7

Unlock the Problem

Related facts are a set of related multiplication and division equations. What related facts can you write for 2, 4, and 8?

- What model can you use to show how multiplication and division are related?

_____

 Activity

Materials ■ square tiles

STEP 1

Use 8 tiles to make an array with 2 equal rows.

Draw the rest of the tiles.

How many tiles are in each row? _____

Write a division equation for the array using the total number of tiles as the dividend and the number of rows as the divisor.

_____ ÷ _____ = _____

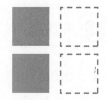

Write a multiplication equation for the array.

_____ × _____ = _____

STEP 2

Now, use 8 tiles to make an array with 4 equal rows.

Draw the rest of the tiles.

How many tiles are in each row? _____

Write a division equation for the array using the total number of tiles as the dividend and the number of rows as the divisor.

_____ ÷ _____ = _____

Write a multiplication equation for the array.

_____ × _____ = _____

So, $8 ÷ 2 =$ _____, $2 × 4 =$ _____, $8 ÷ 4 =$ _____,

and $4 × 2 =$ _____ are related facts.

Try This! **Draw an array with 4 rows of 4 tiles.**

Your array shows the related facts for 4, 4, and 16.

$4 \times 4 =$ _____ $16 \div 4 =$ _____

Since both factors are the same, there are only two equations in this set of related facts.

• **Attend to Precision** Write another set of related facts that has only two equations.

_____

Share and Show

Math Talk MATHEMATICAL PRACTICES 7

Identify Relationships Look at the multiplication and division equations in a set of related facts. What do you notice about the products and dividends?

1. Complete the related facts for this array.

$2 \times 8 = 16$ $16 \div 2 = 8$

_____   _____

Write the related facts for the array.

2.

_____

_____

_____

 3.

_____

_____

_____

 4.

_____

_____

_____

5. Why do the related facts for the array in Exercise 2 have only two equations?

_____

Name _____

Write the related facts for the array.

6.

_____

_____

_____

_____

7.

_____

_____

_____

8.

_____

_____

_____

Write the related facts for the set of numbers.

9. 2, 5, 10

_____

_____

_____

10. 3, 8, 24

_____

_____

_____

11. 6, 6, 36

_____

_____

_____

Complete the related facts.

12. $4 \times 7 =$ _____

$7 \times$ _____ $= 28$

$28 \div$ _____ $= 4$

$28 \div 4 =$ _____

13. $5 \times$ _____ $= 30$

$6 \times$ _____ $= 30$

$30 \div 6 =$ _____

$30 \div 5 =$ _____

14. _____ $\times 9 = 27$

_____ $\times 3 = 27$

_____ $\div 9 = 3$

$27 \div$ _____ $= 9$

15. Write a set of related facts that has only two equations. Draw an array to show the facts.

_____

16.  Maria has an array with 4 rows of 5 tiles. She wants an array that shows the related facts for 5, 5, and 25. What can she do to change her array?

_____

Problem Solving · Applications

Use the table for 17–18.

17. **MATHEMATICAL PRACTICE ③** **Verify the Reasoning of Others** Ty has a package of glitter dough. He says he can give each of 9 friends 5 equal sections. Describe his error.

_____

_____

_____

_____

Clay Supplies	
Item	**Number in Package**
Clay	12 sections
Clay tool set	11 tools
Glitter dough	36 sections

WRITE ▸ *Math*
Show Your Work

18. **THINK SMARTER** Mr. Lee divides 1 package of clay and 1 package of glitter dough equally among 4 students. How many more glitter dough sections than clay sections does each student get?

_____

19. **GO DEEPER** Ms. Cohn divides 21 markers equally among 7 students. Write an equation to show how many markers each student gets. Then write a related fact.

_____

_____

20. **THINK SMARTER** Select the equations that the array represents. Mark all that apply.

(A) $2 \times 10 = 20$ (D) $20 \div 2 = 10$

(B) $20 \div 4 = 5$ (E) $4 \times 5 = 20$

(C) $5 \times 4 = 20$ (F) $20 \div 5 = 4$

Write Related Facts

Common Core **COMMON CORE STANDARD—3.OA.C.7**
Multiply and divide within 100.

Write the related facts for the array.

1.

$2 \times 6 = 12$

$6 \times 2 = 12$

$12 \div 2 = 6$

$12 \div 6 = 2$

2.

_____

_____

_____

_____

3.

_____

_____

_____

_____

Write the related facts for the set of numbers.

4. 3, 7, 21

_____

_____

_____

_____

5. 2, 9, 18

_____

_____

_____

_____

6. 4, 8, 32

_____

_____

_____

_____

Problem Solving • Real World

7. CDs are on sale for $5 each. Jennifer has $45 and wants to buy as many as she can. How many CDs can Jennifer buy?

_____

8. Mr. Moore has 21 feet of wallpaper. He cuts it into sections that are each 3 feet long. How many sections does Mr. Moore have?

_____

9. **WRITE** ▸*Math* Write a division fact. Write the rest of the related facts.

_____

_____

Lesson Check (3.OA.C.7)

1. What number completes the set of related facts?

$5 \times \blacksquare = 40$ $40 \div \blacksquare = 5$

$\blacksquare \times 5 = 40$ $40 \div 5 = \blacksquare$

_____

_____

2. Write the related facts for the set of numbers.

4, 7, 28

_____

_____

Spiral Review (3.OA.A.1, 3.OA.B.5, 3.OA.C.7, 3.NBT.A.3)

3. Beth runs 20 miles each week for 8 weeks. How many miles does Beth run in 8 weeks?

_____

4. Find the product.

5×0

_____

5. Uri's bookcase has 5 shelves. There are 9 books on each shelf. How many books are in Uri's bookcase?

_____

6. There are 6 batteries in one package. How many batteries will 6 packages have?

_____

FOR MORE PRACTICE GO TO THE **Personal Math Trainer**

Name _____

Division Rules for 1 and 0

Essential Question What are the rules for dividing with 1 and 0?

 Common Core **Operations and Algebraic Thinking—**
3.OA.B.5 *Also 3.OA.A.2, 3.OA.A.3, 3.OA.C.7*
MATHEMATICAL PRACTICES
MP6, MP7, MP8

Unlock the Problem

What rules for division can help you divide with 1 and 0?

If there is only 1 fishbowl, then all the fish must go in that fishbowl.

$$4 \div 1 = 4$$

number of fish   number of bowls   number in each bowl

Rule A: Any number divided by 1 equals that number.

Try This! There are 3 fish and 1 fishbowl. Draw a quick picture to show the fish in the fishbowl.

Write the equation your picture shows.

_____ ÷ _____ = _____

Math Talk   MATHEMATICAL PRACTICES ⑦

Identify Relationships Explain how Rule A is related to the Identity Property of Multiplication.

If there is the same number of fish and fishbowls, then 1 fish goes in each fishbowl.

$$4 \div 4 = 1$$

number of fish   number of bowls   number in each bowl

Rule B: Any number (except 0) divided by itself equals 1.

Try This! There are 3 fish and 3 fishbowls. Draw a quick picture to show the fish divided equally among the fishbowls.

Write the equation your picture shows.

_____ ÷ _____ = _____

If there are 0 fish and 4 fishbowls, there will not be any fish in the fishbowls.

0	÷	4	=	0
↑		↑		↑
number of fish		number of bowls		number in each bowl

Rule C: Zero divided by any number (except 0) equals 0.

Try This! There are 0 fish and 3 fishbowls. Draw a quick picture to show the fishbowls.

Write the equation your picture shows.

_____ ÷ _____ = _____

If there are 0 fishbowls, then you cannot separate the fish equally into fishbowls. Dividing by 0 is not possible.

Rule D: You cannot divide by 0.

Share and Show MATH BOARD

1. Use the picture to find 2 ÷ 2. _____

Math Talk MATHEMATICAL PRACTICES ⑧

Generalize What happens when you divide a number (except 0) by itself?

Find the quotient.

2. $7 \div 1 =$ _____   3. $8 \div 8 =$ _____   ✓4. $0 \div 5 =$ _____   ✓5. _____ $= 6 \div 6$

Name _____

Find the quotient.

6. $0 \div 8 =$ _____

7. $5 \div 5 =$ _____

8. $2 \div 1 =$ _____

9. $0 \div 7 =$ _____

10. $5\overline{)0}$

11. $1\overline{)9}$

12. $7\overline{)7}$

13. $10\overline{)10}$

Practice: Copy and Solve **Find the quotient.**

14. $6 \div 1$

15. $25 \div 5$

16. $0 \div 6$

17. $18 \div 3$

18. $14 \div 2$

19. $9 \div 9$

20. $28 \div 4$

21. $8 \div 1$

22. $3\overline{)27}$

23. $5\overline{)10}$

24. $3\overline{)0}$

25. $1\overline{)0}$

Problem Solving • Applications

26. THINK SMARTER Claire has 7 parakeets. She puts 4 of them in a cage. She divides the other parakeets equally among 3 friends to hold. How many parakeets does each friend get to hold?

_____

27. GO DEEPER Lena has 5 parrots. She gives each parrot 1 grape in the morning and 1 grape in the evening. How many grapes does she give to her parrots each day?

_____

28. MATHEMATICAL PRACTICE ⑥ Suppose a pet store has 21 birds that are in 21 cages. Use what you know about division rules to find the number of birds in each cage. **Explain** your answer.

_____

_____

29. $\boxed{\text{THINK SMARTER}}$ For numbers 29a–29c, select True or False for each equation.

29a. $4 \div 4 = 1$ 　　　　　　　◯ True 　　　◯ False

29b. $6 \div 1 = 1$ 　　　　　　　◯ True 　　　◯ False

29c. $1 \div 5 = 1$ 　　　　　　　◯ True 　　　◯ False

Connect to Reading

Compare and Contrast

You have learned the rules for division with 1. Compare and contrast them to help you learn how to use the rules to solve problems.

Compare the rules. Think about how they are *alike*.

Contrast the rules. Think about how they are *different*.

Read:　　Rule A: Any number divided by 1 equals that number.

　　　　　Rule B: Any number (except 0) divided by itself equals 1.

Compare:　How are the rules alike?

　　　　　• Both are division rules for 1.

Contrast:　How are the rules different?

　　　　　• Rule A is about dividing a number by 1.
　　　　　　The quotient is that number.

　　　　　• Rule B is about dividing a number (except 0) by itself.
　　　　　　The quotient is always 1.

Read the problem. Write an equation. Solve.
Write *Rule A* or *Rule B* to tell which rule you used.

30. Jamal bought 7 goldfish at the pet store. He put them in 1 fishbowl. How many goldfish did he put in the fishbowl?

_____

31. Ava has 6 turtles. She divides them equally among 6 aquariums. How many turtles does she put in each aquarium?

_____

Division Rules for 1 and 0

Common Core
COMMON CORE STANDARD—3.OA.B.5
Understand properties of multiplication and the relationship between multiplication and division.

Find the quotient.

1. $3 \div 1 =$ __3__   **2.** $8 \div 8 =$ _____   **3.** _____ $= 0 \div 6$ **4.** $2 \div 2 =$ _____

5. _____ $= 9 \div 1$ **6.** $0 \div 2 =$ _____   **7.** $0 \div 3 =$ _____   **8.** _____ $= 0 \div 4$

9. $7\overline{)7}$ **10.** $1\overline{)6}$ **11.** $9\overline{)0}$ **12.** $1\overline{)5}$

13. $1\overline{)0}$ **14.** $4\overline{)4}$ **15.** $1\overline{)10}$ **16.** $2\overline{)2}$

Problem Solving · Real World

17. There are no horses in the stables. There are 3 stables in all. How many horses are in each stable?

_____

18. Jon has 6 kites. He and his friends will each fly 1 kite. How many people in all will fly a kite?

_____

19. **WRITE** *Math* Compare and contrast the multiplication rules for 1 and 0 with the division rules for 1 and 0.

_____

_____

Lesson Check (3.OA.B.5)

1. Candace has 6 pairs of jeans. She places each pair on its own hanger. How many hangers does Candace use?

_____

2. There are 0 birds and 4 bird cages. What division equation describes how many birds are in each cage?

_____

Spiral Review (3.OA.B.5, 3.MD.B.3)

3. There are 7 plates on the table. There are 0 sandwiches on each plate. How many sandwiches are on the plates?

$$7 \times 0$$

_____

_____

_____

4. Write one way to break apart the array to find the product.

_____

_____

_____

5. Describe a pattern in the table.

Vans	1	2	3	4	5
Students	6	12	18	24	30

_____

_____

6. Use the graph.

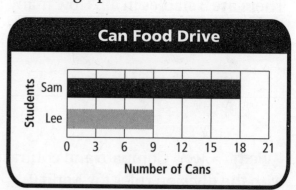

How many more cans did Sam bring in than Lee?

_____

_____

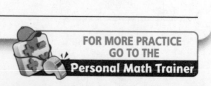

FOR MORE PRACTICE
GO TO THE
Personal Math Trainer

Name _____

Personal Math Trainer
Online Assessment
and Intervention

1. For numbers 1a–1d, select True or False for each equation.

    1a. $3 \div 1 = 1$ ○ True   ○ False

    1b. $0 \div 4 = 0$ ○ True   ○ False

    1c. $7 \div 7 = 1$ ○ True   ○ False

    1d. $6 \div 1 = 6$ ○ True   ○ False

2. Elizabeth has 12 horses on her farm. She puts an equal number of horses in each of 3 pens. How many horses are in each pen?

   Circle a number that makes the sentence true.

   There are
| 4 |
| 9 |
| 36 |
horses in each pen.

3. Chris plants 25 pumpkin seeds in 5 equal rows. How many seeds does Chris plant in each row?

   Make an array to represent the problem. Then solve the problem.

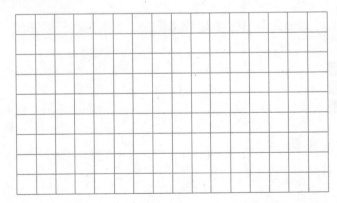

                                   _____ seeds

GO DIGITAL   Assessment Options
Chapter Test

4. Becca spent 24 minutes walking around a track. It took her 3 minutes to walk each time around the track. How many times did Becca walk around the track?

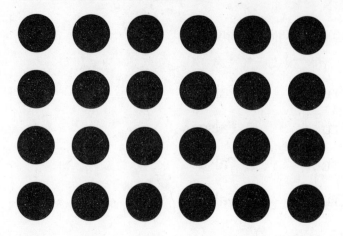

Make equal groups to model the problem. Then explain how you solved the problem.

_____

_____

5. There are 7 cars in an amusement park ride. There are 42 people in the cars. An equal number of people ride in each car. How many people ride in one car?

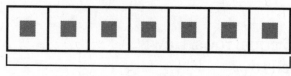

42 people

_____ people

6. Select the equations that the array represents. Mark all that apply.

Ⓐ $3 \times 5 = \blacksquare$

Ⓓ $5 \times \blacksquare = 15$

Ⓑ $2 \times \blacksquare = 12$

Ⓔ $12 \div 3 = \blacksquare$

Ⓒ $\blacksquare \div 3 = 5$

Ⓕ $15 \div 5 = \blacksquare$

Name _____

7. **GO DEEPER** Eduardo visited his cousin for 28 days over the summer. There are 7 days in each week. How long, in weeks, was Eduardo's visit?

Part A
Draw jumps on the number line to model the problem.

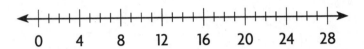

Part B
Write a division equation to represent the model.

_____

_____ weeks

8. A workbook is 64 pages long. If each chapter is 8 pages long, how many chapters are there?

_____ chapters

9. There are 56 apples packed in 7 baskets with the same number of apples in each basket. How many apples are in each basket?

For numbers 9a–9d, choose Yes or No to tell whether the equation represents the problem.

9a. $56 + 7 = \blacksquare$ ○ Yes   ○ No

9b. $7 \times \blacksquare = 56$ ○ Yes   ○ No

9c. $56 \div \blacksquare = 8$ ○ Yes   ○ No

9d. $56 - \blacksquare = 8$ ○ Yes   ○ No

10. Stefan has 24 photos to display on some posters. Select a way that he could display all of the photos in equal groups on the posters. Mark all that apply.

Ⓐ   6 photos on each of 4 posters   Ⓓ   5 photos on each of 5 posters

Ⓑ   7 photos on each of 3 posters   Ⓔ   3 photos on each of 8 posters

Ⓒ   4 photos on each of 6 posters   Ⓕ   7 photos on each of 4 posters

11. Debbie made this array to model a division equation. Which equation could Debbie have modeled? Mark all that apply.

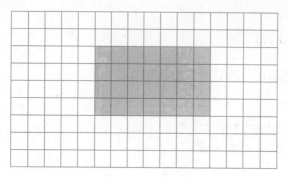

- (A) $14 \div 7 = 2$
- (B) $28 \div 4 = 7$
- (C) $28 \div 7 = 4$
- (D) $14 \div 2 = 7$

12. Mrs. Edwards knitted some gloves. Each glove had 5 fingers. She knitted a total of 40 fingers. How many gloves did Mrs. Edwards knit?

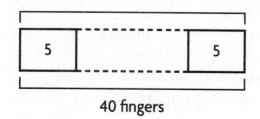

40 fingers

_____ gloves

13. Select a number to complete each equation.

| 0 | 1 | 7 |

$7 \div 7 =$ _____ $7 \div 1 =$ _____ $0 \div 7 =$ _____

14. The coach separated the 18 players at lacrosse practice into 3 equal groups. How many players were in each group?

_____ players

Name _____

15. Write a division equation to represent the repeated subtraction.

$$
\begin{array}{c c c c}
32 & 24 & 16 & 8 \\
-\ 8 & -\ 8 & -\ 8 & -\ 8 \\
\hline
24 & 16 & 8 & 0 \\
\end{array}
$$

_____

16. Write related facts for the array. Explain why there are not more related facts.

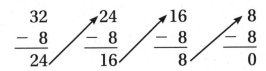

_____

_____

Personal Math Trainer

17. [THINK SMARTER ✚] Darius bakes 18 muffins for his friends. He gives each of his friends an equal number of muffins and has none left over.

Part A

Draw a picture to show how Darius divided the muffins and complete the sentence.

Darius gave muffins to _____

_____ friends.

Part B

Could Darius have given 4 of his friends an equal number of muffins and have none left over? Explain why or why not.

_____

_____

18. Circle numbers to complete the related facts.

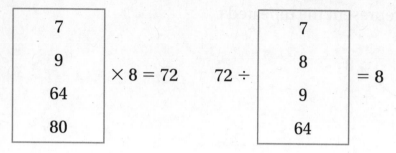

7			7	
9	$\times 8 = 72$	$72 \div$	8	$= 8$
64			9	
80			64	

19. Use the numbers to write related multiplication and division facts.

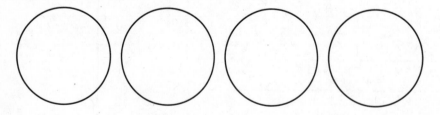

9   45   5

_____

_____

20. Tyrone took 16 pennies from his bank and put them in 4 equal stacks. How many pennies did Tyrone put in each stack? Show your work.

◯   ◯   ◯   ◯

_____ pennies

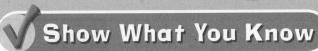

Show What You Know

Personal Math Trainer
Online Assessment
and Intervention

Check your understanding of important skills.

Name _____

▶ **Think Addition to Subtract** Write the missing numbers. (1.OA.B.4)

1. $10 - 3 = \blacksquare$

Think: $3 + \blacksquare = 10$

$3 + \underline{\quad} = 10$

So, $10 - 3 = \underline{\quad}$.

2. $12 - 8 = \blacksquare$

Think: $8 + \blacksquare = 12$

$8 + \underline{\quad} = 12$

So, $12 - 8 = \underline{\quad}$.

▶ **Missing Factors** Write the missing factor. (3.OA.A.4)

3. $2 \times \underline{\quad} = 10$

4. $42 = \underline{\quad} \times 7$

5. $\underline{\quad} \times 6 = 18$

▶ **Multiplication Facts Through 9** Find the product. (3.OA.C.7)

6. $\underline{\quad} = 6 \times 9$

7. $3 \times 8 = \underline{\quad}$

8. $4 \times 4 = \underline{\quad}$

Math in the Real World

On Monday, the students in Mr. Carson's class worked in
pairs. On Tuesday, the students worked in groups of 3.
On Wednesday, the students worked in groups of 4.
Each day the students made equal groups with no
student left out of a group. How many students could
be in Mr. Carson's class?

▶ **Visualize It** •••••••••••••••••••••••••••••••••••

Sort the review words into the Venn diagram.

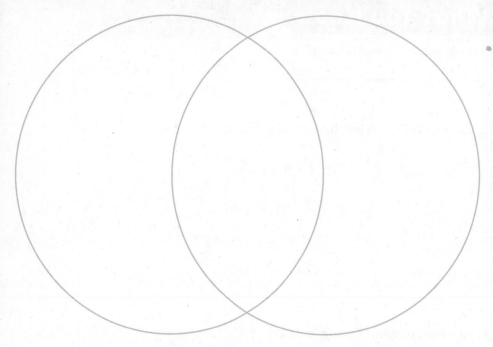

Multiplication Words   **Division Words**

Review Words

divide

dividend

divisor

equation

factor

inverse operations

multiply

product

quotient

related facts

Preview Words

order of operations

▶ **Understand Vocabulary** ••••••••••••••••••••••••••

Complete the sentences by using the review and preview words.

1. An _____ is a number sentence that uses the equal sign to show that two amounts are equal.

2. The _____ is a special set of rules that gives the order in which calculations are done to solve a problem.

3. _____ are a set of related multiplication and division equations.

GO DIGITAL
• **Interactive Student Edition**
• **Multimedia eGlossary**

Chapter 7 Vocabulary

dividend

dividendo

15

divisor

divisor

16

equation

ecuación

22

inverse operations

operaciones inversas

37

order of operations

orden de las
operaciones

55

product

producto

65

quotient

cociente

67

related facts

operaciones
relacionadas

70

The number that divides the dividend

Examples: $32 \div 4 = 8$ $4\overline{)32}\,^{8}$

↑ divisor   ↑ divisor

The number that is to be divided in a division problem

Examples: $32 \div 4 = 8$ $4\overline{)32}\,^{8}$

↑ dividend   ↑ dividend

Opposite operations, or operations that undo one another, such as addition and subtraction or multiplication and division

Examples: $16 + 8 = 24$; $24 - 8 = 16$
$4 \times 3 = 12$; $12 \div 4 = 3$

A number sentence that uses the equal sign to show that two amounts are equal

Example: $9 \times 2 = 18$ is an equation

The answer in a multiplication problem

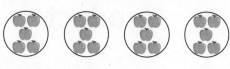

Example: $4 \times 5 = 20$

↑ product

A special set of rules that gives the order in which calculations are done

A set of related addition and subtraction, or multiplication and division, number sentences

Examples: $4 \times 7 = 28$ $28 \div 4 = 7$
$7 \times 4 = 28$ $28 \div 7 = 4$

The number, not including the remainder, that results from division

Example: $35 \div 7 = 5$

↑ quotient

Game

Matchup

For 2–3 players

Materials

- 1 set of word cards

How to Play

1. Put the cards face-down in rows. Take turns to play.

2. Choose two cards and turn them face-up.

   - If the cards show a word and its meaning. it's a match. Keep the pair and take another turn.

   - If the cards do not match, turn them back over.

3. The game is over when all cards have been matched. The players count their pairs. The player with the most pairs wins.

The Write Way

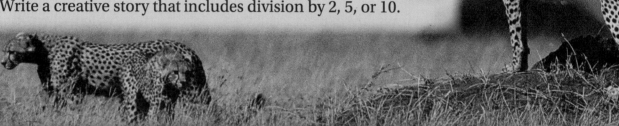

Reflect

Choose one idea. Write about it.

- Do 16 ÷ 8 and 8 ÷ 16 have the same quotient? Explain why or why not.
- Explain the Order of Operations in your own words.
- Write a creative story that includes division by 2, 5, or 10.

Divide by 2

Essential Question What does dividing by 2 mean?

Common Core **Operations and Algebraic Thinking—**
3.OA.A.3 Also 3.OA.A.2, 3.OA.C.7
MATHEMATICAL PRACTICES
MP1, MP2, MP6

Unlock the Problem

There are 10 hummingbirds and 2 feeders in Marissa's backyard. If there are an equal number of birds at each feeder, how many birds are at each one?

- What do you need to find?

_____

- Circle the numbers you need to use.
- What can you use to help solve the

problem? _____

Activity 1

Use counters to find how many in each group.

Materials ■ counters ■ MathBoard

MODEL

- Use 10 counters.
- Draw 2 circles on your MathBoard.
- Place 1 counter at a time in each circle until all 10 counters are used.
- Draw the rest of the counters to show your work.

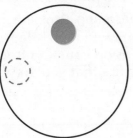 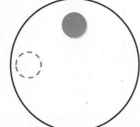

THINK

_____ in all

_____ equal groups

_____ in each group

RECORD

$10 \div 2 = 5$ or $2\overline{)10}^{\,5}$

Read: Ten divided by two equals five.

There are ____ counters in each of the 2 groups.

So, there are ____ hummingbirds at each feeder.

A hummingbird can fly right, left, up, down, ▶ forward, backward, and even upside down!

Math Talk

MATHEMATICAL PRACTICES ❶

Analyze What does each number in $10 \div 2 = 5$ represent from the word problem?

🔒 Activity 2 Draw to find how many equal groups.

There are 10 hummingbirds in Tyler's backyard. If there are 2 hummingbirds at each feeder, how many feeders are there?

MODEL

- Look at the 10 counters.
- Circle a group of 2 counters.
- Continue circling groups of 2 until all 10 counters are in groups.

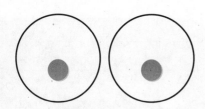

THINK

_____ in all

_____ in each group

_____ equal groups

RECORD

$$10 \div 2 = 5 \text{ or } 2\overline{)10}^{\,5}$$

Read: Ten divided by two equals five.

There are _____ groups of 2 counters.

So, there are _____ feeders.

Share and Show MATH BOARD

1. Complete the picture to find $6 \div 2$. _____

Math Talk MATHEMATICAL PRACTICES ②

Use Reasoning Explain why you can write more than one division equation from the picture that you drew.

Write a division equation for the picture.

2.

✓3.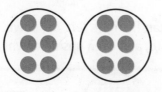

✓4.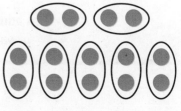

_____   _____   _____

366

Name _____

Write a division equation for the picture.

5.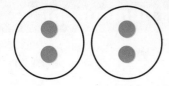

_____

6.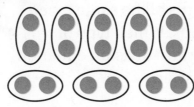

_____

7.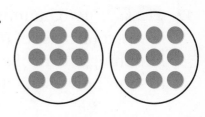

_____

Find the quotient. You may want to draw a quick picture to help.

8. $2 \div 2 =$ _____

9. $16 \div 2 =$ _____

10. $2\overline{)20}$

MATHEMATICAL PRACTICE ② **Reason Abstractly Algebra Find the unknown number.**

11. _____ $\div 2 = 5$

12. _____ $\div 2 = 2$

13. _____ $\div 2 = 3$

14. _____ $\div 2 = 8$

15. Lin makes a tile design with 16 tiles. Half of the tiles are red, and half of the tiles are blue. He takes away 4 red tiles. How many red tiles are in the design now?

_____

16. Go DEEPER Becky made 2 video tapes while a giant hummingbird fed 4 times and a ruby throated hummingbird fed 8 times from her new feeder. Each video tape caught the same number of feedings by the hummingbirds. How many feedings were shown on each video tape? Justify your answer.

_____

_____

Problem Solving • Applications (Real World)

Use the table for 17–18.

17. Go DEEPER Two hummingbirds of the same type have a total mass of 10 grams. Which type of hummingbird are they? Write a division equation to show how to find the answer.

_____

Hummingbirds	
Type	**Mass (in grams)**
Magnificent	7
Ruby-throated	3
Violet-crowned	5

18. THINK SMARTER There are 3 ruby-throated hummingbirds and 2 of another type of hummingbird at a feeder. The birds have a mass of 23 grams in all. What other type of hummingbird is at the feeder? **Explain.**

WRITE Math • **Show Your Work**

_____

_____

_____

_____

19. THINK SMARTER Ryan has 18 socks.

Divisor	Quotient
○ 1	○ 1
○ 2	○ 3
○ 6	○ 9
○ 18	○ 18

Select one number from each column to show the division equation represented by the picture.

$$18 \div \frac{?}{\text{(divisor)}} = \frac{?}{\text{(quotient)}}$$

Divide by 2

Common Core   **COMMON CORE STANDARD—3.OA.A.3**
*Represent and solve problems involving
multiplication and division.*

Write a division equation for the picture.

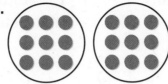

1.

$12 \div 2 = 6$ or _____

$12 \div 6 = 2$

2. _____

_____

3. _____

_____

**Find the quotient. You may want to draw a quick picture
to help.**

4. _____ $= 14 \div 2$

5.

6. $16 \div 2 =$ _____

Problem Solving *Real World*

7. Mr. Reynolds, the gym teacher,
divided a class of 16 students into
2 equal teams. How many students
were on each team?

_____

8. Sandra has 10 books. She divides
them into groups of 2 each. How
many groups can she make?

_____

9. **WRITE** *Math* Explain how to divide an amount by 2. Use the terms *dividend,
divisor,* and *quotient.*

_____

_____

Lesson Check (3.OA.A.3)

1. Ava has 12 apples and 2 baskets. She puts an equal number of apples in each basket. How many apples are in a basket?

_____

2. There are 8 students singing a song in the school musical. Ms. Lang put the students in 2 equal rows. How many students are in each row?

_____

Spiral Review (3.OA.A.2, 3.OA.A.3, 3.OA.D.9)

3. Find the product.

$$2 \times 6$$

_____

4. Jayden plants 24 trees. He plants the trees in 3 equal rows. How many trees are in each row?

_____

5. Describe a pattern in the numbers.

9, 12, 15, 18, 21, 24

_____

6. A tricycle has 3 wheels. How many wheels are there on 4 tricycles?

_____

FOR MORE PRACTICE
GO TO THE
Personal Math Trainer

Name _____

Divide by 10

Essential Question What strategies can you use to divide by 10?

 Common Core **Operations and Algebraic Thinking—3.OA.C.7** *Also 3.OA.A.2, 3.OA.A.3, 3.OA.A.4, 3.OA.B.6*

MATHEMATICAL PRACTICES
MP2, MP3, MP6

Unlock the Problem

There are 50 students going on a field trip to the Philadelphia Zoo. The students are separated into equal groups of 10 students each. How many groups of students are there?

- What do you need to find?

_____

- Circle the numbers you need to use.

One Way Use repeated subtraction.

- Start with 50.
- Subtract 10 until you reach 0.
- Count the number of times you subtract 10.

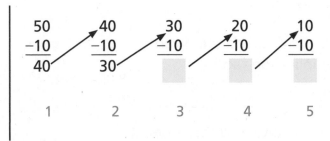

You subtracted 10 five times. $50 \div 10 =$ _____

So, there are _____ groups of 10 students.

Other Ways

A Use a number line.

- Start at 50 and count back by 10s until you reach 0.
- Count the number of times you jumped back 10.

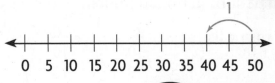

You jumped back by 10 five times.

$50 \div 10 =$ _____

 Math Talk MATHEMATICAL PRACTICES ③

Compare Representations How is counting on a number line to divide by 10 different from counting on a number line to multiply by 10?

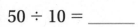

Chapter 7 **371**

B **Use a multiplication table.**

Divide. $50 \div 10 =$ ▨

Since division is the opposite of multiplication, you can use a multiplication table to find a quotient.

Think of a related multiplication fact.

▨ $\times 10 = 50$

STEP 1 Find the factor, 10, in the top row.

STEP 2 Look down to find the product, 50.

STEP 3 Look left to find the unknown

factor, _____.

Since _____ $\times 10 = 50$, then $50 \div 10 =$ _____.

In Step 1, is the divisor or the dividend the given factor in the related multiplication fact?

_____

In Step 2, is the divisor or the dividend the product in the related multiplication fact?

_____

The quotient is the unknown factor.

✕	0	1	2	3	4	5	6	7	8	9	10
0	0	0	0	0	0	0	0	0	0	0	0
1	0	1	2	3	4	5	6	7	8	9	10
2	0	2	4	6	8	10	12	14	16	18	20
3	0	3	6	9	12	15	18	21	24	27	30
4	0	4	8	12	16	20	24	28	32	36	40
5	0	5	10	15	20	25	30	35	40	45	50
6	0	6	12	18	24	30	36	42	48	54	60
7	0	7	14	21	28	35	42	49	56	63	70
8	0	8	16	24	32	40	48	56	64	72	80
9	0	9	18	27	36	45	54	63	72	81	90
10	0	10	20	30	40	50	60	70	80	90	100

Share and Show MATH BOARD

Math Talk MATHEMATICAL PRACTICES ③

Compare Strategies What are some other strategies besides repeated subtraction to solve $30 \div 10$?

1. Use repeated subtraction to find $30 \div 10$. _____

Think: How many times do you subtract 10?

$$\begin{array}{r} 30 \\ -10 \\ \hline 20 \end{array} \qquad \begin{array}{r} 20 \\ -10 \\ \hline 10 \end{array} \qquad \begin{array}{r} 10 \\ -10 \\ \hline \end{array}$$

Find the unknown factor and quotient.

2. $10 \times$ ____ $= 40$ ____ $= 40 \div 10$

☑ 3. $10 \times$ ____ $= 60$ $60 \div 10 =$ ____

Find the quotient.

4. ____ $= 20 \div 10$

5. $10\overline{)50}$

6. $10\overline{)70}$

☑ 7. $90 \div 10 =$ ____

On Your Own

Find the unknown factor and quotient.

8. $10 \times$ ___ $= 70$ $70 \div 10 =$ ___

9. $10 \times$ ___ $= 10$ $10 \div 10 =$ ___

Find the quotient.

10. $50 \div 10 =$ ___

11. ___ $= 60 \div 10$

12. $10\overline{)40}$

13. $10\overline{)80}$

MATHEMATICAL PRACTICE ② Reason Quantitatively **Algebra** Write $<$, $>$, or $=$.

14. $10 \div 1 \bigcirc 4 \times 10$

15. $17 - 6 \bigcirc 18 \div 2$

16. $4 \times 4 \bigcirc 8 + 8$

17. $23 + 14 \bigcirc 5 \times 8$

18. $70 \div 10 \bigcirc 23 - 16$

19. $9 \times 0 \bigcirc 9 + 0$

20. **GO DEEPER** There are 70 pieces of chalk in a box. If each of 10 students gets an equal number of chalk pieces, how many pieces of chalk does each student get?

_____

21. **GO DEEPER** Elijah wrote his name in 15 school shirts. Cora wrote her name in 15 school shirts. Together they labeled 10 shirts each day. On how many days did Elijah and Cora label shirts?

_____

22. **GO DEEPER** Peyton has 32 cubes. Myra has 18 cubes. If both students use all of the cubes to make trains with 10 cubes, how many trains can they make?

_____

Problem Solving • Applications

Use the picture graph for 23–25.

Animal Stickers

Elephants				
Giraffes			
Monkeys				

Key: Each ☐ = 10 stickers.

23. Lyle wants to add penguins to the picture graph. There are 30 stickers of penguins. How many symbols should Lyle draw for penguins?

_____

24. _GO DEEPER_ Write a word problem using information from the picture graph. Then solve your problem.

_____

_____

25. _THINK SMARTER_ **Sense or Nonsense?** Lena wants to put the monkey stickers in an album. She says she will use more pages if she puts 5 stickers on a page instead of 10 stickers on a page. Is she correct? Explain.

_____

_____

_____

WRITE ▸ _Math_ • **Show Your Work**

26. _MATHEMATICAL PRACTICE ⑥_ **Explain** how a division problem is like an unknown factor problem.

_____

_____

_____

27. _THINK SMARTER_ Lilly found 40 seashells. She put 10 seashells in each bucket. How many buckets did Lilly use? Show your work.

_____ buckets

Divide by 10

Common
Core

COMMON CORE STANDARD—3.OA.C.7
Multiply and divide within 100.

Find the unknown factor and quotient.

1. $10 \times \underline{\textbf{2}} = 20$ $20 \div 10 = \underline{\textbf{2}}$

2. $10 \times \underline{\hspace{1cm}} = 70$ $70 \div 10 = \underline{\hspace{1cm}}$

3. $10 \times \underline{\hspace{1cm}} = 80$ $80 \div 10 = \underline{\hspace{1cm}}$

4. $10 \times \underline{\hspace{1cm}} = 30$ $30 \div 10 = \underline{\hspace{1cm}}$

Find the quotient.

5. $60 \div 10 = \underline{\hspace{1cm}}$

6. $\underline{\hspace{1cm}} = 40 \div 4$

7. $20 \div 2 = \underline{\hspace{1cm}}$

8. $50 \div 10 = \underline{\hspace{1cm}}$

9. $10\overline{)40}$

10. $10\overline{)70}$

11. $10\overline{)100}$

12. $10\overline{)20}$

Problem Solving Real World

13. Pencils cost 10¢ each. How many pencils can Brent buy with 90¢?

14. Mrs. Marks wants to buy 80 pens. If the pens come in packs of 10, how many packs does she need to buy?

_____

_____

15. **WRITE** ▸*Math* Write and solve a word problem that involves dividing by 10.

_____

_____

Lesson Check (3.OA.C.7)

1. Gracie uses 10 beads on each necklace she makes. She has 60 beads to use. How many necklaces can Gracie make?

2. A florist arranges 10 flowers in each vase. How many vases does the florist need to arrange 40 flowers?

Spiral Review (3.OA.A.2, 3.OA.A.3, 3.OA.A.4, 3.NBT.A.3)

3. What is the unknown factor?

$$7 \times p = 14$$

4. Aspen Bakery sold 40 boxes of rolls in one day. Each box holds 6 rolls. How many rolls did the bakery sell?

5. Mr. Samuels buys a sheet of stamps. There are 4 rows with 7 stamps in each row. How many stamps does Mr. Samuels buy?

6. There are 56 students going on a field trip to the science center. The students tour the center in groups of 8. How many groups of students are there?

FOR MORE PRACTICE
GO TO THE
Personal Math Trainer

Name _____

Divide by 5

Essential Question What does dividing by 5 mean?

Common Core Operations and Algebraic Thinking—
3.OA.A.3 Also 3.OA.A.2, 3.OA.C.7
MATHEMATICAL PRACTICES
MP1, MP2, MP6, MP7

🔑 Unlock the Problem

Kaley wants to buy a new cage for Coconut, her guinea pig. She has saved 35¢. If she saved a nickel each day, for how many days has she been saving?

> • How much is a nickel worth?
>
> _____

🔑 One Way Count up by 5s.

• Begin at 0.

• Count up by 5s until you reach 35.   0, 5, 10, _____, _____, _____, _____, _____

• Count the number of times you count up.   1 2 3 4 5 6 7

You counted up by 5 seven times. 35 ÷ 5 = _____

So, Kaley has been saving for _____ days.

🔑 Another Way

Count back on a number line.

• Start at 35.

• Count back by 5s until you reach 0. Complete the jumps on the number line.

• Count the number of times you jumped back 5.

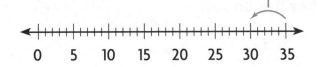

You jumped back by 5 _____ times.

35 ÷ 5 = _____

> **Math Talk** MATHEMATICAL PRACTICES ②
>
> **Reason Abstractly** What if Kaley saved 7¢ each day instead of a nickel? What would you do differently to find how many days she has saved?

Strategies for Multiplying and Dividing with 5

You have learned how to use doubles to multiply. Now you will learn how to use doubles to divide by 5.

 Use 10s facts, and then take half to multiply with 5.

When one factor is 5, you can use a 10s fact.

$5 \times 2 = $ ■

First, multiply by 10.

$10 \times 2 = $ _____

After you multiply, take half of the product.

$20 \div 2 = $ _____

So, $5 \times 2 = $ _____.

 Divide by 10, and then double to divide by 5.

When the divisor is 5 and the dividend is even, you can use a 10s fact.

$30 \div 5 = $ ■

First, divide by 10.

$30 \div 10 = $ _____

After you divide, double the quotient.

$3 + $ _____ $ = $ _____

So, $30 \div 5 = $ _____.

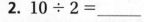 **Share and Show** MATH BOARD

1. Count back on the number line to find $15 \div 5$. _____

Math Talk MATHEMATICAL PRACTICES ⑥

Explain how counting up to solve a division problem is like counting back on a number line.

Use count up or count back on a number line to solve.

2. $10 \div 2 = $ _____

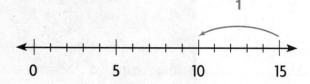

⚲ 3. $20 \div 5 = $ _____

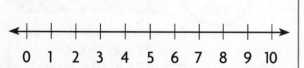

Find the quotient.

4. $50 \div 5 = $ _____   5. $5 \div 5 = $ _____   ⚲ 6. $45 \div 5 = $ _____

Name _____

On Your Own

Use count up or count back on a number line to solve.

7. $30 \div 5 =$ _____

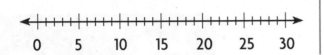

0 5 10 15 20 25 30

8. $25 \div 5 =$ _____

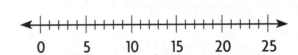

0 5 10 15 20 25

Find the quotient.

9. ___ $= 20 \div 5$

10. $40 \div 5 =$ ___

11. ___ $= 18 \div 2$

12. $0 \div 5 =$ ___

13. $35 \div 5 =$ ___

14. ___ $= 10 \div 5$

15. $40 \div 10 =$ ___

16. ___ $= 4 \div 2$

17. $10\overline{)30}$

18. $2\overline{)16}$

19. $5\overline{)45}$

20. $5\overline{)15}$

MATHEMATICAL PRACTICE ⑦ Look for a Pattern Algebra Complete the table.

21.

×	1	2	3	4	5
10					
5					

22.

÷	10	20	30	40	50
10					
5					

Problem Solving • Applications

23. **MATHEMATICAL PRACTICE ① Evaluate** Guinea pigs eat hay, pellets, and vegetables. If Wonder Hay comes in a 5-pound bag and costs $15, how much does 1 pound of hay cost?

_____

24. **GO DEEPER** Ana picks 25 apples. Pedro picks 20 apples. Ana and Pedro use the apples to make apple pies. They put 5 apples in each pie. How many apple pies can they make?

_____

25. **GO DEEPER** The clerk at a store worked 45 hours one week. He worked an equal number of hours each day on Monday through Friday. He worked an extra 5 hours on Saturday. How many hours did he work on each weekday?

_____

26. *THINK SMARTER* **Pose a Problem** Maddie went to a veterinary clinic. She saw the vet preparing some carrots for the guinea pigs.

Write a division problem that can be solved using the picture of carrots. Draw circles to group the carrots for your problem.

Pose a problem.

_____

_____

_____

_____

Solve your problem.

_____

_____

_____

_____

- Group the carrots in a different way. Then write a problem for the new groups. Solve your problem.

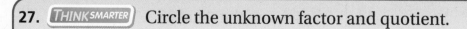

_____

_____

27. *THINK SMARTER* Circle the unknown factor and quotient.

$$5 \times \boxed{\begin{matrix} 5 \\ 6 \\ 7 \end{matrix}} = 35 \qquad \boxed{\begin{matrix} 5 \\ 6 \\ 7 \end{matrix}} = 35 \div 5$$

Divide by 5

Common Core **COMMON CORE STANDARD—3.OA.A.3**
Represent and solve problems involving
multiplication and division.

Use count up or count back on a number line to solve.

1. $40 \div 5 =$ ___8___

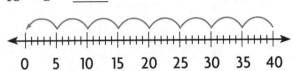

2. $25 \div 5 =$ ____

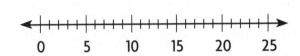

Find the quotient.

3. ____ $= 10 \div 5$

4. ____ $= 30 \div 5$

5. $14 \div 2 =$ ____

6. $5 \div 5 =$ ____

7. ____ $= 0 \div 5$

8. $20 \div 5 =$ ____

9. $25 \div 5 =$ ____

10. ____ $= 35 \div 5$

11. $5\overline{)20}$

12. $10\overline{)70}$

13. $5\overline{)15}$

14. $5\overline{)40}$

Problem Solving Real World

15. A model car maker puts 5 wheels in each kit. A machine makes 30 wheels at a time. How many packages of 5 wheels can be made from the 30 wheels?

_____

16. A doll maker puts a small bag with 5 hair ribbons inside each box with a doll. How many bags of 5 hair ribbons can be made from 45 hair ribbons?

_____

17. **WRITE** ▸*Math* Write about which method you prefer to use to divide by 5—counting up, counting back on a number line, or dividing by 10, and then doubling the quotient. Explain why.

_____

_____

Lesson Check (3.OA.A.3)

1. A model train company puts 5 boxcars with each train set. How many sets can be completed using 35 boxcars?

2. A machine makes 5 buttons at a time. Each doll shirt gets 5 buttons. How many doll shirts can be finished with 5 buttons?

Spiral Review (3.OA.A.3, 3.MD.B.4)

3. Julia earns $5 each day running errands for a neighbor. How much will Julia earn if she runs errands for 6 days in one month?

4. Marcus has 12 slices of bread. He uses 2 slices of bread for each sandwich. How many sandwiches can Marcus make?

Use the line plot for 5–6.

5. How many students have no pets?

6. How many students answered the question "How many pets do you have?"

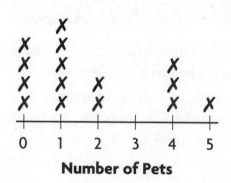

Number of Pets

FOR MORE PRACTICE
GO TO THE
Personal Math Trainer

Name _____

Divide by 3

Essential Question What strategies can you use to divide by 3?

Common Core Operations and Algebraic Thinking—3.OA.C.7 *Also 3.OA.A.2, 3.OA.A.3, 3.OA.A.4, 3.OA.B.6*

MATHEMATICAL PRACTICES
MP1, MP2, MP4

Unlock the Problem

Hands On

For field day, 18 students have signed up for the relay race. Each relay team needs 3 students. How many teams can be made?

One Way Make equal groups.

- Look at the 18 counters below.
- Circle as many groups of 3 as you can.
- Count the number of groups.

- What do you need to find?

  _____

  _____

- Circle the numbers you need to use.

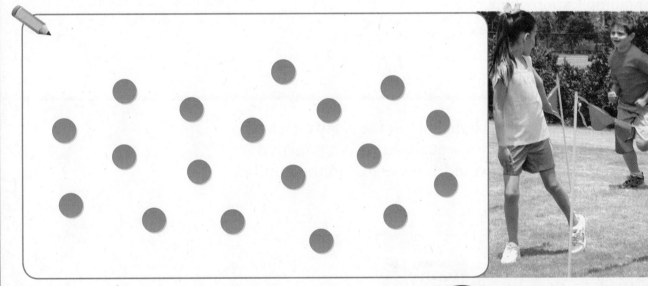

There are _____ groups of 3.

So, _____ teams can be made.

You can write $18 \div 3 =$ _____ or $3\overline{)18}$.

Math Talk

MATHEMATICAL PRACTICES ①

Make Sense of Problems Suppose the question asked how many students would be on 3 equal teams. How would you model 3 equal teams? Would the quotient be the same?

🔓 Other Ways

Ⓐ Count back on a number line.

- Start at 18.
- Count back by 3s as many times as you can. Complete the jumps on the number line.
- Count the number of times you jumped back 3.

⚠️ **ERROR Alert**

Be sure to count back the same number of spaces each time you jump back on the number line.

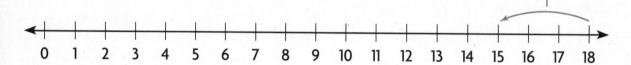

You jumped back by 3 _____ times.

Ⓑ Use a related multiplication fact.

Since division is the opposite of multiplication, think of a related multiplication fact to find $18 \div 3$.

■ $\times 3 = 18$
$6 \times 3 = 18$

Think: What number completes the multiplication fact?

So, $18 \div 3 =$ _____ or $3\overline{)18}$.

- What if 24 students signed up for the relay race and there were 3 students on each team? What related multiplication fact would you use to find the number of teams?

_____

Share and Show

1. Circle groups of 3 to find $12 \div 3$. _____

Math Talk

MATHEMATICAL PRACTICES ④

Model Mathematics What does the number of groups that you circled represent?

Find the quotient.

✓ 2. $6 \div 3 =$ ___

3. ___ $= 14 \div 2$

✓ 4. $21 \div 3 =$ ___

5. ___ $= 30 \div 5$

On Your Own

Practice: Copy and Solve Find the quotient. Draw
a quick picture to help.

6. $9 \div 3$ **7.** $10 \div 5$ **8.** $18 \div 2$ **9.** $24 \div 3$

Find the quotient.

10. ___ $= 12 \div 2$ **11.** $40 \div 5 =$ ___ **12.** $60 \div 10 =$ ___ **13.** ___ $= 20 \div 10$

14. $3\overline{)15}$ **15.** $2\overline{)4}$ **16.** $5\overline{)20}$ **17.** $3\overline{)18}$

MATHEMATICAL PRACTICE ❷ **Use Reasoning** **Algebra** Write $+$, $-$, $\times$, or $\div$.

18. $25 \bigcirc 5 = 10 \div 2$ **19.** $3 \times 3 = 6 \bigcirc 3$ **20.** $16 \bigcirc 2 = 24 - 16$

21. $13 + 19 = 8 \bigcirc 4$ **22.** $14 \bigcirc 2 = 6 \times 2$ **23.** $21 \div 3 = 5 \bigcirc 2$

24. Jem pastes 21 photos and 15 postcards
in a scrap album. She puts 3 items on
each page. How many pages does Jem
fill in the scrap album?

_____

25. **GO DEEPER** Sue plants 18 pink flowers
and 9 yellow flowers in flowerpots.
She plants 3 flowers in each flowerpot.
How many flowerpots does Sue use?

_____

26. **GO DEEPER** Blaine makes an array of 12 red squares and 18 blue squares.
She puts 3 squares in each row. How many rows does Blaine have in the array?

_____

Problem Solving • Applications

Use the table for 27–28.

Field Day Events	
Activity	Number of Students
Relay race	25
Beanbag toss	18
Jump-rope race	27

27. GO DEEPER There are 5 equal teams in the relay race. How many students are on each team? Write a division equation that shows the number of students on each team.

_____

28. THINK SMARTER Students doing the jump-rope race and the beanbag toss compete in teams of 3. How many more teams participate in the jump-rope race than in the beanbag toss? **Explain** how you know.

WRITE ▸ Math
Show Your Work

_____

_____

29. MATHEMATICAL PRACTICE ① **Make Sense of Problems** Michael puts 21 sports cards into stacks of 3. The answer is 7 stacks. What's the question?

_____

_____

30. THINK SMARTER Jorge made $24 selling water at a baseball game. He wants to know how many bottles of water he sold. Jorge used this number line to help him.

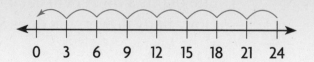

Write the division equation that the number line represents.

_____ ÷ _____ = _____

Divide by 3

Common Core COMMON CORE STANDARD—3.OA.C.7
Multiply and divide within 100.

Find the quotient. Draw a quick picture to help.

1. $12 \div 3 = \underline{\ 4\ }$

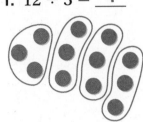

2. $24 \div 3 = \underline{\quad}$

3. $\underline{\quad} = 6 \div 3$

4. $40 \div 5 = \underline{\quad}$

Find the quotient.

5. $\underline{\quad} = 15 \div 3$

6. $\underline{\quad} = 21 \div 3$

7. $16 \div 2 = \underline{\quad}$

8. $27 \div 3 = \underline{\quad}$

9. $0 \div 3 = \underline{\quad}$

10. $9 \div 3 = \underline{\quad}$

11. $\underline{\quad} = 30 \div 3$

12. $\underline{\quad} = 12 \div 4$

13. $3\overline{)12}$

14. $3\overline{)15}$

15. $3\overline{)24}$

16. $3\overline{)9}$

Problem Solving

17. The principal at Miller Street School has 12 packs of new pencils. She will give 3 packs to each third-grade class. How many third-grade classes are there?

_____

18. Mike has $21 to spend at the mall. He spends all of his money on bracelets for his sisters. Bracelets cost $3 each. How many bracelets does he buy?

_____

19. **WRITE** ▸*Math* Explain how to divide an amount by 3.

_____

_____

Lesson Check (3.OA.C.7)

1. There are 18 counters divided equally among 3 groups. How many counters are in each group?

_____

2. Josh has 27 signed baseballs. He places the baseballs equally on 3 shelves. How many baseballs are on each shelf?

_____

Spiral Review (3.OA.A.1, 3.OA.B.5, 3.OA.B.6, 3.MD.B.4)

3. Each bicycle has 2 wheels. How many wheels do 8 bicycles have?

_____

4. How many students watch less than 3 hours of TV a day?

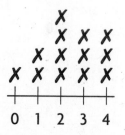

Hours Watching TV

_____

5. Complete the number sentence to show an example of the Distributive Property.

$$3 \times 6 =$$

_____

_____

6. What unknown number completes the equations?

$$3 \times \blacksquare = 21 \qquad 21 \div 3 = \blacksquare$$

_____

_____

_____

388

FOR MORE PRACTICE
GO TO THE
Personal Math Trainer

Name _____

Divide by 4

Essential Question What strategies can you use to divide by 4?

Common Core Operations and Algebraic Thinking—
3.OA.C.7 Also 3.OA.A.2, 3.OA.A.3, 3.OA.A.4, 3.OA.B.6
MATHEMATICAL PRACTICES
MP2, MP4, MP6

🔑 Unlock the Problem (Real World)

A tree farmer plants 12 red maple trees in 4 equal rows. How many trees are in each row?

- • What strategy could you use to solve the problem?

  _____

🔒 One Way Make an array.

- • Look at the array.

- • Continue the array by drawing 1 tile in each of the 4 rows until all 12 tiles are drawn.

- • Count the number of tiles in each row.

There are _____ tiles in each row.

So, there are _____ trees in each row.

Write: _____ ÷ _____ = _____ or $4\overline{)12}$

Read: Twelve divided by four equals three.

🔒 Other Ways

Ⓐ Make equal groups.

- • Draw 1 counter in each group.

- • Continue drawing 1 counter at a time until all 12 counters are drawn.

There are _____ counters in each group.

(Math Talk) **MATHEMATICAL PRACTICES ⑥**
Compare How is making an array to solve the problem like making equal groups?

B **Use factors to find 12 ÷ 4.**

The factors of 4 are 2 and 2.

$$2 \times 2 = 4$$

factors (2, 2) — product (4)

To divide by 4, use the factors.

$12 \div 4 = n$

Divide by 2. $12 \div 2 = 6$

Then divide by 2 again. $6 \div 2 = 3$

$12 \div 4 =$ ____

C **Use a related multiplication fact.**

$12 \div 4 = n$

$4 \times n = 12$

$4 \times 3 = 12$

Think: What number completes the multiplication fact?

$12 \div 4 =$ ____ or $4\overline{)12}$

Remember

A letter or symbol, like *n*, can stand for an unknown number.

Try This! Use factors of 4 to find 16 ÷ 4.

The factors of 4 are 2 and 2. $16 \div 4 = ■$

Divide by 2. $16 \div 2 =$ ____

Then divide by 2 again. $8 \div 2 =$ ____

So, $16 \div 4 =$ ____.

Think: Dividing by the factors of the divisor is the same as dividing by the divisor.

Share and Show MATH BOARD

1. Use the array to find $28 \div 4$. ____

Math Talk MATHEMATICAL PRACTICES 4

Use Models How does using an array help you to find a quotient?

Find the quotient.

2. ____ $= 21 \div 3$

3. $8 \div 4 =$ ____

4. ____ $= 40 \div 5$

5. $24 \div 4 =$ ____

Find the unknown number.

6. $20 \div 4 = a$

   $a =$ ____

7. $12 \div 2 = p$

   $p =$ ____

8. $27 \div 3 = ▲$

   $▲ =$ ____

9. $12 \div 4 = t$

   $t =$ ____

Name _____

Practice: Copy and Solve Draw tiles to make an array.
Find the quotient.

10. $30 \div 10$ **11.** $15 \div 5$ **12.** $40 \div 4$ **13.** $16 \div 2$

Find the quotient.

14. $12 \div 3 =$ ___   **15.** $20 \div 4 =$ ___   **16.** $4\overline{)16}$ **17.** $5\overline{)25}$

Find the unknown number.

18. $45 \div 5 = b$ **19.** $20 \div 10 = e$ **20.** $8 \div 2 = \blacksquare$ **21.** $24 \div 3 = h$

    $b =$ ___ $e =$ ___ $\blacksquare =$ ___ $h =$ ___

Algebra Complete the table.

22.

$\div$	9	12	15	18
3				

23.

$\div$	20	24	28	32
4				

MATHEMATICAL PRACTICE ② **Use Reasoning** **Algebra** Find the unknown number.

24. $14 \div$ ___ $= 7$ **25.** $30 \div$ ___ $= 6$ **26.** $8 \div$ ___ $= 2$ **27.** $24 \div$ ___ $= 8$

28. $36 \div$ ___ $= 9$ **29.** $40 \div$ ___ $= 4$ **30.** $3 \div$ ___ $= 1$ **31.** $35 \div$ ___ $= 7$

32. Mr. Benz arranges 24 music stands in class. He puts the stands in 4 equal rows. How many music stands are in each row?

33. **GO DEEPER** Monty has 16 toy cars in 4 equal groups and 24 toy boats in 3 equal groups. How many more toy boats are in each group than toy cars?

34. **GO DEEPER** Mia puts 15 animal stickers in 3 equal rows in her sticker book. She puts 28 flower stickers in 4 equal rows. How many more flower stickers than animal stickers are in each row?

Problem Solving • Applications

Use the table for 35–36.

35. **GO DEEPER** Douglas planted the birch trees in 4 equal rows. Then he added 2 maple trees to each row. How many trees did he plant in each row?

_____

36. **THINK SMARTER** Mrs. Banks planted the oak trees in 4 equal rows. Mr. Webb planted the dogwood trees in 3 equal rows. Who planted more trees in each row? How many more? Explain how you know.

_____

_____

Trees Planted	
Type	**Number Planted**
Dogwood	24
Oak	28
Birch	16

WRITE ▸ *Math*
Show Your Work

37. **MATHEMATICAL PRACTICE 6** **Use Math Vocabulary** Bryan earns $40 mowing lawns each week. He earns the same amount of money for each lawn. If he mows 4 lawns, how much does Bryan earn for each lawn? Explain how you found your answer.

_____

_____

_____

Personal Math Trainer

38. **THINK SMARTER +** For numbers 38a–38d, select True or False for each equation.

38a. $0 \div 4 = 4$ ○ True ○ False

38b. $4 \div 4 = 1$ ○ True ○ False

38c. $20 \div 4 = 6$ ○ True ○ False

38d. $24 \div 4 = 8$ ○ True ○ False

Divide by 4

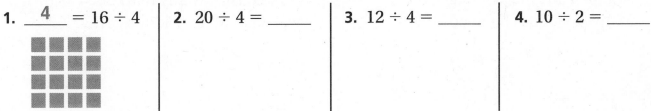

COMMON CORE STANDARD—3.OA.C.7
Multiply and divide within 100.

Draw tiles to make an array. Find the quotient.

1. ___4___ = 16 ÷ 4

2. 20 ÷ 4 = _____

3. 12 ÷ 4 = _____

4. 10 ÷ 2 = _____

Find the quotient.

5. 24 ÷ 3 = _____

6. _____ = 8 ÷ 2

7. 32 ÷ 4 = _____

8. _____ = 28 ÷ 4

9. 4)‾36

10. 4)‾8

11. 4)‾24

12. 3)‾30

Find the unknown number.

13. 20 ÷ 5 = a

14. 32 ÷ 4 = p

15. 40 ÷ 10 = ■

16. 18 ÷ 3 = x

a = _____

p = _____

■ = _____

x = _____

 Problem Solving Real World

17. Ms. Higgins has 28 students in her gym class. She puts them in 4 equal groups. How many students are in each group?

_____

18. Andy has 36 CDs. He buys a case that holds 4 CDs in each section. How many sections can he fill?

_____

19. **WRITE** ▸*Math* Write and solve a word problem that involves dividing by 4.

_____

_____

Lesson Check (3.OA.C.7)

1. Darion picks 16 grapefruits off a tree in his backyard. He puts 4 grapefruits in each bag. How many bags does he need?

2. Tori has a bag of 32 markers to share equally among 3 friends and herself. How many markers will Tori and each of her friends get?

Spiral Review (3.OA.A.2, 3.OA.B.5, 3.OA.C.7, 3.OA.D.9)

3. Find the product.

$$3 \times 7$$

4. Describe a pattern below.

8, 12, 16, 20, 24, 28

5. Use the Commutative Property of Multiplication to write a related number sentence.

$$4 \times 5 = 20$$

6. Jasmine has 18 model horses. She places the model horses equally on 3 shelves. How many model horses are on each shelf?

FOR MORE PRACTICE
GO TO THE
Personal Math Trainer

Divide by 6

Essential Question What strategies can you use to divide by 6?

 Operations and Algebraic Thinking—3.OA.C.7 *Also 3.OA.A.2, 3.OA.A.3, 3.OA.A.4, 3.OA.B.6*

MATHEMATICAL PRACTICES
MP1, MP2, MP3

Unlock the Problem

Ms. Sing needs to buy 24 juice boxes for the class picnic. Juice boxes come in packs of 6. How many packs does Ms. Sing need to buy?

- Circle the number that tells you how many juice boxes come in a pack.
- How can you use the information to solve the problem?

_____

_____

_____

One Way Make equal groups.

- Draw 24 counters.
- Circle as many groups of 6 as you can.
- Count the number of groups.

There are _____ groups of 6.

So, Ms. Sing needs to buy _____ packs of juice boxes.

You can write _____ ÷ _____ = _____ or 6)‾24 .

Math Talk MATHEMATICAL PRACTICES ①

Make Sense of Problems If you divided the 24 counters into groups of 4, how many groups would there be?

🔒 Other Ways

Ⓐ Use a related multiplication fact.

dividend divisor   quotient

$24 \div 6 = \blacksquare$

$\blacksquare \times 6 = 24$ **Think:** What number completes the

$4 \times 6 = 24$ multiplication fact?

$24 \div 6 =$ _____ or $6\overline{)24}$

Ⓑ Use factors to find 24 ÷ 6.

The factors of 6 are 3 and 2.

$3 \times 2 = 6$

factors   product

To divide by 6, use the factors.

$24 \div 6 = \blacksquare$

Divide by 3. $24 \div 3 = 8$

Then divide by 2. $8 \div 2 = 4$

$24 \div 6 =$ _____

- How does knowing $6 \times 9 = 54$ help you find $54 \div 6$?

_____

_____

Share and Show  MATH BOARD

1. Continue making equal groups to find $18 \div 6$. _____

Math Talk

MATHEMATICAL PRACTICES ②

Use Reasoning How can you use factors to find $18 \div 6$?

Find the unknown factor and quotient.

2. ___ $\times 6 = 36$ $36 \div 6 =$ ___

✓3. $6 \times$ ___ $= 12$ $12 \div 6 =$ ___

Find the quotient.

4. ___ $= 0 \div 2$ **5.** $6 \div 6 =$ ___   **6.** ___ $= 28 \div 4$ **✓7.** $42 \div 6 =$ ___

Name _____

Find the unknown factor and quotient.

8. $6 \times$ ____ $= 30$ $30 \div 6 =$ ____   **9.** ____ $\times 6 = 48$ $48 \div 6 =$ ____

Find the quotient.

10. $12 \div 6 =$ ____   **11.** ____ $= 6 \div 1$ **12.** $6\overline{)6}$ **13.** $2\overline{)10}$

Find the unknown number.

14. $24 \div 6 = n$ **15.** $40 \div 5 = \triangle$ **16.** $60 \div 10 = m$ **17.** $18 \div 6 = \blacksquare$

$n =$ ____ $\triangle =$ ____ $m =$ ____ $\blacksquare =$ ____

MATHEMATICAL PRACTICE ② **Use Reasoning** **Algebra** **Find the unknown number.**

18. $20 \div$ ____ $= 4$ **19.** $24 \div$ ____ $= 8$ **20.** $16 \div$ ____ $= 4$ **21.** $3 \div$ ____ $= 3$

22. $42 \div$ ____ $= 7$ **23.** $30 \div$ ____ $= 10$ **24.** $10 \div$ ____ $= 2$ **25.** $32 \div$ ____ $= 4$

26. Mr. Brooks has 36 students in his gym class. He makes 6 teams. If each team has the same number of students, how many students are on each team?

_____

27. **GO DEEPER** Sandy bakes 18 pies. She keeps 2 of the pies. She sells the rest of the pies to 4 people at a bake sale. If each person buys the same number of pies, how many pies does Sandy sell to each person?

_____

28. **THINK SMARTER** Derek has 2 boxes of fruit snacks. There are 12 fruit snacks in each box. If he eats 6 fruit snacks each day, how many days will the fruit snacks last? Explain.

_____

_____

Problem Solving • Applications

29. GO DEEPER Cody baked 12 muffins. He keeps 6 muffins. How many muffins can he give to each of his 6 friends if each friend gets the same number of muffins?

_____

30. MATHEMATICAL PRACTICE ③ **Make Arguments** Mary has 36 stickers to give to 6 friends. She says she can give each friend only 5 stickers. Use a division equation to describe Mary's error.

_____

_____

_____

• WRITE ▸Math • **Show Your Work** • • • •

31. WRITE ▸Math **Pose a Problem** Write and solve a word problem for the bar model.

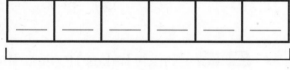

30

_____

_____

_____

_____

Personal Math Trainer

32. THINK SMARTER➕ Each van can transport 6 people. How many vans are needed to transport 48 people to an event? Explain the strategy you used to solve the problem.

_____ vans

Divide by 6

Common Core **COMMON CORE STANDARD—3.OA.C.7**
Multiply and divide within 100.

Find the unknown factor and quotient.

1. $6 \times \underline{\;7\;} = 42$ $42 \div 6 = \underline{\;7\;}$

2. $6 \times \underline{\quad} = 18$ $18 \div 6 = \underline{\quad}$

3. $4 \times \underline{\quad} = 24$ $24 \div 4 = \underline{\quad}$

4. $6 \times \underline{\quad} = 54$ $54 \div 6 = \underline{\quad}$

Find the quotient.

5. $\underline{\quad} = 24 \div 6$

6. $48 \div 6 = \underline{\quad}$

7. $\underline{\quad} = 6 \div 6$

8. $12 \div 6 = \underline{\quad}$

9. $6\overline{)36}$

10. $6\overline{)54}$

11. $6\overline{)30}$

12. $1\overline{)6}$

Find the unknown number.

13. $p = 42 \div 6$

14. $18 \div 3 = q$

15. $r = 30 \div 6$

16. $60 \div 6 = s$

$p = \underline{\quad}$

$q = \underline{\quad}$

$r = \underline{\quad}$

$s = \underline{\quad}$

 Problem Solving Real World

17. Lucas has 36 pages of a book left to read. If he reads 6 pages a day, how many days will it take Lucas to finish the book?

_____

18. Juan has $24 to spend at the bookstore. If books cost $6 each, how many books can he buy?

_____

19. **WRITE** ▸*Math* Which strategy would you use to divide $36 \div 6$? Explain why you chose that strategy.

_____

_____

Lesson Check (3.OA.C.7)

1. Ella earned $54 last week babysitting. She earns $6 an hour. How many hours did Ella babysit last week?

2. What is the unknown factor and quotient?

$$6 \times \blacksquare = 42 \qquad 42 \div 6 = \blacksquare$$

Spiral Review (3.OA.A.1, 3.OA.A.2, 3.OA.C.7, 3.OA.D.8)

3. Coach Clarke has 48 students in his P.E. class. He places the students in teams of 6 for an activity. How many teams can Coach Clarke make?

4. Each month for 7 months, Eva reads 3 books. How many more books does she need to read before she has read 30 books?

5. Each cow has 4 legs. How many legs do 5 cows have?

6. Find the product.

$$3 \times 9$$

© Houghton Mifflin Harcourt Publishing Company

FOR MORE PRACTICE
GO TO THE
Personal Math Trainer

✓ Mid-Chapter Checkpoint

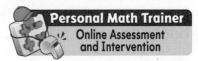

Personal Math Trainer
Online Assessment
and Intervention

Concepts and Skills

1. Explain how to find 20 ÷ 4 by making an array.
(3.OA.A.3)

_____

_____

_____

2. Explain how to find 30 ÷ 6 by making equal groups.
(3.OA.A.3)

_____

_____

_____

Find the unknown factor and quotient. (3.OA.C.7)

3. 10 × ___ = 50   ___ = 50 ÷ 10

4. 2 × ___ = 16   ___ = 16 ÷ 2

5. 2 × ___ = 20   ___ = 20 ÷ 2

6. 5 × ___ = 20   ___ = 20 ÷ 5

Find the quotient. (3.OA.C.7)

7. ___ = 6 ÷ 6   **8.** 21 ÷ 3 = ___   **9.** ___ = 0 ÷ 3   **10.** 36 ÷ 4 = ___

11. 5)‾35   **12.** 4)‾24   **13.** 6)‾54   **14.** 3)‾9

15. Carter has 18 new books. He plans to read 3 of them each week. How many weeks will it take Carter to read all of his new books? (3.OA.C.7)

_____

16. GO DEEPER Gabriella made 5 waffles for breakfast. She has 25 strawberries and 15 blueberries to put on top of the waffles. She will put an equal number of berries on each waffle. How many berries will Gabriella put on each waffle? (3.OA.A.3)

_____

17. There are 60 people at the fair waiting in line for a ride. Each car in the ride can hold 10 people. Write an equation that could be used to find the number of cars needed to hold all 60 people. (3.OA.C.7)

_____

18. Alyssa has 4 cupcakes. She gives 2 cupcakes to each of her cousins. How many cousins does Alyssa have? (3.OA.A.3)

_____

Name _____

Divide by 7

Essential Question What strategies can you use to divide by 7?

Common Core

Operations and Algebraic Thinking—
3.OA.C.7 Also 3.OA.A.2, 3.OA.A.3,
3.OA.A.4, 3.OA.B.6

MATHEMATICAL PRACTICES
MP1, MP6, MP8

Unlock the Problem

Yasmin used 28 large apples to make 7 loaves of apple bread. She used the same number of apples for each loaf. How many apples did Yasmin use for each loaf?

- Do you need to find the number of equal groups or the number in each group?

  _____

- What label will your answer have?

  _____

One Way Make an array.

- Draw 1 tile in each of 7 rows.

- Continue drawing 1 tile in each of the 7 rows until all 28 tiles are drawn.

- Count the number of tiles in each row.

There are _____ tiles in each row.

So, Yasmin used _____ for each loaf.

You can write 28 ÷ 7 = _____ or 7)‾2‾8‾ .

Math Talk

MATHEMATICAL PRACTICES ①

Make Sense of Problems Why can you use division to solve the problem?

1 Other Ways

A Use a related multiplication fact.

$$28 \div 7 = a \qquad 7 \times a = 28$$

$$7 \times 4 = 28$$

Think: What number completes the multiplication fact?

$$28 \div 7 = \underline{\qquad} \text{ or } 7\overline{)28}$$

B Make equal groups.

- Draw 7 circles to show 7 groups.

- Draw 1 counter in each group.

- Continue drawing 1 counter at a time until all 28 counters are drawn.

There are _____ counters in each group.

Share and Show MATH BOARD

1. Use the related multiplication fact to find $42 \div 7$.

   $6 \times 7 = 42$

   $42 \div 7 = \underline{\qquad}$

 Math Talk MATHEMATICAL PRACTICES ⑧

Generalize Why can you use a related multiplication fact to solve a division problem?

Find the unknown factor and quotient.

2. $7 \times \underline{\qquad} = 7 \qquad 7 \div 7 = \underline{\qquad}$

3. $7 \times \underline{\qquad} = 35 \qquad 35 \div 7 = \underline{\qquad}$

Find the quotient.

4. $4 \div 2 = \underline{\qquad}$

5. $56 \div 7 = \underline{\qquad}$

6. $\underline{\qquad} = 20 \div 5$

7. $\underline{\qquad} = 21 \div 7$

On Your Own

Find the unknown factor and quotient.

8. $3 \times$ ____ $= 9$ ____ $= 9 \div 3$

9. $7 \times$ ____ $= 49$ $49 \div 7 =$ ____

Find the quotient.

10. $48 \div 6 =$ ____

11. $7 \div 1 =$ ____

12. $7\overline{)21}$

13. $2\overline{)8}$

Find the unknown number.

14. $60 \div 10 = \blacksquare$

$\blacksquare =$ ____

15. $70 \div 7 = k$

$k =$ ____

16. $m = 63 \div 9$

$m =$ ____

17. $r = 12 \div 6$

$r =$ ____

MATHEMATICAL PRACTICE ⑥ Make Connections Algebra Complete the table.

18.

÷	18	30	24	36
6				

19.

÷	56	42	49	35
7				

20. Clare bought 35 peaches to make peach jam. She uses 7 peaches for each jar of jam. How many jars can Clare make?

_____

21. There are 49 jars of peach salsa packed into 7 gift boxes. If each box has the same number of jars of salsa, how many jars are in each box?

_____

22. **GO DEEPER** There are 31 girls and 25 boys in the marching band. When the band marches, they are in 7 rows. How many people are in each row?

_____

23. **GO DEEPER** Ed has 42 red beads and 28 blue beads. He uses an equal number of all the beads to decorate each of 7 clay sculptures. How many beads are on each sculpture?

_____

🔑 Unlock the Problem

24. THINK SMARTER Gavin sold 21 bagels to 7 different people. Each person bought the same number of bagels. How many bagels did Gavin sell to each person?

a. What do you need to find? _____

_____

b. How can you use a bar model to help you decide which

operation to use to solve the problem? _____

_____

_____

c. Complete the bar model to help you find the number of bagels Gavin sold to each person.

21 bagels

d. What is another way you could have solved the problem?

_____

_____

e. Complete the sentences.

Gavin sold _____ bagels to _____ different people.

Each person bought the same number of _____.

So, Gavin sold _____ bagels to each person.

---

25. GO DEEPER There are 35 plain bagels and 42 wheat bagels on 7 shelves in the bakery. Each shelf has the same number of plain bagels and the same number of wheat bagels. How many bagels are on each shelf?

_____

26. THINK SMARTER Write the correct symbol that makes the equations true.

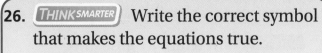

$28 = 7 \boxed{} 4$ $42 \boxed{} 7 = 35$

$7 = 49 \boxed{} 7$

Divide by 7

COMMON CORE STANDARD—3.OA.C.7
Multiply and divide within 100.

Find the unknown factor and quotient.

1. $7 \times \underline{\ 6\ } = 42$ $42 \div 7 = \underline{\ 6\ }$

2. $7 \times \underline{\ \ \ } = 35$ $35 \div 7 = \underline{\ \ \ }$

3. $7 \times \underline{\ \ \ } = 7$ $7 \div 7 = \underline{\ \ \ }$

4. $5 \times \underline{\ \ \ } = 20$ $20 \div 5 = \underline{\ \ \ }$

Find the quotient.

5. $7\overline{)21}$

6. $7\overline{)14}$

7. $6\overline{)48}$

8. $7\overline{)63}$

9. $\underline{\ \ \ } = 35 \div 7$

10. $0 \div 7 = \underline{\ \ \ }$

11. $\underline{\ \ \ } = 56 \div 7$

12. $32 \div 8 = \underline{\ \ \ }$

Find the unknown number.

13. $56 \div 7 = e$

$e = \underline{\ \ \ \ \ }$

14. $k = 32 \div 4$

$k = \underline{\ \ \ \ \ }$

15. $g = 49 \div 7$

$g = \underline{\ \ \ \ \ }$

16. $28 \div 7 = s$

$s = \underline{\ \ \ \ \ }$

 Problem Solving *Real World*

17. Twenty-eight players sign up for basketball. The coach puts 7 players on each team. How many teams are there?

_____

18. Roberto read 42 books over 7 months. He read the same number of books each month. How many books did Roberto read each month?

_____

19. **WRITE** ▸*Math* Describe how to find the number of weeks equal to 56 days.

_____

_____

Lesson Check (3.OA.C.7)

1. Elliot earned $49 last month walking his neighbor's dog. He earns $7 each time he walks the dog. How many times did Elliot walk his neighbor's dog last month?

_____

2. What is the unknown factor and quotient?

$$7 \times \blacksquare = 63$$

$$63 \div 7 = \blacksquare$$

_____

Spiral Review (3.OA.A.3, 3.OA.B.5, 3.OA.B.6, 3.OA.C.7)

3. Maria puts 6 strawberries in each smoothie she makes. She makes 3 smoothies. Altogether, how many strawberries does Maria use in the smoothies?

_____

4. Kaitlyn makes 4 bracelets. She uses 8 beads for each bracelet. How many beads does she use?

_____

5. What is the unknown factor?

$$2 \times 5 = 5 \times \blacksquare$$

_____
_____

6. What division equation is related to the following multiplication equation?

$$3 \times 4 = 12$$

_____
_____

FOR MORE PRACTICE
GO TO THE
Personal Math Trainer

Name _____

Divide by 8

Essential Question What strategies can you use to divide by 8?

Common Core Operations and Algebraic Thinking— 3.OA.A.3, 3.OA.A.4
MATHEMATICAL PRACTICES
MP1, MP2, MP4, MP5, MP6

Unlock the Problem

At Stephen's camping store, firewood is sold in bundles of 8 logs. He has 32 logs to put in bundles. How many bundles of firewood can he make?

> • What will Stephen do with the 32 logs?
>
> _____
>
> _____

One Way Use repeated subtraction.

- Start with 32.
- Subtract 8 until you reach 0.
- Count the number of times you subtract 8.

> **! ERROR Alert**
>
> Continue to subtract the divisor, 8, until the difference is less than 8.

$$
\begin{array}{r} 32 \\ -\ 8 \\ \hline 24 \end{array}
\quad
\begin{array}{r} 24 \\ -\ 8 \\ \hline \end{array}
\quad
\begin{array}{r} \\ -\ 8 \\ \hline \end{array}
\quad
\begin{array}{r} \\ -\ 8 \\ \hline \end{array}
$$

Number of times
you subtract 8:   1   2   3   4

You subtracted 8 _____ times.

So, Stephen can make _____ bundles of firewood.

You can write $32 \div 8 =$ _____ or $8\overline{)32}$.

Another Way Use a related multiplication fact.

$32 \div 8 = \blacksquare$ $\blacksquare \times 8 = 32$

$4 \times 8 = 32$

Think: What number completes the multiplication fact?

$32 \div 8 =$ _____ or $8\overline{)32}$

> **Math Talk** MATHEMATICAL PRACTICES ①
>
> **Make Sense of Problems** How does knowing $4 \times 8 = 32$ help you find $32 \div 8$?

🔑 Example Find the unknown divisor.

Stephen has a log that is 16 feet long. If he cuts the log into pieces that are 2 feet long, how many pieces will Stephen have?

Divide. $16 \div \blacksquare = 2$

You can also use a multiplication table to find the divisor in a division problem.

Think: $\blacksquare \times 2 = 16$

STEP 1 Find the factor, 2, in the top row.

STEP 2 Look down to find the product, 16.

STEP 3 Look left to find the unknown factor.

The unknown factor is _____.

$$\blacksquare = \underline{\hspace{1cm}}$$

$$\underline{\hspace{1cm}} \times 2 = 16$$

$$\underline{\hspace{1cm}} = 16 \checkmark \qquad \text{Check.} \quad \text{The equation is true.}$$

So, Stephen will have ____ pieces.

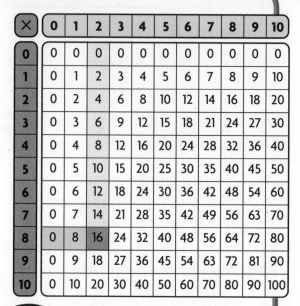

×	0	1	2	3	4	5	6	7	8	9	10
0	0	0	0	0	0	0	0	0	0	0	0
1	0	1	2	3	4	5	6	7	8	9	10
2	0	2	4	6	8	10	12	14	16	18	20
3	0	3	6	9	12	15	18	21	24	27	30
4	0	4	8	12	16	20	24	28	32	36	40
5	0	5	10	15	20	25	30	35	40	45	50
6	0	6	12	18	24	30	36	42	48	54	60
7	0	7	14	21	28	35	42	49	56	63	70
8	0	8	16	24	32	40	48	56	64	72	80
9	0	9	18	27	36	45	54	63	72	81	90
10	0	10	20	30	40	50	60	70	80	90	100

Math Talk MATHEMATICAL PRACTICES ⑤

Use Patterns How do you know how to use the multiplication table to find the unknown dividend for $\blacksquare \div 8 = 5$?

Share and Show 📝 MATH BOARD

Math Talk MATHEMATICAL PRACTICES ⑥

Describe why you subtract 8 from 24 to find $24 \div 8$.

1. Use repeated subtraction to find $24 \div 8$. _____

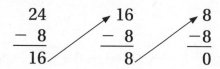

$$\begin{array}{r} 24 \\ -\ 8 \\ \hline 16 \end{array} \qquad \begin{array}{r} 16 \\ -\ 8 \\ \hline 8 \end{array} \qquad \begin{array}{r} 8 \\ -8 \\ \hline 0 \end{array}$$

Think: How many times do you subtract 8?

Find the unknown factor and quotient.

2. $8 \times \underline{\hspace{0.7cm}} = 56$ $\qquad 56 \div 8 = \underline{\hspace{0.7cm}}$ | ⚫3. $\underline{\hspace{0.7cm}} \times 8 = 40$ $\qquad 40 \div 8 = \underline{\hspace{0.7cm}}$

Find the quotient.

4. $18 \div 3 = \underline{\hspace{0.7cm}}$ $\qquad$ 5. $\underline{\hspace{0.7cm}} = 48 \div 8$ $\qquad$ 6. $56 \div 7 = \underline{\hspace{0.7cm}}$ $\qquad$ ⚫7. $\underline{\hspace{0.7cm}} = 32 \div 8$

Name _____

On Your Own

Find the unknown factor and quotient.

8. $6 \times$ ____ $= 18$ $18 \div 6 =$ ____   **9.** $8 \times$ ____ $= 72$ ____ $= 72 \div 8$

Find the quotient.

10. $28 \div 4 =$ ____   **11.** $42 \div 7 =$ ____   **12.** $8\overline{)64}$ **13.** $1\overline{)8}$

Find the unknown number.

14. $16 \div p = 8$ **15.** $t \div 8 = 2$ **16.** $64 \div \triangle = 8$ **17.** $m \div 8 = 10$

$p =$ ____ $t =$ ____ $\triangle =$ ____ $m =$ ____

18. $\triangle \div 2 = 10$ **19.** $40 \div \blacksquare = 8$ **20.** $25 \div k = 5$ **21.** $54 \div n = 9$

$\triangle =$ ____ $\blacksquare =$ ____ $k =$ ____ $n =$ ____

22. (MATHEMATICAL PRACTICE ②) **Connect Symbols and Words** Write a word problem that can be solved by using one of the division facts above.

_____

_____

(MATHEMATICAL PRACTICE ④) **Use Symbols Algebra** Write $+$, $-$, $\times$, or $\div$.

23. $6 \times 6 = 32 \bigcirc 4$ **24.** $12 \bigcirc 3 = 19 - 15$ **25.** $40 \div 8 = 35 \bigcirc 7$

26. GO DEEPER Kyle has 4 packs of baseball cards. Each pack has 12 cards. If Kyle wants to share the cards equally among himself and his 7 friends, how many baseball cards will each person get?

_____

Problem Solving • Applications

Use the table for 27–28.

Tent Sizes	
Type	**Number of People**
Cabin	10
Vista	8
Trail	4

27. **GO DEEPER** There are 32 people who plan to camp over the weekend. Describe two different ways the campers can sleep using 4 tents.

_____

_____

_____

WRITE ▸ *Math* • **Show Your Work**

28. **THINK SMARTER** There are 36 people camping at Max's family reunion. They have cabin tents and vista tents. How many of each type of tent do they need to sleep exactly 36 people if each tent is filled? Explain.

_____

_____

_____

_____

29. Josh is dividing 64 bags of trail mix equally among 8 campers. How many bags of trail mix will each camper get?

_____

30. **THINK SMARTER** Circle the unknown factor and quotient.

$$8 \times \boxed{\begin{array}{c} 6 \\ 7 \\ 8 \end{array}} = 48 \qquad \boxed{\begin{array}{c} 6 \\ 7 \\ 8 \end{array}} = 48 \div 8$$

Name _____

Divide by 8

Common Core

**COMMON CORE STANDARD—3.OA.A.3,
3.OA.A.4** *Represent and solve problems
involving multiplication and division.*

Find the unknown factor and quotient.

1. $8 \times \underline{\ 4\ } = 32$ $32 \div 8 = \underline{\quad}$

2. $3 \times \underline{\quad} = 27$ $27 \div 3 = \underline{\quad}$

3. $8 \times \underline{\quad} = 8$ $8 \div 8 = \underline{\quad}$

4. $8 \times \underline{\quad} = 72$ $72 \div 8 = \underline{\quad}$

Find the quotient.

5. $\underline{\quad} = 24 \div 8$

6. $40 \div 8 = \underline{\quad}$

7. $\underline{\quad} = 56 \div 8$

8. $14 \div 2 = \underline{\quad}$

9. $8\overline{)64}$

10. $7\overline{)28}$

11. $8\overline{)16}$

12. $8\overline{)48}$

Find the unknown number.

13. $72 \div \blacksquare = 9$

14. $25 \div \blacksquare = 5$

15. $24 \div a = 3$

16. $k \div 10 = 8$

$\blacksquare = \underline{\quad}$

$\blacksquare = \underline{\quad}$

$a = \underline{\quad}$

$k = \underline{\quad}$

Problem Solving Real World

17. Sixty-four students are going on
a field trip. There is 1 adult for
every 8 students. How many
adults are there?

_____

18. Mr. Chen spends $32 for tickets to a
play. If the tickets cost $8 each, how
many tickets does Mr. Chen buy?

_____

19. **WRITE** ▸*Math* Describe which strategy you would use to
divide 48 by 8.

_____

_____

Lesson Check (3.OA.A.4)

1. Mrs. Wilke spends $72 on pies for the school fair. Each pie costs $8. How many pies does Mrs. Wilke buy for the school fair?

2. Find the unknown factor and quotient.

$$8 \times \blacksquare = 40$$

$$40 \div 8 = \blacksquare$$

Spiral Review (3.OA.A.3, 3.OA.A.4, 3.OA.B.5)

3. Find the product.

$$(3 \times 2) \times 5$$

4. Use the Commutative Property of Multiplication to write a related multiplication sentence.

$$9 \times 4 = 36$$

5. Find the unknown factor.

$$8 \times \blacksquare = 32$$

6. What multiplication sentence represents the array?

FOR MORE PRACTICE
GO TO THE
Personal Math Trainer

Name _____

Divide by 9

Essential Question What strategies can you use to divide by 9?

Common Core
Operations and Algebraic Thinking—
3.OA.C.7 *Also 3.OA.A.2, 3.OA.A.3,*
3.OA.A.4, 3.OA.B.6
MATHEMATICAL PRACTICES
MP2, MP3, MP4

Unlock the Problem

Becket's class goes to the aquarium. The 27 students from the class are separated into 9 equal groups. How many students are in each group?

• Do you need to find the number of equal groups or the number in each group?

_____

One Way Make equal groups.

• Draw 9 circles to show 9 groups.

• Draw 1 counter in each group.

• Continue drawing 1 counter at a time until all 27 counters are drawn.

There are _____ counters in each group.

So, there are _____ in each group.

You can write $27 \div 9 =$ _____ or $9\overline{)27}$.

Math Talk

MATHEMATICAL PRACTICES ②

Reason Quantitatively
What is another way you could solve the problem?

🔓 Other Ways

Ⓐ Use factors to find 27 ÷ 9.

The factors of 9 are 3 and 3.

$$3 \times 3 = 9$$

factors   product

To divide by 9, use the factors.

$27 \div 9 = s$

Divide by 3. $27 \div 3 = 9$

Then divide by 3 again. $9 \div 3 = 3$

$27 \div 9 = \underline{\hphantom{000}}$

Ⓑ Use a related multiplication fact.

$27 \div 9 = s$

$9 \times s = 27$ **Think:** What number
completes the
$9 \times 3 = 27$ multiplication fact?

$27 \div 9 = \underline{\hphantom{000}}$ or $9\overline{)27}$

- What multiplication fact can you use to find $63 \div 9$? _____

Share and Show   MATH BOARD

1. Draw counters in the groups to find $18 \div 9.$ _____

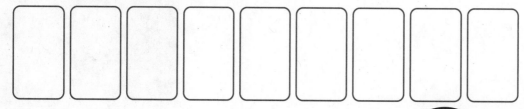

> **Math Talk**
>
> MATHEMATICAL PRACTICES ③
>
> **Apply** How would you use factors to find $18 \div 9$?

Find the quotient.

2. _____ $= 45 \div 9$ **3.** $36 \div 6 =$ _____   **4.** $9 \div 1 =$ _____   ✅**5.** _____ $= 54 \div 9$

6. $7\overline{)28}$ **7.** $9\overline{)9}$ **8.** $5\overline{)40}$ ✅**9.** $9\overline{)36}$

On Your Own

10. _____ = 36 ÷ 4   **11.** _____ = 72 ÷ 9   **12.** 81 ÷ 9 = _____   **13.** _____ = 27 ÷ 9

14. 4)‾1‾2‾   **15.** 9)‾6‾3‾   **16.** 2)‾1‾6‾   **17.** 5)‾2‾5‾

Find the unknown number.

18. 64 ÷ 8 = e **19.** 0 ÷ 9 = g **20.** ■ = 20 ÷ 4   **21.** s = 9 ÷ 9

e = _____ g = _____   ■ = _____ s = _____

MATHEMATICAL PRACTICE ② Use Reasoning Algebra Complete the table.

22.

÷	24	40	32	48
8				

23.

÷	54	45	72	63
9				

24. Baseball games have 9 innings. The Little Tigers played 72 innings last season. How many games did the Little Tigers play last year?

_____

25. **GO DEEPER** Sophie has two new fish. She feeds one fish 4 pellets and the other fish 5 pellets each day. If Sophie has fed her fish 72 pellets, for how many days has she had her fish? Explain.

_____

_____

26. **MATHEMATICAL PRACTICE ④ Write an Equation** Each van going to the aquarium carries 9 students. If 63 third-grade students go to the aquarium, what multiplication fact can you use to find the number of vans that will be needed?

_____

_____

Unlock the Problem (Real World)

27. **THINK SMARTER** Carlos has 28 blue tang fish and 17 yellow tang fish in one large fish tank. He wants to separate the fish so that there are the same number of fish in each of 9 smaller tanks. How many tang fish will Carlos put in each smaller tank?

a. What do you need to find? _____

_____

b. Why do you need to use two operations to solve the problem? _____

_____

c. Write the steps to find how many tang fish Carlos will put in each smaller tank.

d. Complete the sentences.

Carlos has _____ blue tang fish

and _____ yellow tang fish in one large fish tank.

He wants to separate the fish so that there are the same number

of fish in each of _____ smaller tanks.

So, Carlos will put _____ fish in each smaller tank.

28. **THINK SMARTER** Complete the chart to show the quotients.

÷	27	18	45	36
9				

Divide by 9

Common Core

COMMON CORE STANDARD—3.OA.C.7
Multiply and divide within 100.

Find the quotient.

1. __4__ = 36 ÷ 9

2. 30 ÷ 6 = _____

3. _____ = 81 ÷ 9

4. 27 ÷ 9 = _____

5. 9 ÷ 9 = _____

6. _____ = 63 ÷ 7

7. 36 ÷ 6 = _____

8. _____ = 90 ÷ 9

9. $9\overline{)63}$

10. $9\overline{)18}$

11. $7\overline{)49}$

12. $9\overline{)45}$

Find the unknown number.

13. 48 ÷ 8 = g

14. s = 72 ÷ 9

15. m = 0 ÷ 9

16. 54 ÷ 9 = n

g = _____

s = _____

m = _____

n = _____

Problem Solving Real World

17. A crate of oranges has trays inside that hold 9 oranges each. There are 72 oranges in the crate. If all trays are filled, how many trays are there?

18. Van has 45 new baseball cards. He puts them in a binder that holds 9 cards on each page. How many pages does he fill?

_____

_____

19. **WRITE** ▸Math Explain which division facts were the easiest for you to learn.

_____

_____

Lesson Check (3.OA.C.7)

1. Darci sets up a room for a banquet. She has 54 chairs. She places 9 chairs at each table. How many tables have 9 chairs?

_____

2. Mr. Robinson sets 36 glasses on a table. He puts the same number of glasses in each of 9 rows. How many glasses does he put in each row?

_____

Spiral Review (3.OA.A.2, 3.OA.C.7, 3.OA.D.8)

3. Each month for 9 months, Jordan buys 2 sports books. How many more sports books does he need to buy before he has bought 25 sports books?

_____

4. Find the product.

$$\begin{array}{r} 8 \\ \times\,7 \\ \hline \end{array}$$

5. Adriana made 30 pet collars to bring to the pet fair. She wants to display 3 pet collars on each hook. How many hooks will Adriana need to display all 30 pet collars?

_____

6. Carla packs 4 boxes of books. Each box has 9 books. How many books does Carla pack?

_____

FOR MORE PRACTICE
GO TO THE
Personal Math Trainer

Name _____

Problem Solving • Two-Step Problems

Essential Question How can you use the strategy *act it out* to solve two-step problems?

 Common Core — **Operations and Algebraic Thinking—3.OA.D.8**

MATHEMATICAL PRACTICES
MP1, MP3, MP6

Unlock the Problem

Madilyn bought 2 packs of pens and a notebook for $11. The notebook cost $3. Each pack of pens cost the same amount. What is the price of 1 pack of pens?

Read the Problem

What do I need to find?

I need to find the price of

1 pack of _____.

What information do I need to use?

Madilyn spent _____ in all.

She bought _____ packs of

pens and _____ notebook.

The notebook cost _____.

How will I use the information?

I will use the information to

_____ out the problem.

Solve the Problem

Describe how to act out the problem.

Start with 11 counters. Take away 3 counters.

total cost ↓		cost of notebook ↓		p, cost of 2 packs of pens ↓
_____	−	_____	=	p
		_____	=	p

Now I know that 2 packs of pens cost _____.

Next, make _____ equal groups with the 8 remaining counters.

p, cost of 2 packs of pens ↓		number of packs ↓		c, cost of 1 pack of pens ↓
$8	÷	_____	=	c
		_____	=	c

So, the price of 1 pack of pens is _____.

 Math Talk

MATHEMATICAL PRACTICES ①

Make Sense of Problems Why do you need to use two operations to solve the problem?

🔒 Try Another Problem

Chad bought 4 packs of T-shirts. He gave 5 T-shirts to his brother. Now Chad has 19 shirts. How many T-shirts were in each pack?

Read the Problem	Solve the Problem
What do I need to find?	**Describe how to act out the problem.**
What information do I need to use?	
How will I use the information?	

- How can you use multiplication and subtraction to check your answer?

_____

_____

_____

Math Talk

MATHEMATICAL PRACTICES ❸

Apply What is another strategy you could use to solve this problem?

Name _____

Unlock the Problem
√ Circle the question.
√ Underline the important facts.
√ Choose a strategy you know.

1. Mac bought 4 packs of toy cars. Then his friend gave him 9 cars. Now Mac has 21 cars. How many cars were in each pack?

Act out the problem by using counters or the picture and by writing equations.

First, subtract the cars Mac's friend gave him.

total cars ↓		cars given to Mac ↓		c, cars in 4 packs ↓
21	−	_____	=	c
		_____	=	c

Then, divide to find the number of cars in each pack.

c, cars in 4 packs ↓		number of packs ↓		p, number in each pack ↓
12	÷	_____	=	p
		_____	=	p

So, there were _____ cars in each pack.

2. **THINK SMARTER** What if Mac bought 8 packs of toy boats, and then he gave his friend 3 boats? If Mac has 13 boats now, how many boats were in each pack?

_____

On Your Own

3. **THINK SMARTER** Ryan gave 7 of his model cars to a friend. Then he bought 6 more cars. Now Ryan has 13 cars. How many cars did Ryan start with?

_____

4. **Go DEEPER** Chloe bought 5 sets of books. Each set has the same number of books. She donated 9 of her books to her school. Now she has 26 books. How many books were in each set?

_____

5. Hilda cuts a ribbon into 2 equal pieces. Then she cuts 4 inches off one piece. That piece is now 5 inches long. What was the length of the original ribbon?

_____

6. **Go DEEPER** Teanna has 2 boxes of color pencils. One box has 20 color pencils and the other box has 16 color pencils. She gives her brother 3 of the color pencils. She wants to put the color pencils that she has left into 3 equal groups. How many color pencils will Teanna put in each group?

_____

WRITE ▸ Math
Show Your Work

7. **MATHEMATICAL PRACTICE 6** Rose saw a movie, shopped, and ate at a restaurant. She did not see the movie first. She shopped right after she ate. In what order did Rose do these activities? **Explain** how you know.

_____

_____

_____

_____

Personal Math Trainer

8. **THINK SMARTER +** Eleni bought 3 packs of crayons. Each pack contains the same number of crayons. She then found 3 crayons in her desk. Eleni now has 24 crayons. How many crayons were in each pack she bought? Explain how you solved the problem.

_____

Problem Solving • Two-Step Problems

Common Core **COMMON CORE STANDARD—3.OA.D.8**
Solve problems involving the four operations, and
identify and explain patterns in arithmetic.

Solve the problem.

1. Jack has 3 boxes of pencils with the same
   number of pencils in each box. His mother gives
   him 4 more pencils. Now Jack has 28 pencils.
   How many pencils are in each box?

   Think: I can start with 28 counters
   and act out the problem.   **8 pencils**

2. The art teacher has 48 paintbrushes. She puts
   8 paintbrushes on each table in her classroom.
   How many tables are in her classroom?   _____

3. Ricardo has 2 cases of video games with the
   same number of games in each case. He gives
   4 games to his brother. Ricardo has 10 games
   left. How many video games were in each case?
                                                               _____

4. Patty has $20 to spend on gifts for her friends.
   Her mother gives her $5 more. If each gift
   costs $5, how many gifts can she buy?
                                                               _____

5. Joe has a collection of 35 DVD movies. He
   received 8 of them as gifts. Joe bought the rest
   of his movies over 3 years. If he bought the
   same number of movies each year, how many
   movies did Joe buy last year?
                                                               _____

6. **WRITE** ▸*Math* Write a division word problem and
   explain how to solve it by *acting it out*.

   _____

   _____

Lesson Check (3.OA.D.8)

1. Gavin saved $16 to buy packs of baseball cards. His father gives him $4 more. If each pack of cards costs $5, how many packs can Gavin buy?

2. Chelsea buys 8 packs of markers. Each pack contains the same number of markers. Chelsea gives 10 markers to her brother. Then, she has 54 markers left. How many markers were in each pack?

Spiral Review (3.OA.A.1, 3.OA.A.3, 3.OA.A.4, 3.OA.D.8)

3. Each foot has 5 toes. How many toes do 6 feet have?

4. Each month for 5 months, Sophie makes 2 quilts. How many more quilts does she need to make before she has made 16 quilts?

5. Meredith practices the piano for 3 hours each week. How many hours will she practice in 8 weeks?

6. Find the unknown factor.

$$9 \times \blacksquare = 36$$

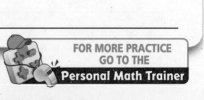

FOR MORE PRACTICE
GO TO THE
Personal Math Trainer

Order of Operations

Essential Question Why are there rules such as the order of operations?

Common Core — **Operations and Algebraic Thinking—3.OA.D.8**
MATHEMATICAL PRACTICES
MP4, MP7, MP8

Investigate

CONNECT You can use what you know about acting out a two-step problem to write one equation to describe and solve a two-step problem.

- If you solved a two-step problem in a different order, what do you think might happen?

_____

Use different orders to find $4 + 16 \div 2$.

A. Make a list of all the possible orders you can use to find the answer to $4 + 16 \div 2$.

_____

B. Use each order in your list to find the answer. Show the steps you used.

_____

_____

Draw Conclusions

1. Did following different orders change the answer? _____

2. **MATHEMATICAL PRACTICE 8** **Draw Conclusions** If a problem has more than one type of operation, how does the order in which you perform the operations affect the answer?

_____

3. Explain the need for setting an order of operations that everyone follows.

_____

Make Connections

When solving problems with more than one type of operation, you need to know which operation to do first. A special set of rules, called the **order of operations**, gives the order in which calculations are done in a problem.

First, multiply and divide from left to right.

Then, add and subtract from left to right.

Meghan buys 2 books for $4 each. She pays with a $10 bill. How much money does she have left?

You can write $\$10 - 2 \times \$4 = c$ to describe and solve the problem.

Use the order of operations to solve $\$10 - 2 \times \$4 = c$.

STEP 1

Multiply from left to right.

$$\$10 - 2 \times \$4 = c$$
$$\$10 - \quad \$8 \quad = c$$

STEP 2

Subtract from left to right.

$$\$10 - \$8 = c$$
$$\$2 \quad = c$$

So, Meghan has _____ left.

• Does your answer make sense? Explain.

_____

_____

_____

Math Talk

MATHEMATICAL PRACTICES ⑦

Identify Relationships What operation should you do first to find: $12 - 6 \div 2$ and $12 \div 6 - 2$? What is the answer to each problem?

Share and Show

Write *correct* if the operations are listed in the correct order. If not correct, write the correct order of operations.

1. $4 + 5 \times 2$ multiply, add

_____

✓ 2. $8 \div 4 \times 2$ multiply, divide

_____

3. $12 + 16 \div 4$ add, divide

_____

4. $9 + 2 \times 3$ add, multiply

_____

5. $4 + 6 \div 3$ divide, add

_____

6. $36 - 7 \times 3$ multiply, subtract

_____

Name _____

**Follow the order of operations to find the unknown number.
Use your MathBoard.**

7. $63 \div 9 - 2 = f$

$f =$ _____

8. $7 - 5 + 8 = y$

$y =$ _____

☑**9.** $3 \times 6 - 2 = h$

$h =$ _____

10. $80 - 64 \div 8 = n$

$n =$ _____

11. $3 \times 4 + 6 = a$

$a =$ _____

12. $2 \times 7 \div 7 = c$

$c =$ _____

Problem Solving • Applications

MATHEMATICAL PRACTICE ④ Write an Equation **Algebra** **Use the numbers listed to
make the equation true.**

13. 2, 6, and 5

_____ + _____ × _____ = 16

14. 4, 12, and 18

_____ − _____ ÷ _____ = 15

15. 8, 9, and 7

_____ × _____ − _____ = 47

16. 2, 4, and 9

_____ ÷ _____ + _____ = 11

17. **WRITE** ▸*Math* **Pose a Problem** Write a word problem
that can be solved by using $2 \times 5 \div 5$. Solve your problem.

_____

_____

_____

_____

18. *THINK SMARTER* Is $4 + 8 \times 3$ equal to $4 + 3 \times 8$? Explain
how you know without finding the answers.

_____

_____

_____

19. THINK SMARTER For numbers 19a–19d, select True or False for each equation.

19a. $24 \div 3 + 5 = 13$ ○ True ○ False

19b. $5 + 2 \times 3 = 21$ ○ True ○ False

19c. $15 - 3 \div 3 = 14$ ○ True ○ False

19d. $18 \div 3 \times 2 = 12$ ○ True ○ False

Connect to Social Studies

Picture Book Art

The Eric Carle Museum of Picture Book Art in Amherst, Massachusetts, is the first museum in the United States that is devoted to picture book art. Picture books introduce literature to young readers.

The museum has 3 galleries, a reading library, a café, an art studio, an auditorium, and a museum shop. The exhibits change every 3 to 6 months, depending on the length of time the picture art is on loan and how fragile it is.

The table shows prices for some souvenirs in the bookstore in the museum.

Souvenir Prices	
Souvenir	**Price**
Firefly Picture Frame	$25
Exhibition Posters	$10
Caterpillar Note Cards	$8
Caterpillar Pens	$4
Sun Note Pads	$3

20. Kallon bought 3 Caterpillar note cards and 1 Caterpillar pen. How much did he spend on souvenirs?

_____

21. GO DEEPER Raya and 4 friends bought their teacher 1 Firefly picture frame. They shared the cost equally. Then Raya bought an Exhibition poster. How much money did Raya spend in all? Explain.

_____

_____

_____

Order of Operations

COMMON CORE STANDARD—3.OA.D.8
Solve problems involving the four operations, and identify and explain patterns in arithmetic.

Write *correct* if the operations are listed in the correct order. If not correct, write the correct order of operations.

1. $45 - 3 \times 5$ subtract, multiply

         multiply, subtract
_____

2. $3 \times 4 \div 2$ divide, multiply

_____

3. $5 + 12 \div 2$ divide, add

_____

4. $7 \times 10 + 3$ add, multiply

_____

Follow the order of operations to find the unknown number.

5. $6 + 4 \times 3 = n$

   $n =$ _____

6. $8 - 3 + 2 = k$

   $k =$ _____

7. $24 \div 3 + 5 = p$

   $p =$ _____

Problem Solving

8. Shelley bought 3 kites for $6 each. She gave the clerk $20. How much change should Shelley get?

_____

9. Tim has 5 apples and 3 bags with 8 apples in each bag. How many apples does Tim have in all?

_____

10. **WRITE** ▸*Math* Give a description of the rules for the order of operations in your own words.

_____

_____

Lesson Check (3.OA.D.8)

1. Natalie is making doll costumes. Each costume has 4 buttons that cost 3¢ each and a zipper that costs 7¢. How much does she spend on buttons and a zipper for each costume?

_____

2. Leonardo's mother gave him 5 bags with 6 flower bulbs in each bag to plant. He has planted all except 3 bulbs. How many flower bulbs has Leonardo planted?

_____

Spiral Review (3.OA.C.7, 3.OA.D.9, 3.NBT.A.3)

3. Each story in Will's apartment building is 9 feet tall. There are 10 stories in the building. How tall is the apartment building?

_____

_____

4. Describe a pattern in the table.

Tables	1	2	3	4
Chairs	4	8	12	16

_____

_____

5. For decorations, Meg cut out 8 groups of 7 snowflakes each. How many snowflakes did Meg cut out in all?

_____

6. A small van can hold 6 students. How many small vans are needed to take 36 students on a field trip to the music museum?

_____

© Houghton Mifflin Harcourt Publishing Company

FOR MORE PRACTICE
GO TO THE
Personal Math Trainer

Name _____

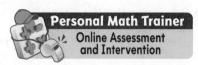
1. Ming shared 35 marbles among 7 different friends. Each friend received the same number of marbles. How many marbles did Ming give to each friend?

$$35 \div 7 = a$$
$$7 \times a = 35$$

(A) 4   (C) 6

(B) 5   (D) 7

2. Mrs. Conner has 16 shoes.

Select one number from each column to show the division equation represented by the picture.

$$16 \div \frac{?}{\text{(divisor)}} = \frac{?}{\text{(quotient)}}$$

Divisor	Quotient
○ 1	○ 1
○ 2	○ 4
○ 4	○ 8
○ 16	○ 16

3. Twenty boys are going camping. They brought 5 tents. An equal number of boys sleep in each tent. How many boys will sleep in each tent?

_____ boys

GO DIGITAL
Assessment Options
Chapter Test

4. Circle a number for the unknown factor and quotient that makes the equation true.

$4 \times \boxed{\begin{matrix} 6 \\ 7 \\ 8 \end{matrix}} = 28$ $\boxed{\begin{matrix} 6 \\ 7 \\ 8 \end{matrix}} = 28 \div 4$

5. Mrs. Walters has 30 markers. She gives each student 10 markers. How many students received the markers?

$$\begin{matrix} 30 \\ -10 \\ \hline 20 \end{matrix} \quad \begin{matrix} 20 \\ -10 \\ \hline 10 \end{matrix} \quad \begin{matrix} 10 \\ -10 \\ \hline 0 \end{matrix}$$

Write a division equation to represent the repeated subtraction.

_____ ÷ _____ = _____

6. Complete the chart to show the quotients.

÷	27	36	45	54
9				

7. For numbers 7a–7e, select True or False for each equation.

7a. $12 \div 6 = 2$ ○ True   ○ False

7b. $24 \div 6 = 3$ ○ True   ○ False

7c. $30 \div 6 = 6$ ○ True   ○ False

7d. $42 \div 6 = 7$ ○ True   ○ False

7e. $48 \div 6 = 8$ ○ True   ○ False

Name _____

8. Alicia says that $6 \div 2 + 5$ is the same as $5 + 6 \div 2$.
   Is Alicia correct or incorrect? Explain.

   _____

   _____

   _____

   _____

   _____

9. Keith arranged 40 toy cars in 8 equal rows. How many
   toy cars are in each row?

   _____ toy cars

10. Bella made $21 selling bracelets. She wants to know how
    many bracelets she sold. Bella used this number line.

    Write the division equation that the number
    line represents.

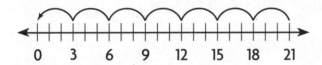

    _____ ÷ _____ = _____

11. Each picnic table seats 6 people. How many picnic tables
    are needed to seat 24 people? Explain the strategy you
    used to solve the problem.

    _____

    _____

    _____

12. Finn bought 2 packs of stickers. Each pack had the same number of stickers. A friend gave him 4 more stickers. Now he has 24 stickers in all. How many stickers were in each pack? Explain how you solved the problem.

_____

_____

_____

13. Ana used 49 strawberries to make 7 strawberry smoothies. She used the same number of strawberries in each smoothie. How many strawberries did Ana use in each smoothie?

_____ strawberries

14. For numbers 14a–14e, use the order of operations. Select True or False for each equation.

14a. $81 \div 9 + 2 = 11$ ○ True ○ False

14b. $6 + 4 \times 5 = 50$ ○ True ○ False

14c. $10 + 10 \div 2 = 15$ ○ True ○ False

14d. $12 - 3 \times 2 = 6$ ○ True ○ False

14e. $20 \div 4 \times 5 = 1$ ○ True ○ False

15. A flower shop sells daffodils in bunches of 9 daffodils. The shop sells 27 daffodils. How many bunches of daffodils does the shop sell?

_____ bunches

© Houghton Mifflin Harcourt Publishing Company

Personal Math Trainer

16. *THINK SMARTER ✛* Aviva started a table showing a division pattern.

÷	20	30	40	50
10				
5				

Part A

Complete the table.

Compare the quotients when dividing by 10 and when dividing by 5. Describe a pattern you see in the quotients.

_____

_____

Part B

Find the quotient, *a*.

$70 \div 10 = a$

a = _____

How could you use *a* to find the value of *n*? Find the value of *n*.

$70 \div 5 = n$

n = _____

_____

_____

17. Ben needs 2 oranges to make a glass of orange juice. If oranges come in bags of 10, how many glasses of orange juice can he make using one bag of oranges?

_____ glasses

18. For numbers 18a–18e, select True or False for each equation.

18a. $0 \div 9 = 0$ ○ True   ○ False

18b. $9 \div 9 = 1$ ○ True   ○ False

18c. $27 \div 9 = 4$ ○ True   ○ False

18d. $54 \div 9 = 6$ ○ True   ○ False

18e. $90 \div 9 = 9$ ○ True   ○ False

19. Ellen is making gift baskets for four friends. She has 16 prizes she wants to divide equally among the baskets. How many prizes should she put in each basket?

_____ prizes

20. **GO DEEPER** Emily is buying a pet rabbit. She needs to buy items for her rabbit at the pet store.

Part A

Emily buys a cage and 2 bowls for $54. The cage costs $40. Each bowl costs the same amount. What is the price of 1 bowl? Explain the steps you used to solve the problem.

_____

_____

_____

Part B

Emily also buys food and toys for her rabbit. She buys a bag of food for $20. She buys 2 toys for $3 each. Write one equation to describe the total amount Emily spends on food and toys. Explain how to use the order of operations to solve the equation.

_____

_____

_____

Glossary

Pronunciation Key

a	add, map	f	fit, half	n	nice, tin	p	pit, stop	û(r)	burn, term
ā	ace, rate	g	go, log	ng	ring, song	r	run, poor	yo͞o	fuse, few
â(r)	care, air	h	hope, hate	o	odd, hot	s	see, pass	v	vain, eve
ä	palm, father	i	it, give	ō	open, so	sh	sure, rush	w	win, away
b	bat, rub	ī	ice, write	ô	order, jaw	t	talk, sit	y	yet, yearn
ch	check, catch	j	joy, ledge	oi	oil, boy	th	thin, both	z	zest, muse
d	dog, rod	k	cool, take	ou	pout, now	th	this, bathe	zh	vision, pleasure
e	end, pet	l	look, rule	o͝o	took, full	u	up, done		
ē	equal, tree	m	move, seem	o͞o	pool, food	ù	pull, book		

ə the schwa, an unstressed vowel representing the sound spelled *a* in *above*, *e* in *sicken*, *i* in *possible*, *o* in *melon*, *u* in *circus*

Other symbols:
• separates words into syllables
′ indicates stress on a syllable

A

addend [a′dend] **sumando** Any of the numbers that are added in addition
Examples: 2 + 3 = 5
                ↑   ↑
            addend addend

addition [ə•dish′ən] **suma** The process of finding the total number of items when two or more groups of items are joined; the opposite operation of subtraction

A.M. [ā•em] **a.m.** The time after midnight and before noon

analog clock [an′ə•log kläk] **reloj analógico** A tool for measuring time, in which hands move around a circle to show hours and minutes
Example:

angle [ang′gəl] **ángulo** A shape formed by two rays that share an endpoint
Example:

Word History

When the letter *g* is replaced with the letter *k* in the word **angle**, the word becomes *ankle*. Both words come from the same Latin root, *angulus*, which means "a sharp bend."

area [âr′ē•ə] **área** The measure of the number of unit squares needed to cover a surface
Example:

Area = 6 square units

array [ə•rā′] **matriz** A set of objects arranged in rows and columns
Example:

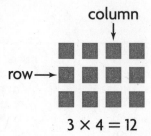

column

row →

$3 \times 4 = 12$

Associative Property of Addition [ə•sō′shē•āt•iv präp′ər•tē əv ə•dish′ən] **propiedad asociativa de la suma** The property that states that you can group addends in different ways and still get the same sum
Example:
$4 + (2 + 5) = 11$
$(4 + 2) + 5 = 11$

Associative Property of Multiplication [ə•sō′shē•āt•iv präp′ər•tē əv mul•tə•pli•kā′shən] **propiedad asociativa de la multiplicación** The property that states that when the grouping of factors is changed, the product remains the same
Example:
$(3 \times 2) \times 4 = 24$
$3 \times (2 \times 4) = 24$

 B

bar graph [bär graf] **gráfica de barras** A graph that uses bars to show data
Example:

Favorite Food

Number of Votes

12 10 8 6 4 2 0

Tacos Pizza Chili Pasta
Food

 C

capacity [kə•pas′i•tē] **capacidad** The amount a container can hold
Example:
1 liter = 1,000 milliliters

cent sign (¢) [sent sīn] **símbolo de centavo** A symbol that stands for *cent* or *cents*
Example: 53¢

centimeter (cm) [sen′tə•mēt•ər] **centímetro (cm)** A metric unit that is used to measure length or distance
Example:

1 cm

circle [sûr′kəl] **círculo** A round closed plane shape
Example:

closed shape [klōzd shāp] **figura cerrada** A shape that begins and ends at the same point
Examples:

Commutative Property of Addition [kə•myōōt′ə•tiv präp′ər•tē əv ə•dish′ən] **propiedad conmutativa de la suma** The property that states that you can add two or more numbers in any order and get the same sum
Example: $6 + 7 = 13$
$7 + 6 = 13$

Commutative Property of Multiplication [kə•myōōt′ə•tiv präp′ər•tē əv mul•tə•pli•kā′shən] **propiedad conmutativa de la multiplicación** The property that states that you can multiply two factors in any order and get the same product
Example: $2 \times 4 = 8$
$4 \times 2 = 8$

compare [kəm•pâr′] **comparar** To describe whether numbers are equal to, less than, or greater than each other

compatible numbers [kəm•pat′ə•bəl num′bərz] **números compatibles** Numbers that are easy to compute with mentally

cone [kōn] **cono** A three-dimensional, pointed shape that has a flat, round base
Example:

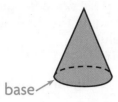

base

counting number [kount´ing num´bər] **número natural** A whole number that can be used to count a set of objects (1, 2, 3, 4 . . .)

cube [kyo̅o̅b] **cubo** A three-dimensional shape with six square faces of the same size
Example:

cylinder [sil´ən•dər] **cilindro** A three-dimensional object that is shaped like a can
Example:

 D

data [dāt´ə] **datos** Information collected about people or things

decagon [dek´ə•gän] **decágono** A polygon with ten sides and ten angles
Example:

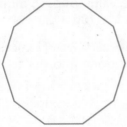

decimal point [des´ə•məl point] **punto decimal** A symbol used to separate dollars from cents in money
Example: $4.52

↑ decimal point

denominator [dē•näm´ə•nāt•ər] **denominador** The part of a fraction below the line, which tells how many equal parts there are in the whole or in the group
Example: $\frac{3}{4}$ ← denominator

difference [dif´ər•əns] **diferencia** The answer to a subtraction problem
Example: $6 - 4 = 2$

↑ difference

digital clock [dij´i•təl kläk] **reloj digital** A clock that shows time to the minute, using digits
Example:

digits [dij´its] **dígitos** The symbols 0, 1, 2, 3, 4, 5, 6, 7, 8, and 9

dime [dīm] **moneda de 10¢** A coin worth 10 cents and with a value equal to that of 10 pennies; 10¢
Example:

Distributive Property [di•strib´yo̅o̅•tiv präp´ər•tē] **propiedad distributiva** The property that states that multiplying a sum by a number is the same as multiplying each addend by the number and then adding the products
Example:
$$5 \times 8 = 5 \times (4 + 4)$$
$$5 \times 8 = (5 \times 4) + (5 \times 4)$$
$$5 \times 8 = 20 + 20$$
$$5 \times 8 = 40$$

divide [də•vīd´] **dividir** To separate into equal groups; the opposite operation of multiplication

dividend [div´ə•dend] **dividendo** The number that is to be divided in a division problem
Example: $35 \div 5 = 7$

↑ dividend

division [də•vizh′ən] **división** The process of sharing a number of items to find how many groups can be made or how many items will be in a group; the opposite operation of multiplication

divisor [de•vī′zər] **divisor** The number that divides the dividend
Example: 35 ÷ 5 = 7

divisor

dollar [däl′ər] **dólar** Paper money worth 100 cents and equal to 100 pennies; $1.00
Example:

edge [ej] **arista** A line segment formed where two faces meet

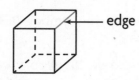
edge

eighths [ātths] **octavos**

These are eighths

elapsed time [ē•lapst′ tīm] **tiempo transcurrido** The time that passes from the start of an activity to the end of that activity

endpoint [end′point] **extremo** The point at either end of a line segment

equal groups [ē′kwəl grōōpz] **grupos iguales** Groups that have the same number of objects

equal parts [ē′kwəl pärts] **partes iguales** Parts that are exactly the same size

equal sign (=) [ē′kwəl sīn] **signo de igualdad** A symbol used to show that two numbers have the same value
Example: 384 = 384

equal to (=) [ē′kwəl tōō] **igual a** Having the same value
Example: 4 + 4 is equal to 3 + 5.

equation [ē•kwā′zhən] **ecuación** A number sentence that uses the equal sign to show that two amounts are equal
Examples:
  3 + 7 = 10
  4 − 1 = 3
  6 × 7 = 42
  8 ÷ 2 = 4

equivalent [ē•kwiv′ə•lənt] **equivalente** Two or more sets that name the same amount

equivalent fractions [ē•kwiv′ə•lənt frak′shənz] **fracciones equivalentes** Two or more fractions that name the same amount
Example:

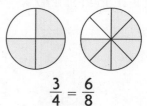

$$\frac{3}{4} = \frac{6}{8}$$

estimate [es′tə•māt] *verb* **estimar** To find about how many or how much

estimate [es′tə•mit] *noun* **estimación** A number close to an exact amount

even [ē′vən] **par** A whole number that has a 0, 2, 4, 6, or 8 in the ones place

expanded form [ek•span′did fôrm] **forma desarrollada** A way to write numbers by showing the value of each digit
Example: 721 = 700 + 20 + 1

experiment [ek•sper′ə•mənt] **experimento** A test that is done in order to find out something

face [fās] **cara** A polygon that is a flat surface of a solid shape

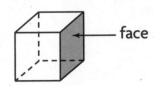

— face

factor [fak'tər] **factor** A number that is multiplied by another number to find a product
Examples: 3 × 8 = 24
↑   ↑
factor   factor

foot (ft) [fŏŏt] **pie** A customary unit used to measure length or distance;
1 foot = 12 inches

fourths [fôrths] **cuartos**

These are fourths

fraction [frak'shən] **fracción** A number that names part of a whole or part of a group
Examples:

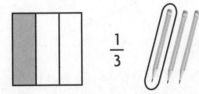

$\frac{1}{3}$

fraction greater than 1 [frak'shən grāt'ər <u>th</u>an wun] **fracción mayor que 1** A number which has a numerator that is greater than its denominator
Examples:

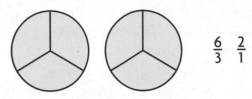

$\frac{6}{3}$ $\frac{2}{1}$

frequency table [frē'kwən•sē tā'bəl] **tabla de frecuencia** A table that uses numbers to record data
Example:

Favorite Color	
Color	**Number**
Blue	10
Green	8
Red	7
Yellow	4

G

gram (g) [gram] **gramo (g)** A metric unit that is used to measure mass;
1 kilogram = 1,000 grams

greater than (>) [grāt'ər <u>th</u>an] **mayor que** A symbol used to compare two numbers when the greater number is given first
Example:
Read 6 > 4 as "six is greater than four."

Grouping Property of Addition [grŏŏp'ing präp'ər•tē əv ə•dish'ən] **propiedad de agrupación de la suma** *See* Associative Property of Addition.

Grouping Property of Multiplication [grŏŏp'ing präp'ər•tē əv mul•tə•pli•kā'shən] **propiedad de agrupación de la multiplicación** *See* Associative Property of Multiplication.

half dollar [haf dol'ər] **moneda de 50¢**
A coin worth 50 cents and with a value
equal to that of 50 pennies; 50¢
Example:

half hour [haf our] **media hora** 30 minutes
Example: Between 4:00 and 4:30 is one
half hour.

halves [havz] **mitades**

These are halves

hexagon [hek'sə•gän] **hexágono** A polygon
with six sides and six angles
Examples:

horizontal bar graph [hôr•i•zänt'l bär graf]
gráfica de barras horizontales A bar graph
in which the bars go from left to right
Examples:

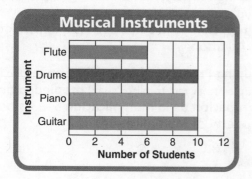

hour (hr) [our] **hora (h)** A unit used to measure
time; in one hour, the hour hand on an analog
clock moves from one number to the next;
1 hour = 60 minutes

hour hand [our hand] **horario** The short hand on
an analog clock

Identity Property of Addition [ī•den'tə•tē
präp'ər•tē əv ə•dish'ən] **propiedad de
identidad de la suma** The property that
states that when you add zero to a number,
the result is that number
Example: 24 + 0 = 24

Identity Property of Multiplication [ī•den'tə•tē
präp'ər•tē əv mul•tə•pli•kā'shən] **propiedad de
identidad de la multiplicación** The property
that states that the product of any number
and 1 is that number
Examples: 5 × 1 = 5
1 × 8 = 8

inch (in.) [inch] **pulgada (pulg.)** A customary
unit used to measure length or distance
Example:

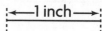

intersecting lines [in•tər•sekt'ing līnz] **líneas
secantes** Lines that meet or cross
Example:

inverse operations [in'vûrs äp•ə•rā'shənz]
operaciones inversas Opposite operations,
or operations that undo one another, such
as addition and subtraction or multiplication
and division

key [kē] **clave** The part of a map or graph
that explains the symbols

kilogram (kg) [kil'ō•gram] **kilogramo (kg)**
A metric unit used to measure mass;
1 kilogram = 1,000 grams

© Houghton Mifflin Harcourt Publishing Company

H6 Glossary

L

length [lengkth] **longitud** The measurement of the distance between two points

less than (<) [les <u>than</u>] **menor que** A symbol used to compare two numbers when the lesser number is given first
Example:
Read 3 < 7 as "three is less than seven."

line [līn] **línea** A straight path extending in both directions with no endpoints
Example:

⟷

Word History

The word *line* comes from *linen*, a thread spun from the fibers of the flax plant. In early times, thread was held tight to mark a straight line between two points.

line plot [līn plät] **diagrama de puntos** A graph that records each piece of data on a number line
Example:

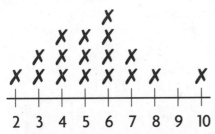

**Height of Bean Seedlings
to the Nearest Centimeter**

line segment [līn seg′mənt] **segmento** A part of a line that includes two points, called endpoints, and all of the points between them
Example:

●————————●

liquid volume [lik′wid väl′yo͞om] **volumen de un líquido** The amount of liquid in a container

liter (L) [lēt′ər] **litro (L)** A metric unit used to measure capacity and liquid volume;
1 liter = 1,000 milliliters

M

mass [mas] **masa** The amount of matter in an object

meter (m) [mēt′ər] **metro (m)** A metric unit used to measure length or distance;
1 meter = 100 centimeters

midnight [mid′nīt] **medianoche** 12:00 at night

milliliter (mL) [mil′i•lēt•ər] **mililitro (mL)** A metric unit used to measure capacity and liquid volume

minute (min) [min′it] **minuto (min)** A unit used to measure short amounts of time; in one minute, the minute hand on an analog clock moves from one mark to the next

minute hand [min′it hand] **minutero** The long hand on an analog clock

multiple [mul′tə•pəl] **múltiplo** A number that is the product of two counting numbers
Examples:

				counting
6	6	6	6	
× 1	× 2	× 3	× 4	← numbers
6	12	18	24	← multiples of 6

multiplication [mul•tə•pli•kā′shən] **multiplicación** The process of finding the total number of items in two or more equal groups; the opposite operation of division

multiply [mul′tə•plī] **multiplicar** To combine equal groups to find how many in all; the opposite operation of division

N

nickel [nik′əl] **moneda de 5¢** A coin worth 5 cents and with a value equal to that of 5 pennies; 5¢
Example:

noon [no͞on] **mediodía** 12:00 in the day

© Houghton Mifflin Harcourt Publishing Company

number line [num′bər līn] **recta numérica**
A line on which numbers can be located
Example:

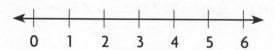

number sentence [num′bər sent′ns] **enunciado numérico** A sentence that includes numbers, operation symbols, and a greater than symbol, a less than symbol, or an equal sign
Example: $5 + 3 = 8$

numerator [nōō′mər·āt•ər] **numerador** The part of a fraction above the line, which tells how many parts are being counted
Example: $\frac{3}{4}$ ← numerator

octagon [äk′tə•gän] **octágono** A polygon with eight sides and eight angles
Examples:

odd [od] **impar** A whole number that has a 1, 3, 5, 7, or 9 in the ones place

open shape [ō′pən shāp] **figura abierta** A shape that does not begin and end at the same point
Examples:

order [ôr′dər] **orden** A particular arrangement or placement of numbers or things, one after another

order of operations [ôr′dər əv äp•ə•rā′shənz] **orden de las operaciones** A special set of rules that gives the order in which calculations are done

Order Property of Addition [ôr′dər präp′ər•tē əv ə•dish′ən] **propiedad de orden de la suma** *See* Commutative Property of Addition.

Order Property of Multiplication [ôr′dər präp′ər•tē əv mul•tə•pli•kā′shən] **propiedad de orden de la multiplicación** *See* Commutative Property of Multiplication.

parallel lines [pâr′ə•lel līnz] **líneas paralelas** Lines in the same plane that never cross and are always the same distance apart
Example:

pattern [pat′ərn] **patrón** An ordered set of numbers or objects in which the order helps you predict what will come next
Examples:
2, 4, 6, 8, 10

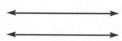

pentagon [pen′tə•gän] **pentágono** A polygon with five sides and five angles
Examples:

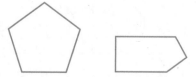

perimeter [pə•rim′ə•tər] **perímetro** The distance around a figure
Example:

perpendicular lines [pər•pən•dik′yōō•lər līnz] **líneas perpendiculares** Lines that intersect to form right angles
Example:

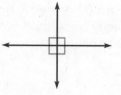

picture graph [pik'chər graf] **gráfica con dibujos** A graph that uses pictures to show and compare information
Example:

How We Get to School	
Walk	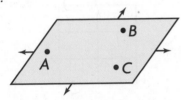 ✹ ✹ ✹
Ride a Bike	✹ ✹ ✹ ✹
Ride a Bus	✹ ✹ ✹ ✹ ✹ ✹
Ride in a Car	✹ ✹
Key: Each ✹ = 10 students.	

place value [plās val'yōō] **valor posicional** The value of each digit in a number, based on the location of the digit

plane [plān] **plano** A flat surface that extends without end in all directions
Example:

plane shape [plān shāp] **figura plana** A shape in a plane that is formed by curves, line segments, or both
Example:

P.M. [pē•em] **p.m.** The time after noon and before midnight

point [point] **punto** An exact position or location

polygon [päl'i•gän] **polígono** A closed plane shape with straight sides that are line segments
Examples:

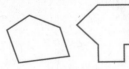 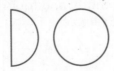

polygons   not polygons

© Houghton Mifflin Harcourt Publishing Company

Word History

Did you ever think that a *polygon* looks like a bunch of knees that are bent? This is how the term got its name. *Poly-* is from the Greek word *polys*, which means "many." The ending *-gon* is from the Greek word *gony*, which means "knee."

product [präd'əkt] **producto** The answer in a multiplication problem
Example: $3 \times 8 = 24$
                        ↑ product

Q

quadrilateral [kwäd•ri•lat'ər•əl] **cuadrilátero** A polygon with four sides and four angles
Example:

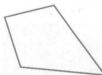

quarter [kwôrt'ər] **moneda de 25¢** A coin worth 25 cents and with a value equal to that of 25 pennies; 25¢
Example:

quarter hour [kwôrt'ər our] **cuarto de hora** 15 minutes
Example: Between 4:00 and 4:15 is one quarter hour.

quotient [kwō'shənt] **cociente** The number, not including the remainder, that results from division
Example: $8 \div 4 = 2$
                        ↑ quotient

R

ray [rā] **semirrecta** A part of a line, with one endpoint, that is straight and continues in one direction
Example:

rectangle [rek'tang•gəl] **rectángulo**
A quadrilateral with two pairs of parallel sides, two pairs of sides of equal length, and four right angles
Example:

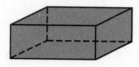

rectangular prism [rek•tang'gyə•lər priz'əm]
prisma rectangular A three-dimensional shape with six faces that are all rectangles
Example:

regroup [rē•grōop'] **reagrupar** To exchange amounts of equal value to rename a number
Example: 5 + 8 = 13 ones or 1 ten 3 ones

related facts [ri•lāt'id fakts] **operaciones relacionadas** A set of related addition and subtraction, or multiplication and division, number sentences
Examples: 4 × 7 = 28   28 ÷ 4 = 7
           7 × 4 = 28   28 ÷ 7 = 4

remainder [ri•mān'dər] **residuo** The amount left over when a number cannot be divided evenly

results [ri•zults'] **resultados** The answers from a survey

rhombus [räm'bəs] **rombo** A quadrilateral with two pairs of parallel sides and four sides of equal length
Example:

right angle [rīt ang'gəl] **ángulo recto** An angle that forms a square corner
Example:

round [round] **redondear** To replace a number with another number that tells about how many or how much

S

scale [skāl] **escala** The numbers placed at fixed distances on a graph to help label the graph

side [sīd] **lado** A straight line segment in a polygon

sixths [siksths] **sextos**

These are sixths

skip count [skip kount] **contar salteado** A pattern of counting forward or backward
Example: 5, 10, 15, 20, 25, 30, . . .

solid shape [sä'lid shāp] **cuerpo geométrico**
See three-dimensional shape.

sphere [sfir] **esfera** A three-dimensional shape that has the shape of a round ball
Example:

square [skwâr] **cuadrado** A quadrilateral with two pairs of parallel sides, four sides of equal length, and four right angles
Example:

square unit [skwâr yoo′nit] **unidad cuadrada** A unit used to measure area such as square foot, square meter, and so on

standard form [stan′dərd fôrm] **forma normal** A way to write numbers by using the digits 0–9, with each digit having a place value
Example: 345 ← standard form

subtraction [səb•trak′shən] **resta** The process of finding how many are left when a number of items are taken away from a group of items; the process of finding the difference when two groups are compared; the opposite operation of addition

sum [sum] **suma o total** The answer to an addition problem
Example: 6 + 4 = 10
           ↑—sum

survey [sûr′vā] **encuesta** A method of gathering information

tally table [tal′ē tā′bəl] **tabla de conteo** A table that uses tally marks to record data
Example:

Favorite Sport	
Sport	**Tally**
Soccer	卌 |||
Baseball	|||
Football	卌
Basketball	卌	

thirds [thûrdz] **tercios**

These are thirds

three-dimensional shape [thrē də•men′shə•nəl shāp] **figura tridimensional** A shape that has length, width, and height
Example:

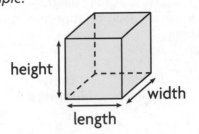

time line [tīm līn] **línea cronológica** A drawing that shows when and in what order events took place

trapezoid [trap′i•zoid] **trapecio** A quadrilateral with at least one pair of parallel sides
Example:

triangle [trī′ang•gəl] **triángulo** A polygon with three sides and three angles
Examples:

two-dimensional shape [too də•men′shə•nəl shāp] **figura bidimensional** A shape that has only length and width
Example:

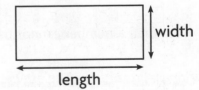

unit fraction [yoo′nit frak′shən] **fracción unitaria** A fraction that has 1 as its top number, or numerator
Examples: $\frac{1}{2}$ $\frac{1}{3}$ $\frac{1}{4}$

unit square [yoo′nit skwâr] **cuadrado de una unidad** A square with a side length of 1 unit, used to measure area

Venn diagram [ven dĭ′ə•gram] **diagrama de Venn** A diagram that shows relationships among sets of things
Example:

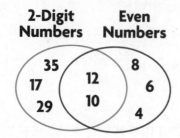

2-Digit Numbers   **Even Numbers**

35   17   29 | 12   10 | 8   6   4

vertex [vûr′teks] **vértice** The point at which two rays of an angle or two (or more) line segments meet in a plane shape or where three or more edges meet in a solid shape
Examples:

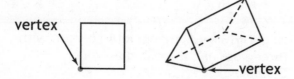

vertex

vertex

vertical bar graph [vûr′ti•kəl bär graf] **gráfica de barras verticales** A bar graph in which the bars go up from bottom to top

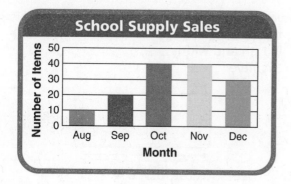

School Supply Sales

Number of Items

50
40
30
20
10
0

Aug   Sep   Oct   Nov   Dec
Month

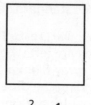

whole [hōl] **entero** All of the parts of a shape or group
Example:

$\frac{2}{2} = 1$

This is one whole.

whole number [hōl num′bər] **número entero** One of the numbers 0, 1, 2, 3, 4, . . . The set of whole numbers goes on without end

word form [wûrd fôrm] **en palabras** A way to write numbers by using words
Example: The word form of 212 is two hundred twelve.

Zero Property of Multiplication [zē′rō präp′ər•tē əv mul•tə•pli•kā′shən] **propiedad del cero de la multiplicación** The property that states that the product of zero and any number is zero
Example: $0 \times 6 = 0$

Correlations

COMMON CORE STATE STANDARDS

Standards You Will Learn

Mathematical Practices		Some examples are:
MP1	Make sense of problems and persevere in solving them.	Lessons 1.2, 2.1, 2.4, 5.3, 6.3, 7.1, 9.3, 10.7, 11.2
MP2	Reason abstractly and quantitatively.	Lessons 1.1, 1.5, 3.7, 5.5, 6.4, 7.2, 10.9, 11.4, 12.8
MP3	Construct viable arguments and critique the reasoning of others.	Lessons 2.5, 4.7, 5.3, 7.2, 9.7, 10.4, 10.5, 11.1, 12.6
MP4	Model with mathematics.	Lessons 1.12, 2.2, 3.2, 5.2, 6.2, 8.2, 10.3, 11.3, 12.9
MP5	Use appropriate tools strategically.	Lessons 1.6, 2.7, 3.5, 4.9, 6.7, 7.8, 9.5, 10.6, 11.4
MP6	Attend to precision.	Lessons 1.1, 1.4, 2.6, 5.2, 6.8, 7.1, 9.2, 10.1, 12.6
MP7	Look for and make use of structure.	Lessons 1.1, 3.3, 3.6, 5.1, 6.5, 7.11, 11.5, 11.7, 12.6
MP8	Look for and express regularity in repeated reasoning.	Lessons 2.2, 3.6, 4.5, 5.4, 6.9, 7.7, 9.5, 11.4, 12.3
Domain: Operations and Algebraic Thinking		**Student Edition Lessons**
Represent and solve problems involving multiplication and division.		
3.OA.A.1	Interpret products of whole numbers, e.g., interpret 5×7 as the total number of objects in 5 groups of 7 objects each.	Lessons 3.1, 3.2
3.OA.A.2	Interpret whole-number quotients of whole numbers, e.g., interpret $56 \div 8$ as the number of objects in each share when 56 objects are partitioned equally into 8 shares, or as a number of shares when 56 objects are partitioned into equal shares of 8 objects each.	Lessons 6.2, 6.3, 6.4

Standards You Will Learn

Domain: Operations and Algebraic Thinking

Represent and solve problems involving multiplication and division.

3.OA.A.3	Use multiplication and division within 100 to solve word problems in situations involving equal groups, arrays, and measurement quantities, e.g., by using drawings and equations with a symbol for the unknown number to represent the problem.	Lessons 3.3, 3.5, 4.1, 4.2, 4.3, 6.1, 6.5, 6.6, 7.1, 7.3, 7.8
3.OA.A.4	Determine the unknown whole number in a multiplication or division equation relating three whole numbers.	Lessons 5.2, 7.8

Understand properties of multiplication and the relationship between multiplication and division.

3.OA.B.5	Apply properties of operations as strategies to multiply and divide. *Examples: If 6 × 4 = 24 is known, then 4 × 6 = 24 is also known (Commutative property of multiplication.) 3 × 5 × 2 can be found by 3 × 5 = 15, then 15 × 2 = 30, or by 5 × 2 = 10, then 3 × 10 = 30. (Associative property of multiplication.) Knowing that 8 × 5 = 40 and 8 × 2 = 16, one can find 8 × 7 as 8 × (5 + 2) = (8 × 5) + (8 × 2) = 40 + 16 = 56. (Distributive property.)*	Lessons 3.6, 3.7, 4.4, 4.6, 6.9
3.OA.B.6	Understand division as an unknown-factor problem.	Lesson 6.7

Multiply and divide with 100.

3.OA.C.7	Fluently multiply and divide within 100, using strategies such as the relationship between multiplication and division (e.g., knowing that 8 × 5 = 40, one knows 40 ÷ 5 = 8) or properties of operations. By the end of Grade 3, know from memory all products of two one-digit numbers.	Lessons 4.5, 4.8, 4.9, 6.8, 7.2, 7.4, 7.5, 7.6, 7.7, 7.9

Domain: Operations and Algebraic Thinking		
Solve problems involving the four operations, and identify and explain patterns in arithmetic.		
3.OA.D.8	Solve two-step word problems using the four operations. Represent these problems using equations with a letter standing for the unknown quantity. Assess the reasonableness of answers using mental computation and estimation strategies including rounding.	Lessons 1.12, 2.1, 2.6, 3.4, 4.10, 7.10, 7.11
3.OA.D.9	Identify arithmetic patterns (including patterns in the addition table or multiplication table), and explain them using properties of operations.	Lessons 1.1, 4.7, 4.10, 5.1
Domain: Number and Operations in Base Ten		
Use place value understanding and properties of operations to perform multi-digit arithmetic.		
3.NBT.A.1	Use place value understanding to round whole numbers to the nearest 10 or 100.	Lessons 1.2, 1.3, 1.8
3.NBT.A.2	Fluently add and subtract within 1000 using strategies and algorithms based on place value, properties of operations, and/or the relationship between addition and subtraction.	Lessons 1.4, 1.5, 1.6, 1.7, 1.9, 1.10, 1.11, 2.2, 2.3, 2.4, 2.5, 2.7
3.NBT.A.3	Multiply one-digit whole numbers by multiples of 10 in the range 10–90 (e.g., 9×80, 5×60) using strategies based on place value and properties of operations.	Lessons 5.3, 5.4, 5.5

Domain: Number and Operations—Fractions

Develop understanding of fractions as numbers.

3.NF.A.1	Understand a fraction 1/b as the quantity formed by 1 part when a whole is partitioned into b equal parts; understand a fraction a/b as the quantity formed by a parts of size 1/b.	Lessons 8.1, 8.2, 8.3, 8.4, 8.7, 8.8, 8.9
3.NF.A.2	Understand a fraction as a number on the number line; represent fractions on a number line diagram.	
	a. Represent a fraction 1/b on a number line diagram by defining the interval from 0 to 1 as the whole and partitioning it into b equal parts. Recognize that each part has size 1/b and that the endpoint of the part based at 0 locates the number 1/b on the number line.	Lesson 8.5
	b. Represent a fraction a/b on a number line diagram by marking off a lengths 1/b from 0. Recognize that the resulting interval has size a/b and that its endpoint locates the number a/b on the number line.	Lesson 8.5

Domain: Number and Operations—Fractions

Develop understanding of fractions as numbers.

3.NF.A.3	Explain equivalence of fractions in special cases, and compare fractions by reasoning about their size.	
	a. Understand two fractions as equivalent (equal) if they are the same size, or the same point on a number line.	Lesson 9.6
	b. Recognize and generate simple equivalent fractions, e.g., 1/2 = 2/4, 4/6 = 2/3. Explain why the fractions are equivalent, e.g., by using a visual fraction model.	Lesson 9.7
	c. Express whole numbers as fractions, and recognize fractions that are equivalent to whole numbers.	Lesson 8.6
	d. Compare two fractions with the same numerator or the same denominator by reasoning about their size. Recognize that comparisons are valid only when the two fractions refer to the same whole. Record the results of comparisons with the symbols >, =, or <, and justify the conclusions, e.g., by using a visual fraction model.	Lessons 9.1, 9.2, 9.3, 9.4, 9.5

Domain: Measurement and Data

Solve problems involving measurement and estimation of intervals of time, liquid volumes, and masses of objects.

3.MD.A.1	Tell and write time to the nearest minute and measure time intervals in minutes. Solve word problems involving addition and subtraction of time intervals in minutes, e.g., by representing the problem on a number line diagram.	Lessons 10.1, 10.2, 10.3, 10.4, 10.5
3.MD.A.2	Measure and estimate liquid volumes and masses of objects using standard units of grams (g), kilograms (kg), and liters (l). Add, subtract, multiply, or divide to solve one-step word problems involving masses or volumes that are given in the same units, e.g., by using drawings (such as a beaker with a measurement scale) to represent the problem.	Lessons 10.7, 10.8, 10.9

Represent and interpret data.

3.MD.B.3	Draw a scaled picture graph and a scaled bar graph to represent a data set with several categories. Solve one- and two-step "how many more" and "how many less" problems using information presented in scaled bar graphs.	Lessons 2.1, 2.2, 2.3, 2.4, 2.5, 2.6
3.MD.B.4	Generate measurement data by measuring lengths using rulers marked with halves and fourths of an inch. Show the data by making a line plot, where the horizontal scale is marked off in appropriate units—whole numbers, halves, or quarters.	Lessons 2.7, 10.6

Domain: Measurement and Data

Geometric measurement: understand concepts of area and relate area to multiplication and to addition.

3.MD.C.5	Recognize area as an attribute of plane figures and understand concepts of area measurement.	Lesson 11.4
	a. A square with side length 1 unit, called "a unit square," is said to have "one square unit" of area, and can be used to measure area.	Lesson 11.4
	b. A plane figure which can be covered without gaps or overlaps by *n* unit squares is said to have an area of *n* square units.	Lesson 11.5
3.MD.C.6	Measure areas by counting unit squares (square cm, square m, square in, square ft, and improvised units).	Lesson 11.5
3.MD.C.7	Relate area to the operations of multiplication and addition.	Lesson 11.6
	a. Find the area of a rectangle with whole-number side lengths by tiling it, and show that the area is the same as would be found by multiplying the side lengths.	Lesson 11.6, 11.8
	b. Multiply side lengths to find areas of rectangles with whole-number side lengths in the context of solving real world and mathematical problems, and represent whole-number products as rectangular areas in mathematical reasoning.	Lesson 11.7
	c. Use tiling to show in a concrete case that the area of a rectangle with whole-number side lengths a and $b + c$ is the sum of $a \times b$ and $a \times c$. Use area models to represent the distributive property in mathematical reasoning.	Lesson 11.8
	d. Recognize area as additive. Find areas of rectilinear figures by decomposing them into non-overlapping rectangles and adding the areas of the non-overlapping parts, applying this technique to solve real world problems.	Lesson 11.8

Domain: Measurement and Data		
Geometric measurement: recognize perimeter as an attribute of plane figures and distinguish between linear and area measures.		
3.MD.D.8	Solve real world and mathematical problems involving perimeters of polygons, including finding the perimeter given the side lengths, finding an unknown side length, and exhibiting rectangles with the same perimeter and different areas or with the same area and different perimeters.	Lessons 11.1, 11.2, 11.3, 11.9, 11.10
Domain: Geometry		
Reason with shapes and their attributes.		
3.G.A.1	Understand that shapes in different categories (e.g., rhombuses, rectangles, and others) may share attributes (e.g., having four sides), and that the shared attributes can define a larger category (e.g., quadrilaterals). Recognize rhombuses, rectangles, and squares as examples of quadrilaterals, and draw examples of quadrilaterals that do not belong to any of these subcategories.	Lessons 12.1, 12.2, 12.3, 12.4, 12.5, 12.6, 12.7, 12.8
3.G.A.2	Partition shapes into parts with equal areas. Express the area of each part as a unit fraction of the whole.	Lesson 12.9

Common Core State Standards © Copyright 2010. National Governors Association Center for Best Practices and Council of Chief State School Officers. All rights reserved. This product is not sponsored or endorsed by the Common Core State Standards Initiative of the National Governors Association Center for Best Practices and the Council of Chief State School Officers.

Index

A

Act It Out, 301–304, 421–424, 507–510

Activities

Activity, 5, 6, 126, 139, 165, 166, 171, 209, 229, 230, 281, 287, 307, 319, 320, 345, 365, 366, 467, 487, 533, 534, 594, 599, 600, 605, 606, 612, 631, 643, 649, 650, 669, 675, 681, 704, 729, 735

Cross-Curricular Activities and Connections. *See* Cross-Curricular Activities and Connections

Investigate, 301–304, 421–424, 507–510

Math in the Real World, 3, 85, 137, 189, 259, 299, 363, 441, 505, 559, 623, 695

Addition

with addition tables, 5–6

bar models, 73–76

break apart strategy, 25, 35–38, 42, 56

with compatible numbers, 17–20, 24–25

draw a diagram, 73–76

elapsed time, 573–576

estimate sums, 17–20

with friendly numbers, 24–26

as inverse operations, 61, 637

of liquid volume, 611–614

of mass, 612–614

mental math strategies, 23–26

on number lines, 23–26, 573–574, 579–581, 585–587

place value strategy, 41–44

properties of
Associative, 29–32, 223
Commutative, 6, 29–32
Identity, 5, 29–32

regrouping, 41–43

related to area, 655–658, 669–672

related to multiplication, 145–148

rounding and, 17–20

three-digit numbers, 17–20, 23–26, 35–38, 41–44

of time intervals, 573–576, 579–582, 585–587

two-digit numbers, 23–26, 29–32

Addition tables, 5, 6

Algebra

addition
Associative Property of Addition, 29–32, 223
Commutative Property of Addition, 6, 29–32
describe a number pattern, 5–8, 261–264
Identity Property of Addition, 5, 29–32
patterns on the addition table, 5–8
related to area, 655–658, 669–672
related to multiplication, 145–148
unknown digits, 43

area, 275–278, 643–646, 655–658

division
factors, 389–392, 396–397, 415–418
related facts, 345–348
related to subtraction, 325–328
relate multiplication to division, 339–342, 345–348, 372–374, 384–386, 390–392, 396–398, 404–406, 409–412, 416–418
rules for one and zero, 351–354
unknown divisor, 410

equations, 267–270, 585

input/output tables, 261–264

inverse operations, 61, 339–342

multiplication
area models, 275–278, 655–658, 663–666
arrays, 165–168, 209–212, 223, 267–268, 340–342
Associative Property of Multiplication, 223–226, 236
Commutative Property of Multiplication, 171–174, 215, 224
describe a number pattern, 229–232, 261–264
Distributive Property, 209–212, 215, 241, 275–278, 669–672
factors, 145–148, 267–270
Identity Property of Multiplication, 177–180
number pattern, 229–232, 261–264
with one and zero, 177–180
order of operations, 427–430
patterns on a multiplication table, 229–232

© Houghton Mifflin Harcourt Publishing Company

E

Ⓖ

problem solving, 73–74, 87–88, 159–160,
247–248, 275–276, 301–302, 421–424,
493–494, 507–508, 585–586, 663–664,
741–742

Tree Map, 138, 190, 260, 696

Venn diagram, 4, 364, 624

Graphs

bar graphs

analyzing and constructing, 107–110,
113–116

defined, 107

horizontal bar graphs, 107–108,
110–113, 116–121

scale, 107–110, 113–116

vertical bar graphs, 108–109, 114–115,
120–121, 122

key, 93–96, 99–102, 114, 162, 374

line plots

analyzing and constructing, 125–128

defined, 125

generating measurement data, 126,
593–596

picture graphs

analyzing and constructing, 93–96,
99–102, 113–116

defined, 93

key, 93

solving problems, 119–122

Greater than (>)

angles and, 703–706

fractions and, 507–510, 513–516,
519–522, 525–528

Grouping Property of Multiplication,
223–226

Groups

equal groups. *See* Equal groups

fractions of, 481–484, 487–490, 493–496

Half hours, 579, 585

Half symbol, 94

Halves, 443–446

measure to the nearest half inch, 593–596

Hexagons

angles of, 710–712

sides of, 710–712

Horizontal bar graphs, 107–108, 110–113,
116–121

Hour hand, 561–564

Hours

half, 559, 567–570, 579, 585

minutes after hour, 562

minutes before hour, 562

Hundreds

place value, 11–14, 18–20, 41–44, 50–52,
61–64, 67–70, 282–284, 288

round to nearest, 11–14

Identity Property

Addition, 5, 29–32

Multiplication, 177–180

Inches

as customary unit, 593–596

generating data in, 126, 593–596

measure to nearest fourth inch, 593–596

measure to nearest half inch, 593–596

measure to nearest inch, 126

Intersecting lines, 715–718

Inverse operations, 61, 339

Investigate, 333–336, 427–430, 539–542,
625–628, 747–750

K

Keys, 93–96, 99–102, 114, 162, 374

Kilograms

defined, 605

as metric unit, 605–608

solving problems in, 605–608, 611–614

L

Length

customary units for

feet, 151, 633, 637–640

inches, 593–596, 633

measure in centimeters, 631–634

measure to nearest fourth inch, 593–596

measure to nearest half inch, 593–596

measure to nearest inch, 126

metric units for

centimeters, 89, 631–634

© Houghton Mifflin Harcourt Publishing Company

with counters, 191–194, 301–304,
        307–310, 313–316, 319–322, 365–368,
        383–386, 395–396, 415–416, 481–484,
        487–490, 493–496
    division with arrays, 333–336, 340–342,
        389–391, 403–406
    equivalent fractions, 539–542, 545–548
    fractions
        with fraction circles, 508, 519–522,
            525–528
        with fraction strips, 467–470, 507,
            513–516, 520–522, 533–536, 540
    fractions greater than 1, 475–478,
        482–483
    multiplication, 159–162
    multiplication with arrays, 165–168,
        209–212, 340–342
    multiplication with base-ten blocks, 281,
        287
    with number lines. *See* Number lines
    part of a group, 481–484, 487–490
    perimeter, 625–628
    with square tiles, 165–168, 171–174,
        267–268, 333–336, 345–348, 386, 403,
        649, 669
    triangles, 735–738
Money, 90, 142, 198, 226, 250, 262,270, 278,
    283, 342, 377, 392, 421, 428, 430
Multiples
    defined, 197
    of ten, 275–278, 281–284, 287–290
Multiplication
    area models, 275–278, 655–658, 663–666
    as inverse operation, 339–342
    bar models, 159–161, 197–200, 339–342
    describe a number pattern, 229–232
    doubles, 191–194, 204, 235
    draw a diagram, 159–162, 275–278
    factors, 146
        eight, 235–238
        five, 197–200, 204
        four, *179*, 191–194
        nine, 241–244
        one, 177–180
        seven, 215–218
        six, 203–206
        ten, 197–200
        three, *179*, 203–206
        two, 191–194
        unknown factors, 173, 205, 225,
            267–270, 396–397, 415–418
        zero, 177–180

of equal groups, 139–142, 145–148,
        151–154, 301–304, 307–310
    of liquid volume, 611–614
    of mass, 611–614
    place value strategy, 281–284
    products, 146
    properties of
        Associative Property of Multiplication,
            223–226, 236
        Commutative Property of
            Multiplication, 171–174, 215, 224
        Distributive Property, 209–212, 215,
            241, 275–278, 669–672
        Grouping Property of Multiplication,
            223–226
        Identity Property of Multiplication,
            177–180
        Zero Property of Multiplication,
            177–180
    regrouping, 287–290
    related facts, 345–348
    related to addition, 145–148
    related to area, 655–658, 663–666,
        669–672
    related to division, 339–342
    related to perimeter, 638
    strategies, 281–284
    with arrays, 165–168, 209–212, 223,
        267–268, 339–342
    with measurement quantities, 611–614
    with multiples of ten, 275–278, 281–284,
        287–290
    with multiplication table, 204
    with number lines, 151–154, 197–198,
        235, 281–283
Multiplication tables, 204
    find unknown divisor, 410
    find unknown factor, 267–270
    make a table, 247–250
    patterns on the, 229–232
Multiply, 146

N

Nickels, 377
Noon, 568
Number lines
    add and subtract minutes, 573, 580
    adding with, 23–26, 573–576, 579
    comparing fractions on, 514–515

© Houghton Mifflin Harcourt Publishing Company

© Houghton Mifflin Harcourt Publishing Company

Products, 146

Projects, 1–2, 439–440, 557–558, 693–694

Properties

Associative Property of Addition, 29–32, 223

Associative Property of Multiplication, 223–226, 236

Commutative Property of Addition, 6, 29–32

Commutative Property of Multiplication, 171–174, 215, 224

Distributive Property, 209–212, 215, 241, 275–278, 669–672

Grouping Property of Multiplication, 223–226

Identity Property of Addition, 5, 29–32

Identity Property of Multiplication, 177–180

Zero Property of Multiplication, 177–180

Q

Quadrilaterals

angles of, 710–712, 723–726

classifying, 723–726, 741

comparing, 723–726, 741

defined, 710

describing, 710–715, 723–726

drawing, 729–732

sides of, 710–712, 723–726

Quick pictures, 171–174, 177–180, 287–290, 443–446, 449–452

Quotients, 320

R

Rays, 697

Reading

Connect to Reading, 58, 128, 218, 354, 542, 678, 726

Read/Solve the Problem, 73–74, 87–88, 159–160, 247–248, 275–276, 301–302, 421–422, 493–494, 507–508, 585–586, 663–664, 741–742

Strategies

Cause and Effect, 678

Compare and Contrast, 58, 354, 726

Make an Inference, 128

Summarize, 218, 542

Visualize It, 4, 86, 138, 190, 260, 300, 364, 442, 506, 560, 624, 696

Real World

Problem Solving, In most lessons. Some examples are: 14, 52, 374, 412, 732, 750

Unlock the Problem, In most lessons. Some examples are: 11, 41, 377, 409, 681, 741

Reasonableness of an answer, 36, 41, 61, 67, 74, 561, 586

Rectangles

angles of, 723–726

area of, 649–652, 655–658, 663–666, 669–672, 675–678, 681–684

drawing, 675–678, 729–732

find unknown side length, 638

perimeter of, 675–678

sides of, 723–726

Related facts

defined, 345

multiplication and division facts, 345–348

using, 345–348, 372, 384, 390, 396, 404, 409, 416

Relationships, mathematical

addition to multiplication, 145–148

area to fractions and shapes, 747–750

area to multiplication, 655–658, 663–666, 669–672

area to perimeter, 643–646

division

to multiplication, 339–342, 371, 384, 390, 396

to subtraction, 325–328, 371–374, 409–412

fractions to shapes and area, 747–750

multiplication

to addition, 145–148

to division, 339–342, 371, 384, 390, 396

number of equal parts in a whole

to size of the parts, 443–446, 449–452, 455–458, 461–464, 475–478, 487–490

part-whole, 443–446, 455–458, 461–464, 487–490

perimeter to area, 643–646

shapes to fractions and area, 747–750

subtraction to division, 325–328, 371–374, 409–412

metric units
for area
square centimeters, 650–651
square meters, 655–657, 681
for length, centimeters, 89, 627, 631–634
for liquid volume and capacity, liters, 599–602
for mass
grams, 605–608
kilograms, 605–608
square units, 643–646, 649–652, 655–658, 663–666, 669–672, 675–678, 681–684

Unlock the Problem, In most lessons. Some examples are: 5, 41, 377, 409, 715, 741

Unlock the Problem Tips, 75, 277, 303, 423, 495, 509, 587

Variables
using letters and symbols, 267–270, 390, 637–640

Venn diagrams, 4, 364, 624, 741–744

Vertical bar graphs, 108

Vertices (vertex)
of angles, 703

Visualize It, 4, 86, 138, 190, 260, 300, 364, 442, 506, 560, 624, 696

Vocabulary
Chapter Vocabulary Cards, At the beginning of every chapter
Mid-Chapter Checkpoint, 47–48, 105–106, 157–158, 221–222, 273–274, 331–332, 401–402, 473–474, 531–532, 591–592, 661–662, 721–722
Multimedia eGlossary, 4, 86, 138, 190, 260, 300, 364, 442, 506, 560, 624, 696
Understand Vocabulary, 4, 86, 138, 190, 260, 300, 364, 442, 506, 560, 624, 696

Vocabulary Games, 4A, 86A, 138A, 190A, 260A, 300A, 364A, 442A, 506A, 560A, 624A, 696A

Vocabulary Builder, 4, 86, 138, 190, 260, 300, 364, 442, 506, 560, 624, 696

Weight, 52, 148

What if, 58, 70, 75, 89, 93, 101, 102, 107, 109, 120, 121, 139, 140, 151, 161, 174, 177, 206, 248, 249, 270, 277, 303, 314, 339, 377, 384, 423, 487, 495, 509, 548, 564, 587, 602, 664, 665, 678, 712, 743, 750

What's the Error?, 38, 95, 200, 212, 398, 478, 516, 527, 602, 628, 700

What's the Question?, 52, 121, 180, 283, 484, 510

Wholes, 443–446, 455–458, 461–464, 513, 525, 747–750

Whole numbers
unknown, 63, 193, 267–270, 367, 390–391, 397, 405, 411, 417, 429
using place value, 11–14, 17–20, 23–26, 29–32, 35–38, 49–52, 55–58, 61–64, 67–70, 281–284, 287–290
writing, as fractions, 461–464, 475–478, 482–484

Write Math, In every Student Edition lesson. Some examples are: 15, 143, 374, 471, 727

Writing
Write Math, In every Student Edition lesson.
Some examples are: 15, 143, 374, 471, 727

Zero Property of Multiplication, 177–180

Table of Measures

METRIC	CUSTOMARY

Length

1 centimeter (cm) = 10 millimeters (mm)	
1 decimeter (dm) = 10 centimeters (cm)	1 foot (ft) = 12 inches (in.)
1 meter (m) = 100 centimeters	1 yard (yd) = 3 feet, or 36 inches
1 meter (m) = 10 decimeters	1 mile (mi) = 1,760 yards, or 5,280 feet
1 kilometer (km) = 1,000 meters	

Capacity and Liquid Volume

1 liter (L) = 1,000 milliliters (mL)	1 pint (pt) = 2 cups (c)
	1 quart (qt) = 2 pints
	1 gallon (gal) = 4 quarts

Mass/Weight

| 1 kilogram (kg) = 1,000 grams (g) | 1 pound (lb) = 16 ounces (oz) |

TIME

1 minute (min) = 60 seconds (sec)	1 year (yr) = 12 months (mo), or about 52 weeks
1 hour (hr) = 60 minutes	1 year = 365 days
1 day = 24 hours	1 leap year = 366 days
1 week (wk) = 7 days	1 decade = 10 years
	1 century = 100 years

MONEY

1 penny = 1 cent (¢)
1 nickel = 5 cents
1 dime = 10 cents
1 quarter = 25 cents
1 half dollar = 50 cents
1 dollar ($) = 100 cents

SYMBOLS

< is less than
> is greater than
= is equal to